RICHARD WILBUR'S CREATION

D1249973

UNDER DISCUSSION
Donald Hall, General Editor

Elizabeth Bishop and Her Art
   Edited by Lloyd Schwartz and Sybil P. Estess

Richard Wilbur's Creation
   Edited and with an Introduction by Wendy Salinger

Richard Wilbur's Creation

Edited and with an Introduction
by Wendy Salinger

Ann Arbor
THE UNIVERSITY OF MICHIGAN PRESS

For my father—poet, translator, teacher
1905–83

Library of Congress Cataloging in Publication Data
Main entry under title:

Richard Wilbur's creation.

   (Under discussion)
   Bibliography: p.
   1. Wilbur, Richard, 1921–   —Criticism and
interpretation—Addresses, essays, lectures.
I. Salinger, Wendy.   II. Series.
PS3545.I32165Z85   1983   811'.52   83-10313
ISBN 0-472-09348-7
ISBN 0-472-06348-0 (pbk.)

Acknowledgments

Grateful acknowledgment is made to the following authors, publishers, and journals for permission to reprint previously published material:

Atlantic Monthly for "Technique and Inspiration: A Year of Poetry" by Peter Viereck, *Atlantic Monthly,* January 1952. Copyright © 1951, R 1952, by The Atlantic Monthly Company, Boston, Mass. Reprinted with permission from publisher and author.

Joseph Brodsky for his "On Richard Wilbur," *American Poetry Review* 2, no. 1 (January–February 1972). Reprinted with permission from the author and publisher.

John Ciardi for his "Our Most Melodic Poet," *Saturday Review,* August 1956.

Concerning Poetry and Charles Duffy for "Intricate Neural Grace: The Esthetic of Richard Wilbur" by Charles Duffy, *Concerning Poetry* 4, no. 1 (Spring 1971).

Contemporary Literature for "The Beautiful Changes in Richard Wilbur's Poetry" by John P. Farrell, *Contemporary Literature* 12, no. 1 (Winter 1971). Copyright © 1971 by the Board of Regents of the University of Wisconsin System.

Contemporary Poetry: A Journal of Criticism for "Richard Wilbur's Critical Condition" by Charles R. Woodard, *Contemporary Poetry* 2, no. 2 (Autumn 1977).

Farrar, Straus and Giroux for an excerpt from "Fifty Years of American Poetry" by Randall Jarrell, from his *Third Book of Criticism.* Copyright © 1963, 1965, by Randall Jarrell. Reprinted with permission from Farrar, Straus and Giroux, Inc., and Mary Jarrell, executrix of the estate of Randall Jarrell.

David R. Godine for "What Was Modern Poetry?" from *Figures of Thought* by Howard Nemerov. Copyright © 1978 by Howard Nemerov. Reprinted with permission from David R. Godine, Publisher, Inc.

Contents

Introduction

It is the intention of this book to survey the critical reception given Richard Wilbur's poetry since his first book, *The Beautiful Changes,* was published in 1947 and, in doing so, to analyze the nature of his talent and his vision. Since the perception of a phenomenon is related to the position of the observer, however, it's necessary first to reverse the looking glass: to understand with what eyes Richard Wilbur has been measured. The revolution of one generation provides the next with its orthodoxy, and it's sometimes astonishing to realize how complete the inversion has been.

American poets in the years following the Second World War felt a particular kind of freedom—a liberation from the need for revolt. The work of revolution, they believed, had been accomplished. Eliot, Pound, Williams—rebels of an earlier generation—had revitalized the materials of an art form previously grown stale with gentility. Now all the richness of literary tradition, all the resources of poetic device were once again available to their successors. This included rhyme and meter, which were seen as "the companions not the causes" of the decline of old.[1] The ideal for the new generation of poets was a virtuoso craftsmanship. Their professor-mentors, the New Critics, encouraged them to embrace the dilemmas of modern existence with this totality of expressive powers: as Wilbur described it, "to feel that the most convincing poetry is that which accommodates mixed feelings, clashing ideas, and incongruous images. Poetry could not be honest, we thought, unless it began by acknowledging the full discordancy of modern life and consciousness."[2] The young Wilbur, who was twenty-four when his first book was published, was recognized at once as the peerless craftsman in this endeavor.

The formal renaissance for poetry was accompanied by a social one. Once an exile, the poet was now patronized by universities, literary magazines, and audiences for live readings. While there were some admonitory grumblings (from such quarters as *Time* magazine) about the dangers respectability might hold for a society's prophets, the prospect was rich with promise: the learned and original talents of such young writers as Wilbur, Robert Lowell, Theodore Roethke, Elizabeth Bishop, given full literary and social license.

Like all critical prospects, however, this one can be viewed almost as easily in reverse. What expands in one geometry contracts in another. This generation came out of the Second World War, and its preoccupation with craftsmanship also was seen by some critics—and by some of the poets themselves—as a retrenchment, an effort at containment. As one fifties critic suggested, the members of this war generation were unlike the post–First World War poets, who in their disillusion turned to the rebellious act of innovation. The survivors of the Second World War were faced immediately with the A-bomb and new threats of annihilation. In reaction their instincts were toward preservation, perpetuation: the entrenchments of tradition, the securities of the academic job, the grant, and so forth.[3] Wilbur himself acknowledges such a conservative impulse:

> My first poems were written in answer to the inner and outer disorders of the Second World War and they helped me, as poems should, to take ahold of raw events and convert them, provisionally, into experience.[4]

If art is always in some sense a rage for order, in times of greatest disorder the rage must burn brightest. "One does not use poetry for its major purposes, as a means of organizing oneself and the world," Wilbur wrote of his work that came out of the war, "until one's world somehow gets out of hand."[5] And the British poet John Wain saw something of the same lesson in the precision and control of craft so highly valued by his generation of poets:

> We wrote like that because we had seen too much in the preceding five (1940–45) years of the energy that loses itself in display, the large gesture that indicates nothing. If we were

cautious it was because we knew that we had to be better than our immediate elders, and the best way seemed to be to go to work humbly and patiently, as craftsmen, and build upwards from the ground.[6]

Whatever its source, it was clear to the critics of the 1950s that the constraint of craftsmanship in Wilbur's case produced some dazzling effects. The words most frequently used to describe his gifts were: *precise, graceful, delicate, elegant*. Although this last was later to resound like something of an accusation from some Wilbur critics, it aptly characterizes his genius when used in the sense preferred by one reviewer,

> as it is used in the physical sciences, where elegance is a measure of rightness: an explanation is elegant when, in the most economical and coherent fashion possible, it explains everything that then needs to be explained.[7]

No one exceeded Wilbur in rightness of eye and ear. "No one since Herrick," wrote Donald Hall, "has written more exactly."[8]

Critics saw in the early Wilbur the influences of the metaphysical poets, of the ear and eye of Hopkins, of Marianne Moore in her particularity, of the poetic stance of Eliot, of the elegant John Crowe Ransom, and of that "voluptuary of the mind,"[9] Wallace Stevens. While some found these voices intrusive, others praised the young Wilbur for absorbing and transforming his influences. Wilbur himself described his position as that of "the grateful inheritor of all that my talent can employ."[10]

The subject of Wilbur's relation to particular literary traditions is an interesting and a complex one, as I hope the selection of essays in this book indicates. Some critics believe Wilbur writes out of a metaphysical, post-Symbolist tradition, while others place him in the line of a poetry of experience reaching from Whitman through Pound to such contemporaries as Gary Snyder and William Stafford. The distinction is significant for what it reveals about the creative tension at the heart of Wilbur's work.

Things, objects, "thingness" are a central concern in his poetry. In this he has an affinity with Hopkins that is both thematic and stylistic. Both poets have the gift of realizing in the aural and visual properties of language the "thisness" of things. Wilbur also is connected to a poet like William Carlos Williams; he too is a believer in the credo: "no ideas but in things." It's an admonishment he repeats to himself often—particularly in the early poetry. He is constantly dethroning his own vision from its "ruddy gallows," calling himself back to the green tree, the burrowing mole and the vaulting sparrow, to the "steam of beasts" and the "beautiful, heavy, unweary, loud, obvious thing!" He is, like Williams and like Whitman, a wooer of the world. And he shares with them, and with the other great American nature poet, Frost, an essential identification with the natural world. As Robert Sayre says (see pp. 153–61), like them Wilbur feels that it's the commitment to nature that brings self-knowledge.

But for Wilbur *things* are irrepressibly suggestive—have "legerity." The beautiful world changes—not only in time ("the lively wasting sun") but also in expression (sundered "for a second finding"). And Wilbur's poetry is as much a measure of that pulse, the volatility of things, as of their thisness. Things have unwedded valences, are impelled. They ramify and rarify, are transformed and transfigured. They are impermanent and permeable. While Wilbur holds the imagist reverence for things of a William Carlos Williams, Williams' objects have a bare simplicity to which Wilbur can't confine himself—because his deepest instincts are metaphoric.

So enters the problem of *mind*. That it *is* a problem for Wilbur is clearly indicated in the familiar tone of self-chastisement with which he so frequently reins in his burgeoning fantasy. He asks if mind "perverts our praise to uncreation." Would mind substitute itself for the world, wrench reality awry, remake creation in its own image? Is he writing out of the rich suggestiveness of things or from the self-immured world of fantasy? Wilbur mistrusts the imagination that would be a world to itself—it is in this sense that he has described his work as a continuing quarrel with the aesthetics of Edgar Allen Poe, who extolled the transcendent escape into the otherworld of the imagination. Wilbur's deep love of earth things denies him such a flight. Yet his eye beholds a world constantly ramifying outward and upward. (Wilbur, it happens, has described a similar paradox in discussing Emily Dickinson and Gerard Manley Hopkins, in whose poems, he feels, "the object is spiritually possessed, not merely for itself, but more truly as an index of the All."[11])

This central tension in Wilbur's poetry between the eye—the observer—and the (love) object is analyzed in several essays in this book. Both Howard Nemerov and Raymond Benoit describe a split in modern Western consciousness between subjective and objective. Since Plato and Descartes, Benoit says, truth has become a matter of perception rather than one of being. He sees in the history of American poetry a developing poetry of experience in which "the eye focusing on event replaces the mind building in metaphor." It's interesting that he places Wilbur directly in the line of this development: from Romantic and Victorian sources (Keats, Coleridge, Browning) through Pound and Eliot to Nemerov, Stafford, Snyder, and Wilbur. Truth *is* the beauty of things. The things of the world are not merely a pretext for the ideal. It is the world the poet must immerse himself or herself in.

Certainly it is this lesson that Wilbur repeats to himself.

Nemerov's essay too sees a modern world in which mind has been "read out of the universe along with gods, devils, spirits, and so much else." Imagism he regards as a step in that development. But Wilbur is not a direct descendant of the imagists, Nemerov believes, because his world is intellectual and intuitive as well; he struggles with the paradox of object and subject and finally unites the terms. He recovers a harmony in which self and world are experienced through one another. It's a union such as Nemerov sees in Lévi-Strauss' description of the primitive and artistic minds, "definable both by a consuming symbolic ambition . . . and by scrupulous attention directed entirely toward the concrete, and finally by the implicit conviction that these two attitudes are one." ("The object is . . . possessed . . . as an index of the All.")

Charles Woodard (pp. 221–31) also recognizes the union of opposites—of existence with essence—in Wilbur's vision but in a thoroughly twentieth-century context. He defends Wilbur's epistemology and questions those who, like the followers of William Carlos Williams, would omit mind from "the reality-equation." "Mind is as good a model of reality as we have," Woodard says. It's folly to believe we can render the thing-in-itself except as the mind's testimony. Thus, all evidence of the nature of reality is evidence of the nature of mind as well. Further, it becomes especially clear that there is no way to use *language* as "pre-reflective cognition," as Woodard believes Williams' followers would use it. In effect, one cannot render *things* totally free from *ideas*. There is no purely denotative vocabulary, and syntax itself is a revelation of the formal properties of the mind.

I think the resolution of these dichotomies has always been an implicit part of Wilbur's vision even as he has struggled with them. This is covertly expressed, for instance, in his statement about the transformation of raw event into experience. We do not *possess* experience except as it is processed through the mind. It is "raw," undigested and therefore uncaptured—unrecaptured in the Proustian sense—until won to us by the labors of the imagination.

The self-sameness of mind and world is the text, for example, of Wilbur's "Advice to a Prophet." The world is the expression of our humanity; it is what "calls our natures forth." The "live tongue" is the self *in* the world, that only knows itself so. We ourselves are natural things, and so the world's body is our own: it speaks "the rose of our love and the clean / horse of our courage."

In Wilbur's later poetry there is a growing directness, a simplicity of tone which, I think, is the voice of this reconciliation of the pull of things with their spiritual/intellectual suggestiveness. Michael Benedikt says (see pp. 101–5) that Wilbur has progressed from a visual to a visionary stance, that in the more recent poetry he begins to look *into* rather than *at* the things of the world. Mind is *in* the world—there has been a merging. (As physicists have discovered in this century: observer plus object equals, not the object, but the interaction that takes place between the two. The act of looking creates a new thing.) Wilbur has shifted, says Benedikt, from an objective to a subjective stance. A peace has been won. The voice of this peace may have the sound of an earlier, innocent lyric poetry, but it is also a modern voice speaking out of a world view that recognizes that the nature of the mind and the nature of reality are inseparable.

If the terms of Wilbur's art are in this way thoroughly contemporary, he is nonetheless counted out of several recent poetic fashions. His later work is indeed more personal and direct than the earlier, but he was not a part of the "confessional" movement whose ur-voice was Robert Lowell's and whose resonances are still strong in the work of a succeeding generation of poets. Surely many things are a matter of temperament. It is through the exploration of *things* that Wilbur discovers the nature of the self. But temperament is nurtured by context. Confessionalism, which was a revolt against the restraint and virtuoso control of post–Second World War verse, later became the orthodoxy of American poetry. Similarly, the virtuoso poets of the fifties originally were rebels themselves. In 1955 Britisher David Daiches described "the revolution in poetic taste that has taken place in the last 30 years or so" as one "associated with the repudiation of self-expression as a poetic ideal."[12] The Second World War generation, although it declared all stylistic revolutions accomplished and so repudiated Eliot the innovator, accepted the poetic stance which produced the theory of the "objective correlative."

It's not my purpose here to defend one school of thought against the other. When original statement grows stale with repetition and imitation, it's refreshed by contradiction. My intention is to understand how the terms change in time. From the beginning, Wilbur sought to engage "the full discordance of modern life and consciousness" with all the resources of the traditions he had mastered. He has been a poet who believes in remaining *in the world,* "in becoming a poet-citizen rather than an alienated artist."[13] He is wary of the seductions of "a personal system of imagery."

> It is the province of poems to make some order in the world, but the poets can't afford to forget that there is a reality of

things which survives all orders great and small. Things *are*. The cow is there. No poetry can have any strength unless it continually bashes itself against the reality of things.[14]

Such a stance is both personal to Wilbur and indicative of the context which nurtured him. He and his contemporaries of the postwar years spoke from a command of time—the full resources of tradition—and place: the poet was a citizen valued by a community; he was empowered by context.

But in the eyes of their critics such securities began to endanger this generation of poets. They warned them against the conformist seductions of suburbia. Poetry was becoming too correct and well-behaved, worn smooth by the desire to charm and please,

> characterized by a uniform style, a uniform subject matter, a uniform evasion of personal anguish and joy, a uniform broad range of erudition, and a uniform high level of technical excellence—impressive but somehow more than a little depressing.[15]

The model fifties poem was, Donald Hall said, the *poème bien fait*. It was a Wilbur imitation—that "was usually not that damned *bien fait*."[16] It was out of this context that a counter-cult of the personal arose.

Of course, the dynamic of thesis and antithesis is neither so simple nor so direct as retrospect may make it appear. Lowell, whose *Life Studies* came out in 1959, had always, even before his confessional flowering, a voice of passionate intensity.[17] Sylvia Plath insisted that the personal be connected to larger issues like the bombing of Hiroshima and the Nazi persecutions of the Jews. Ginsberg and the Beats, who were the first to rebel against "the poetry of suburbia," were in their own way highly allusive in their work and not without traditional ties—although the traditions they chose were in deliberate opposition to the Eliotic heritage of the academics. And it was, in fact, the poets of academe whom some critics accused of being too personal, of having a limited, insular vision that began and ended with suburban and university life. They rejected public concerns in favor of private ones. Domestic replaced historical issues.

It's even possible to see the confessional mode as a further development of fifties privatism rather than as a counteraction. Some critics explained it as the response of the individual sensibility to a meaningless world: when the historical process begins to alienate the individual rather than enrich his life sense, he turns to what is local and intimate.[18] Or one might see two roads diverging from the main thoroughfare, the thruway of the fifties: one leading deeper into a private sensibility and one traveling outward to meet public event, war and social revolution. And there were poets who worked both routes—Bly, Wright, Kinnell, and other so-called deep image poets, for example. Their form of privatism, however, was less confessional and personal than it was psychic and surreal—in fact, impersonal.

However these developments are presented, Richard Wilbur clearly wasn't completely at home in either the confessional or the political camp. This is interesting not as a question of popularity, which is obviously a sometime thing, but of poetic stance. Wilbur is not by nature drawn to personal confession because for him it is artifice that is the essential expression of the artist's relation to reality. It's by indirection—attention to the world as well as to language—that one finds out the directions of the self. There can be no direct confrontation. Wilbur once explained this using the metaphor of the rain dancer's relation to the rain, quoting Suzanne Langer's observation that "the most important virtue of the rite is not so much its practical as its religious success . . . its power to articulate a relation between man and nature . . . ."[19] The dancer doesn't merely imitate the motions of the rain, which can't in any case be faithfully reproduced. The dance attempts what Wilbur calls "a magic borrowing of the powers it wants to approach, and a translation of what is borrowed into the language of the dancing, human body."[20]

> The relation between an artist and reality is always an oblique one, and indeed there is no good art which is not consciously oblique. If you respect the reality of the world, you know that

you can approach that reality only by indirect means. The painter who throws away the frame and rebels at composition is not a painter any more: he thinks the world is himself, and that there is no need of a devious and delimited struggle with it. He lacks that feeling of inadequacy which must precede every genuine act of creation.

So that paradoxically it is respect for reality which makes a necessity of artifice.[21]

As Joseph Brodsky says (see his essay, pp. 203–6), "in the physical world only resistance is possible."

(It's clear, of course, that even the confessional voice involves artifice: the poet selects only particular events in a life for attention and a particular—often only one—tone or stance toward those events. As informal as the voice may seem, he or she creates a *persona* as surely as the more "formal" poet does.)

Wilbur is no more at ease with the unmediated response in the political realm than he is in the personal. In fact, those poems which try to approach events in such a manner—"A Miltonic Sonnet for Mr. Johnson," "For the Student Strikers"—have a conspicuous rhetorical stiffness. It's interesting to me that Wilbur's most successful "political" poem is "Advice to a Prophet." The poem works because Wilbur frames its political question in his own deeply religious terms. He speaks from love of nature and love of language. Wilbur has never been a political poet in the usual sense of the word. And to many his work seemed to lose "relevance" during the years of the sixties and seventies when that term was so important. Yet as a true nature poet, he has and always has had a kind of ecological prophecy to deliver. His reverence for life—not as an abstraction but in its very holy and delectable particulars—makes his voice timely.

Several of the essays in this book deal with the question of Wilbur's "relevance." Because of his interest in the formal properties of language and because he is not a topical poet, he has often been accused of remoteness and slightness. Because he is witty, he has been charged with frivolity. Because his love of things is ebullient, he has been chastised for ignoring the harsh realities of modern existence.

But is Wilbur's lushness "merely" formal? No, says critic

John Farrell (see pp. 187–202). In Wilbur's poems "beauty is realized only upon the exercise of man's intellectual and moral faculties." The experience of beauty must be earned—just as "raw event" can be captured only by the transforming labors of the imagination. Beauty is realized only through a serious confrontation with the questions of man's relation to the world and to the infinite: with history and with religion. As a poem like Wilbur's "Looking into History" shows, for example, history requires a creative act from us. We discover our own identities by understanding its metamorphoses. In "Merlin Enthralled," the retreat from history into dream robs the world of its "natural magic": art—the realization of beauty—must be an entry, not an escape.

Nor is Wilbur's world view the one of simplistic cheerfulness he's been charged with, argues Ejner Jensen (pp. 243–64), but a complex and paradoxical one. Unlike those poets who reject modern society and extoll instinctual man, Wilbur struggles with the problem of the rational consciousness as it lives in nature. This is the more profound awareness, Jensen feels, producing a deeper understanding of both the potential for evil and the potential for beauty and love in the universe.

Too, Wilbur's seriousness is clear by virtue of the fact that he is also in a fundamental way a religious poet, as various critics have noticed. Beauty is spiritual for him, as it is for Hopkins. When again and again Wilbur recalls himself to reality, it is the Incarnation, a *spiritual* reality, to which he returns: the incarnate world is "the spirit's right oasis." "The things of this world are not in themselves exalted in Wilbur's poetry; it is the god in them."[22] And creation, like history, asks of the poet-observer an analogous act. Only through the poet's own creative labors is the god experienced, incarnated. Art, in this sense, is an act of worship.

Is Wilbur then, as a poet of serious, contemporary concerns, a major poet of the age? Whether or not that is a useful question, it's one that critics ask. It's hard not to ask it about someone who by the age of thirty-five had published three books of poetry and won the Pulitzer Prize and the National Book Award, who went on to publish three more collections, translate Molière for the stage, write the lyrics to a Broadway musical, and so on and on. Auden said there were these criteria for major status: original vision and style, mastery of verse technique, range, prolificity, and a continual process of maturation.[23] Certainly, Wilbur fulfills the first three of these. Regarding prolificity, it must be said that Wilbur's volumes of poetry are usually slim—and, some complain, the number of original poems in proportion to the number of translations has grown less with each volume. Yet when one adds up the accomplishments of Wilbur's career, it's hard not to recognize a major achievement.

But has Wilbur's work changed over the years? Has he grown? Critics have had differing views of the progress of his career. Some saw a crucial thematic shift away from asceticism and toward involvement with reality in the poems of *Things of This World*. For others that book was, rather, in terms of themes and style, a culmination of all the early Wilbur, and it was with *Advice to a Prophet* that they saw a new openness and even an awkwardness hinting at the deeper vision that came with *Walking to Sleep*. But there have always been critics who have said Wilbur has failed to change at all, that the later poems are very like the earliest.

It must be asked, of course, whether change is an adequate measure of literary greatness. When Auden decided that, according to his criteria, Housman was a minor poet, Wilbur responded in an essay: "I wonder if an alternative measure of stature might not be the extent to which any poet has given sustained, forceful, and original treatment to a theme of some consequence?"[24]

Wilbur's own themes are certainly consequential, and he has devoted to them a scrupulous and persistent attention over the years. Perhaps it isn't so much his persistence in these themes that some of his critics have objected to as it is the certainty of their resolutions. He is "a rational teacher in a rational world,"[25] and the powerful closure of his conclusions is a familiar signature of many of the poems. The question is whether his rage for order, mentioned earlier, sometimes inhibits the development of his material.

Some critics would think better of the poems if the struggle were carried on nearer the surface, revealing itself more clearly in whirlpools and bubbles. They find his countermeasures almost too successful, his usual poise an indication that disorder is no match for him. Others see in this poise not only a technical but a spiritual strength.[26]

It's a tribute to Wilbur's seriousness that, as Gerald Reedy observed in 1969, he is not just a poet of effects but one who has a serious moral judgment to make upon the world.[27] But moral instruction can distance if not estrange a reader from a poem. It's the difference between instruction and experience, between being told about something and being immersed in it. Wilbur has won from the world some convincing and convinced moral conclusions; the danger is that he may use the world's things as texts for his treatises. Sometimes there is that sense of pulling back—particularly at the end of a poem, if not in the fundamental arrangements made with the material through the initial choices of metaphor. As one critic said, at times Wilbur comes "close to denying raw events in the interests of a general truth"[28]—although his descriptions are so fertile that the effects are usually minimized.

It's in reaction to this, I think, that Wilbur's critics have often wished he would take greater risks.

> The truth is that Mr. Wilbur has never allowed his gifts the freedom they deserve . . . . His brilliant descriptive powers are never stretched so far as to indulge the poet at the risk of tiring the reader. Perhaps they might be.[29]

The critics seem to ask that Wilbur venture out beyond his usual borders. It's not, of course, advice which one can simply follow or not. If such indulgence would mean for Wilbur the kind of imaginative negation of reality that he finds abhorrent, he can't be so untrue to himself. "What I must not do," Wilbur once wrote, "is to attempt a manner which might satisfy my critics; there is nothing to do in art but to persevere hopefully in one's peculiarities."[30]

But one *can* see stylistic changes in Wilbur's work. Over the years he has shifted his attention from the "ironic meditative lyric" to the dramatic poem, a movement toward a more direct, freer expression of feeling.[31] And both he and his critics recognize that his style has grown simpler, less ornate with each volume of poetry. Wilbur says that the greater decorativeness of his early work was often a result of pure exuberance, although, he admits, those poems "may at moments have taken refuge from events in language itself—in wordplay, in the coinage of new words, in a certain preciosity."[32]

There are those who regret what they see as the loss of Wilbur's early lushness.[33] But others find that Wilbur's work has emerged from this process of simplification with a new strength, a roughness and sexuality that are evidence of deeper resolutions of subject matter.[34] I've talked earlier about the sense of reconciliation in Wilbur's later poems that is part of this development. Surely this is an important sign of growth. And there is also something to be said for pursuing the *difficulty* in one's work. It's necessary, as Robert Bly once said, to develop one's weak functions and not to lean wholly on the stronger. Wilbur may have felt it as necessary to struggle *against* the abundance of his linguistic gifts as to indulge them (as his comment about his early preciosity indicates). It's the struggle to speak the truth always more clearly and cleanly. Everything must be sacrificed to it.

> . . . When I was putting down those simple lines—lines like "It is always a matter, my darling, of life or death, as I had forgotten"—I was excited by their very simplicity.[35]

Nonetheless, it's a discussion of Wilbur's linguistic genius that I'd like to end with—because it is unrivaled. And to understand Richard Wilbur's place in his generation is to praise his music.

Musicality is, I think, something of a lost value in contemporary American poetry. First, it's been lost through the fear of poeticizing, the wish to make the language of poetry real and not genteel or superfluous. Various poets in the past several decades, from William Carlos Williams to Robert Bly, have hailed the death of traditional forms, declaring them not only boring but possibly dangerous. These antiformalist statements arise naturally from the Romantic, Wordsworthian idea that poetry should embrace the ordinary modes of language. The process of demystification has been a healthy and historically logical development in literature throughout the past century: the poet has rejected traditional formal restraints to find a greater range in subject and expression.

Perhaps another reason for the de-emphasis on the formal properties of our language has been the great interest in translations over the past several decades. Magazines like *The Fifties, The Sixties,* and *The Seventies* from Bly, and later (despite its name) *The American Poetry Review,* have devoted a large proportion of their contents to the work of foreign-language poets. There is no question of the vitality of the influence this has had on American writers: the introduction to great voices and to new vocabularies of psychic and political experience. (Wilbur himself is recognized as one of the finest living translators, his sensitivity to linguistic nuance unsurpassed.) But another result of the translation boom has been the importation of a surrealist mode into American poetry of the sixties and seventies. If the typical poem of the fifties literary journal was the well-made poem, in the late sixties and seventies it was the well-dreamt poem. As Bly himself described it, writing for *Kayak* magazine about that magazine, "as long as there are a few skeletons of fossil plants . . . or some horses floating in the mind, or a flea whispering in Norwegian, in it goes!"[36] (The confessional poem also typical of the era often incorporates such surrealist elements.)

I don't want to deny the emergence during this period of fine surrealist talents. What I want to point out is a general effect of the increased interest in translated poetry. I think much of the original poetry published during this time is written in a kind of "translation language." Since even the best-translated poem has to do not with the special properties of the English language but with those of another language, this means that the poem written in translation language has no interest in *sound* and therefore none of the intimacy between sound and meaning which is the particular mystery of poetry.

A term like *onomatopoeia* only suggests this powerful mystery. Like the term *alliteration, onomatopoeia* refers to the principle of repetition. And repetition—or, repetition-and-variation—is of the deep structure of things. (Variation recalls its complement and so is itself a reminder of the repetition principle.) It is characteristic of the probabilities of the outer universe as well as of the motions of the psyche, of inner psychological space. In poetry, word repeats world (*onomatopoeia*) and word recalls word (*alliteration*). Richard Wilbur is a poet wonderfully sensitive to this echoic fabric. His poems constantly conjure mirages of the world:

> Tables and earth were riding
>
> Back and forth in the minting shade of the trees.
> There were whiffs of anise, a clear clinking
> Of coins and glasses, a still crepitant sound
> Of the earth in the garden drinking
>
> The late rain . . .
>
> "Part Of A Letter"

An analysis of the crisp minting of that scene—of how the vaporous puff of the short *i* ("whiffs of anise") is quickly toned between consonants to a finer vibration (*clinking, still, drinking*)—must be as tentative as a discussion of the meaning of music. Yet in both cases it is world repetition which is performed. Plato observed that if the laws of music change, the laws of society must also; this is true because music (musical law) reiterates the structure of reality. That is, music is simply the playing out of the laws of the things of the world.

In the process of freeing poetry of those formal habits which may have become ossified, we can't afford to forget: poetry is still and always about this, about medium, about *language,* as much as it's about anything else. And, further: this doesn't limit poetry, doesn't make it merely fabulous. On the contrary. Our sense of language and our sense of reality are inextricably bound. This is the great mystery and joy of writing.

Not surprisingly, this mystery has always been at the heart of Richard Wilbur's work. He writes *about* it as well as *from* it: the interaction of the self, as it learns to see, to know, to love—that is, to write—the reality that both forms the self and is formed by it. (This is also the paradox that twentieth-century physics teaches us: reality is only what we know of reality, therefore reality is *how* we know it.)

One of Wilbur's poems is called "Lamarck Elaborated" and bears the epigraph, "The environment creates the organ."

> It was the song of doves begot the ear
> And not the ear that first conceived of sound:
> That organ bloomed in vibrant atmosphere,
> As music conjured Ilium from the ground.
>
> The yielding water, the repugnant stone,
> The poisoned berry and the flaring rose
> Attired in sense the tactless finger-bone
> And set the taste-buds and inspired the nose.

It's easy to see from this that the word-and-world correspondence in Wilbur's poetry is a manifestation of the intimate connection he sees between self and world. His linguistic sensitivities correspond to his moral vision. ("Lamarck Elaborated" doesn't *effect* the linguistic correlation so well as other Wilbur poems, but it is a clear description of the principle which operates implicitly in other poems.) In Wilbur's work the self is understood through the world; the world evokes the self. The self encounters itself by first conjuring the world. Remembering Wilbur's use of the rain-dance metaphor, we see that *he* is not the world, but his medium is the articulation of his relation *to* the world.

It's this that connects love of nature with love of language in such a poem as "Advice to a Prophet." Human existence is only conceivable in the language of the natural world, the poem says. The death of that world would mean the loss of the images, the words ("lofty," "longstanding") through which we imagine ourselves. The final, urgent plea of "Advice to a Prophet" is that we not destroy *vocabulary*! Wilbur's most moving political poem is at its heart about language.

Of course. Language is for Wilbur scarcely a superfluous matter. It is "re-creative," Bruce Michelson says (see pp. 265–81). Wilbur's craft is his mantra, evoking the deity it embodies. Its properties are holy. To neglect any of the functions of language would be to lessen the efficacy of that mantra. Thus: the consummate craftsman, the master worshipper. Language is his most sensitive receptor; through it, he receives and interprets the world.

John Ciardi (pp. 52–56) explains Wilbur's gift for physical description, for conjuring world with word, by saying that in the poetry, "physical punctualities are precisely *that which is thought with*." Wilbur's metaphors are "physically suggestive yet alive with idea." There is a congruence of the physical and the mental worlds. Idea and meaning are of the same texture as the physical; they arise with or from a sense of it.

Wilbur is so impressible. In the least shift of real air he records overtones of consonant and vowel which in turn intone a series of their own suggestions:

> The balked water tossed its froth. . . .
> > "Thyme Flowering Among Rocks"

> . . . the sound of rim-struck stones.
> > "The Agent"

> Backtrack of sea, the baywater goes; flats
> Bubble in sunlight, running with herringbone streams;
> Sea-lettuce lies in oily mats. . . .
> > "Conjuration"

As one critic noticed of Wilbur's use of assonance, a sound may linger "like a silent third in music" throughout a line:[37]

> . . . as the slightest shade of you
> Valleys my mind in fabulous blue Lucernes.
> > "The Beautiful Changes"

Rhyme, which in its purest state is repetition, is the affinity of thing for thing (in the universe). The true "rhymer" has a vision which says: "only connect."

The physical, of course, is not simply aural in Wilbur's poems. As Babette Deutsch (using a term of Joyce's) pointed out, Wilbur is "ear-sighted."[38] Ear sense and eye sense are scarcely distinguishable. Such synesthesia is not surprising in so reciprocal a universe as Wilbur's where sensation animates idea. Sound is light-producing; image is an evocative concurrence:

> . . . the ping-pong balls
> Scatter their hollow knocks
> Like crazy clocks.
> > "My Father Paints the Summer"

> The packet's smooth approach, the slip,
> Slip of the silken river past the sides. . . .
> > "A Simile for Her Smile"

> Gold ranks of temples flank the dazzled street.
> > "October Maples, Portland"

To Wilbur's ear for sonorities is added a supple rhythmic sense. Anthony Hecht (pp. 123–31) calls Wilbur's poetry kinetic. Wilbur is not dominated by form; form becomes sensitive in his hands.

> But for a brief
> Moment, a poised minute,
> He paused on the chicory leaf;
> Yet within it

> The sprung perch
> Had time to absorb the shock,
> Narrow its pitch and lurch,
> Cease to rock.
> > "A Grasshopper"

> The woodlands are morose and reek of punk,
> These gobbets grow—
> Tongue, lobe, hand, hoof or butchered toe
> Amassing on the fallen branch half-sunk
> In leaf-mold, or the riddled trunk.
> > "Children of Darkness"

It's been suggested, in fact, that in his poems Wilbur has been able to revive a rhythmic subtlety that was lost when the iambic foot began to dominate and finally, at the end of the nineteenth century, to tyrannize American poetry.[39] And Ciardi credits Wilbur with a further reanimation of the language by pointing out that "the Latin root sense . . . shines through so much of Wilbur's diction." His language reverberates to the level of primary meanings. His wordplay—as Michelson explains—is serious business, uniting through its connotative range the realm of the diverse with the transcendent. He gives us a fundamental sense of the functions of language, of the full range of harmonies possible. He restores full responsiveness to the instrument.

A more responsive instrument is capable of a greater range of observation as well as thought and feeling. Deutsch once pointed out, for example, that Wilbur's rhythmic sense is not only physical but also theological.[40] In his poems, bird's nest, juggling balls, milkweed pods, a sunhat, the imagination of a mind-reader—all are "risk-hallowed" with the impulse toward transformation which is essential to him.

He has always been praised for his virtuosity but too often praised and *dismissed* because of it. This is a mistake. In the best poems, Wilbur's virtuosity is one with his vision. It is a function of intimacy, not formalism. As it should be. For, language is the profound expression of our relation to reality. Its subtleties are holy, not precious. Even as we work as poets to liberate the deepest mysteries of the psyche, we will encounter language: in the *expression* of the psyche. (Interestingly, despite his protests against poems that are to him "crystallized flower formations,"[41] Bly, and other "deep image" poets, don't pursue a more realistic, proletarian verse. They are interested in a suprareality, the unconscious, which can be summoned only by an indirect, magical language.) From the deepest levels of the unconscious what we will emerge with is diastole and systole, the dilation and delay of the vowel, the concentration of the consonant. I think, in fact, we can't have a native surrealist idiom except through a deep grasp of the workings of our own language, reaching to the primitive level where nonmeaning becomes meaning, where guttural becomes vocable and reverberates upward with the transformations of the unconscious.

We can't afford to undervalue the *bel canto* of our language.

Richard Wilbur justly has been called a poet's poet,[42] the Mozart of his generation,[43] because he wakens the language. And language is all we can "say" about reality. We can only intimate. Truth can only be embodied in parable. Metaphor, the physicists tell us, is what we know. Poetry is "refined" language because it's the purest form of that intimation. It is, in this way, the sense of language speaking to itself.

This survey of the critical response Wilbur's work has received is organized chronologically. Part 1, "Under Review," contains a representative sampling of the reviews that followed the publication of each of Wilbur's volumes of poetry—through *The Mind-Reader* (1976). A review of Wilbur's children's book, *Opposites,* and a review of *Responses—Prose Pieces: 1953–1976* (which offers comment on the poetry) are also included here. In part 2, the "Under Discussion" section, the articles examine particular critical issues involved in Wilbur's artistic development through the decades. Since his gifts as a translator are highly regarded and since they bear upon the development of his original verse, I have included in this section an article on Wilbur's translation work.

The selection of reviews and essays is biased to the extent that I am interested in those critics who have enough sympathy with Wilbur's work to offer access to its subtleties. Yet I have tried to give a place to dissenting voices as well, particularly to those whose themes have been repeated over the years.

I am indebted to Dr. Jack W. C. Hagstrom for generously providing me with his extensive Wilbur bibliography—an invaluable aid to my work; to Patricia Collins for her time and trouble in reproducing those materials; and to Donald Hall for his unfailing support and counsel.

NOTES

1. Donald Hall, "American Poets Since the War," part 1, *World Review,* n.s. 41 (December 1952): 31.

2. Richard Wilbur, "On My Own Work," *Responses—Prose Pieces: 1953–1976* (New York: Harcourt Brace Jovanovich, 1976), pp. 118–19.

3. See Francis W. Warlow, "Richard Wilbur," *Bucknell Review* 7 (May 1958): 217–33.

4. Wilbur, "On My Own Work," *Responses,* p. 118.

5. Wilbur, quoted in Paul F. Cummins, *Richard Wilbur—A Critical Essay* (Grand Rapids, Mich.: Eerdmans, 1971), p. 8.

6. Quoted in Cummins, p. 39.

7. William Dickey, "A Place In The Country," *The Hudson Review* 22 (Summer 1969): 347.

8. Donald Hall, "The New Poetry: Notes on the Past Fifteen Years in America," *New World Writing* (New York: New American Library, 1955), p. 242.

9. Babette Deutsch, *Poetry in Our Time* (Garden City, N.Y.: Doubleday, Anchor, 1963), p. 283.

10. Wilbur, "On My Own Work," *Responses,* p. 123.

11. Wilbur, "'Sumptuous Destitution,'" *Responses,* p. 11.

12. David Daiches, "The Anglo-American Difference: Two Views," part 2, *The Anchor Review,* no. 1 (Garden City, N.Y.: Doubleday, 1955), p. 232.

13. Wilbur, "On My Own Work," *Responses,* p. 116. "There are risks of corruption . . . in becoming a poet-citizen rather than an alienated artist, but I myself would consider them risks well taken, because it seems to me that poetry is sterile unless it arises from a sense of community or, at least, from the hope of community."

14. Wilbur, "The Bottles Become New, Too," *Responses,* p. 217.

15. Leslie Fiedler, "A Kind of Solution: The Situation of Poetry Now," *The Kenyon Review* 26 (Winter 1964): 54.

16. Donald Hall, "Introduction," in his *Contemporary American Poetry* (Baltimore: Penguin, 1962), p. 20.

17. Donald Hall, "The New Poetry," p. 242: "When suffering is a subject in a Wilbur poem, it is understood and discussed, not presented in the act. Robert Lowell's poems often seem to have been squeezed out of him, foot by foot, by the pressure of his suffering."

18. See A. Poulin, Jr., "Contemporary American Poetry: The Radical Tradition," *Contemporary American Poetry* (Boston: Houghton Mifflin, 1975), p. 391.

19. Wilbur, "The Bottles," *Responses,* p. 219.

20. Ibid.

21. Ibid., p. 220.

22. Edgar Bogardus, "The Flights of Love," *The Kenyon Review* 19 (Winter 1957): 143.

23. See Mary S. Mattfield, "Some Poems of Richard Wilbur," *Ball State University Forum* 11 (Summer 1970): 10.

24. Wilbur, "Poetry's Debt to Poetry," *Responses,* p. 171.

25. Victor Contoski, untitled review of *The Mind-Reader, The Denver Quarterly* 13 (Summer 1978): 156.

26. Donald Hill, *Richard Wilbur* (New York: Twayne, 1967), p. 21.

27. Gerald Reedy, S. J., "The Senses of Richard Wilbur," *Renascence* 21 (Spring 1969): 145.

28. Karl Malkoff, "Richard Wilbur," *Crowell's Handbook of Contemporary American Poetry* (New York: Crowell, 1973), p. 327.

29. "In Search of An Audience," anonymous review of *Walking to Sleep* and other books of poetry, *The Times Literary Supplement,* no. 3612 (May 21, 1971): 580.

30. Wilbur in *The Contemporary Poet as Artist and Critic,* ed. Anthony Ostroff (Boston: Little, Brown, 1964), p. 20.

31. Wilbur, "On My Own Work," *Responses,* p. 118.

32. Ibid. See also Wilbur in Ostroff, p. 187.

33. See J. D. McClatchy, "Dialects of the Tribe," *Poetry* 130 (April 1977): 41–53.

34. See Bruce Michelson, "Richard Wilbur's *The Mind-Reader,*" *The Southern Review* 15 (July 1979): 763–68. Reprinted here.

35. Wilbur, "The Art of Poetry," *Paris Review* 19 (Winter 1977): 83.

36. Robert Bly, "The First Ten Issues of *Kayak,*" *Kayak,* no. 12 (1967): 46.

37. J. W. Lambert, "A Songster in the Wilderness," *The Sunday Times* (London), July 17, 1977, p. 40.

38. Babette Deutsch, pp. 346–47. According to Deutsch, Hopkins has influenced "those moderns who have what Joyce called 'an earsighted view of things.'"

39. James G. Southworth, "The Poetry of Richard Wilbur," *College English* 22 (October 1960): 25.

40. Deutsch, p. 347.

41. Bly, p. 47.

42. George Greene, "Four Campus Poets," *Thought* 35 (Summer 1960): 227.

43. Victor Howes, "Cool Crystals from Wilbur," *The Christian Science Monitor,* July 31, 1969, p. 11.

BIBLIOGRAPHY

Bly, Robert. "The First Ten Issues of Kayak." *Kayak,* no. 12 (1967): 45–49.

Bogardus, Edgar. "The Flights of Love." *The Kenyon Review* 19 (Winter 1957):137–44.

Contoski, Victor. "Review." *Denver Quarterly* 13 (Summer 1978): 156–57.

Cummins, Paul F. *Richard Wilbur—A Critical Essay*. Grand Rapids, Mich.: Eerdmans, 1971.

Daiches, David. "The Anglo-American Difference: Two Views," part 2. In *The Anchor Review*, no. 1, edited by Melvin J. Lasky, pp. 219–33. Garden City, N.Y.: Doubleday, 1955.

Deutsch, Babette. *Poetry in Our Time*. Garden City, N.Y.: Doubleday, Anchor, 1963.

Dickey, William. "A Place in the Country." *The Hudson Review* 22 (Summer 1969):347–68.

Fiedler, Leslie A. "A Kind of Solution: The Situation of Poetry Now." *The Kenyon Review* 26 (Winter 1964):54–79.

Foster, Richard. "Debauch by Craft: Problems of the Younger Poets." *Perspective* 12 (Spring–Summer 1960):3–17.

Greene, George. "Four Campus Poets." *Thought* 35 (Summer 1960):223–46.

Gregory, Horace. "The Poetry of Suburbia." *The Partisan Review* 23 (Fall 1956):545–53.

Hall, Donald. "Ah, Love, Let Us Be True: Domesticity and History in Contemporary Poetry." *The American Scholar* 28 (Summer 1959):310–19.

———. "American Poets Since the War," part 1. *World Review*, n.s. 46 (December 1952):28–32.

———. "American Poets Since the War," part 2. *World Review*, n.s. 47 (January 1953):48–54.

———. "Claims on the Poet." *Poetry* 88 (September 1956):398–403. (Reprinted here.)

———. "Introduction." In *Contemporary American Poetry*, edited by Donald Hall, pp. 17–26. Baltimore: Penguin, 1962.

———. "The New Poetry: Notes on the Past Fifteen Years in America." In *New World Writing*, pp. 231–47. New York: New American Library, 1955.

Hill, Donald L. *Richard Wilbur*. New York: Twayne, 1967.

Howes, Victor. "Cool Crystals from Wilbur." *The Christian Science Monitor*, July 31, 1969, p. 11.

"In Search of an Audience." *Times Literary Supplement*, no. 3612 (May 21, 1971):580.

Jarrell, Randall. "Fifty Years of American Poetry." *Prairie Schooner* 37

(Spring 1963):1–27. Reprinted in his *Third Book of Criticism*. New York: Farrar, Straus and Giroux, 1969.

Lambert, J. W. "A Songster in the Wilderness." *The Sunday Times* (London), July 17, 1977, p. 40.

Malkoff, Karl. "Richard Wilbur." In *Crowell's Handbook of Contemporary American Poetry,* pp. 325–31. New York: Crowell, 1973.

Mattfield, Mary S. "Some Poems of Richard Wilbur." *Ball State University Forum* 11 (Summer 1970):10–24.

McClatchy, J. D. "Dialects of the Tribe." *Poetry* 130 (April 1977): 41–53.

Michelson, Bruce. "Richard Wilbur's *The Mind-Reader*." *The Southern Review* 15 (July 1979):763–68. (Reprinted here.)

Ostroff, Anthony. *The Contemporary Poet as Artist and Critic,* pp. 2–21. Boston: Little, Brown, 1964.

Packard, William, ed. *The Craft of Poetry: Interviews from the New York Quarterly*. New York: Doubleday, 1974.

Poulin, A., Jr. "Contemporary American Poetry: The Radical Tradition." In his *Contemporary American Poetry,* pp. 459–73. Boston: Houghton Mifflin, 1975.

Reedy, Gerald, S. J. "The Senses of Richard Wilbur." *Renascence* 21 (Spring 1969):145–50.

Rosenthal, M. L. "Speak the Whole Mind." *New York Herald Tribune Books,* March 21, 1948, p. 8. (Reprinted here.)

———. "An Unfair Question." *The Reporter* 26 (February 15, 1962):48, 50–51.

Southworth, James G. "The Poetry of Richard Wilbur." *College English* 22 (October 1960):24–29.

Stauffer, Donald Barlow. *A Short History of American Poetry*. New York: Dutton, 1974.

Summers, Joseph H. "Richard (Purdy) Wilbur." In *Great Writers of the English Language,* edited by James Vinson, pp. 1075–77. New York: St. Martin's Press, 1979.

Taylor, Henry. "Two Worlds Taken as They Come: Richard Wilbur's *Walking to Sleep*." *The Hollins Critic* 6 (July 1969):1–12. (Reprinted here.)

Warlow, Francis W. "Richard Wilbur." *Bucknell Review* 7 (May 1958):217–33.

Wilbur, Richard. *Advice to a Prophet and Other Poems*. New York: Harcourt, Brace & World, 1961.

———. "The Art of Poetry," an interview by P. Still, E. C. High, and H. M. Ellison. *Paris Review* 19 (Winter 1977):69–105.

_____. *The Beautiful Changes and Other Poems*. New York: Reynal & Hitchcock, 1947.

_____. *Ceremony and Other Poems*. New York: Harcourt Brace, 1950.

_____. *The Mind-Reader*. New York: Harcourt Brace Jovanovich, 1976.

_____. *Opposites*. New York: Harcourt Brace Jovanovich, 1973.

_____. *Responses—Prose Pieces: 1953–1976*. New York: Harcourt Brace Jovanovich, 1976.

_____. *Things of This World*. New York: Harcourt Brace, 1956.

_____. *Walking to Sleep—New Poems and Translations*. New York: Harcourt, Brace & World, 1969.

PART ONE *Under Review*

THE BEAUTIFUL CHANGES
AND OTHER POEMS
1947

LOUISE BOGAN

From "Verse"

What is now called the war generation continues to turn out poetry, and although some of its productions, taken singly, are rather inconsiderable, the over-all effect is interesting. This new and crucial age group is again appearing in numbers; we now have a larger basis for comparing these poets with their elders, and with each other. This review will deal with four of these young writers and one slightly older one.

The youngest, Richard Wilbur, is twenty-six. His publishers have felt impelled to use the words "romantic" and "emotional" in describing his volume of verse, *The Beautiful Changes* (Reynal & Hitchcock), and they are quite right; in the best senses of these words, it is both. Wilbur is still quite plainly entangled with the technical equipment of his favorite poetic forerunners, specifically Marianne Moore, Eliot, Rilke, and Hopkins, from whose work he has pretty well absorbed certain lessons. He has had the wit, however, to point up these influences from time to time with the invisible quotation marks of near-parody. Wilbur surpasses the majority of his contemporaries in range of imaginative reference and depth of feeling. He has a remarkable variety of interest and mood, and he can contemplate his subjects without nervousness, explore them with care, and then let them drop at the exact moment that the organization of a poem is complete. This ease of pace, this seemingly effortless advance to a resolute conclusion, is rare at his age; the young usually yield to tempting inflation and elaboration. Wilbur's gift of fitting the poetic pattern to the material involves all sorts of delicate adjustments of

The New Yorker, November 15, 1947, pp. 130, 133–34. Other poets reviewed in the article: Howard Nemerov, *The Image and The Law* (Holt); William Jay Smith, *Poems* (Banyan Press); John Ciardi, *Other Skies* (Little, Brown); Karl Shapiro, *Trial of a Poet* (Reynal & Hitchcock).

the outward senses to the inner ear. Fidelity to Nature (that old-fashioned virtue) underlies every word, and this fidelity is directed by intelligence and taste. Wilbur is a talent so sure of its bases that using the despised words "the beautiful," which he employs not as an adjective but as a noun in his title, does not harm it in the least. Let us watch Richard Wilbur. He is composed of valid ingredients.

F. C. GOLFFING

A Remarkable New Talent

This first book of verse by a young poet is a very remarkable if not entirely satisfying job of work. Mr. Wilbur too often spoils his chances by concessions to modishness ("on heilignüchterne lakes of memory"—a gratuitous loan from Hölderlin, quite meaningless in the context; "legerty begs no quarter"; the whole of "Water Walker") and by attempts at genres that are outside his range ("The Regatta," "Superiorities"). It seems a pity, for his range is sufficiently wide, his craftsmanship sufficiently fine, to secure him serious attention within his proper competence. He apprehends sharply and justly; his metrical structures are often of great beauty; his diction combines cleanness with elegance. But he lacks wit and, when tapping the lighter vein, is capable of jejuneness such as this:

> The hotel guests make joking bets,
> And Mrs. Vane has turned, inquired
> If Mr. Vane is feeling "tired."
> He means to answer, but forgets.

Wit of the kind he is aiming at—the Swiftian or Eliotesque kind—demands more intellectual incisiveness and emotional "blackness" than Mr. Wilbur is at present able to muster. His true domain is the borderland between natural and moral perception, his special gift for the genteel, non-metaphysical conceit which illuminates the hidden correspondences between natural and moral phenomena. Characteristically, two of Mr. Wilbur's favorite devices stem from Marianne Moore: the lingering over minute particulars and the sudden introduction of anecdotal units into straight narrative or meditative sequences, e.g.—

Poetry 71 (January 1948):221–23.

> This thin uncomprehended song it is
> springs healing questions into binding air
> *Fabre, by firing all the municipal cannon*
> *under a piping tree, found out*
> *cigales cannot hear*[1]

where the "anecdote," so far from merely winding up the poem, both climaxes and clinches it. (Compare Miss Moore's use of the *terminal* anecdote in such poems as "The Monkeys" and "Light is Speech.")

There is yet another point of contact with Marianne Moore: the main interest of Mr. Wilbur's verse lies in the progressions, which are quick, subtle, seemingly inconsequent and, in nine cases out of ten, right. A good example of his method is "Grace," a set of variations on a theme by Hopkins, where the discourse shifts from the notion of naive animal grace to that of routine nimbleness, bordering on legerdemain, thence to the scholar's halting grace-in-awkwardness and alights, finally, on the paradox of graceful reserve—the minimum holding back—in rapid action.

The most successful pieces in this book are "Bell Speech"; "Poplar, Sycamore"; "Cigales"; "For Ellen"; "Grace" and "The Beautiful Changes"—the last two as good as any poetry written in English today, save Eliot and Stevens at their best.

NOTE

1. The emphasis is Golffing's. —Ed.

M. L. ROSENTHAL

From "Speak the Whole Mind"

"The beautiful," writes Richard Wilbur in his title poem, "changes as a forest is changed / By a chameleon's tuning his skin to it; / As a mantis, arranged / On a green leaf, grows / Into it, makes the leaf leafier, and proves / Any greenness is deeper than anyone knows." This is to be Marianne Moore's "literalist of the imagination," and also to be "influenced" without being overwhelmed by the master. Richard Wilbur learns from many, but in the manner of the true original who seeks to master all techniques which will help him say just what he wants to on any level. The art of deliberately juxtaposing images of diverse connotation and clashing rhythms has been carefully studied. It can be used subtly, as in the poem that develops the theme that war "hits childhood more than churches" or in the one that describes with Imagist precision the first snow of an Alsace winter, yet finds time to note how "this snowfall fills the eyes / Of soldiers dead a little while." It can turn a simple impression of evening in the Place Pigalle, where "the soldiers come, the boys with ancient faces, / Seeking their ancient friends," into one of those romantic outbursts of Pound's which loose a flood of light on past and present. In short, Wilbur is one of those rare poets who not only can think in verse but who are also a pure joy to read. The promise is part of the pleasure, and he should soon strike out on new and independent paths.

The New York Herald Tribune Books, March 21, 1948, p. 8. Other poets reviewed in the article: John Ciardi, *Other Skies* (Little, Brown); Conrad Aiken, *The Kid* (Duell, Sloan and Pearce).

CEREMONY AND OTHER POEMS
1950

BABETTE DEUTSCH

Scenes Alive with Light

Here, as in Richard Wilbur's earlier book, are the landscapes, the seascapes and the interiors, the vistas and the intimacies that render tolerable our duller and more cruel hours. Beyond that, these pages give the pleasure that shines wherever one remarks a draftsman in control of his material.

Some of these poems are pieces of pure gaiety, some present uncrossed felicity. Most of them are about gratifying objects. All of them are charged with responsiveness to the lusters, the tones, of the physical world, and show the poet alert to less apparent matters. The scenes are alive with light, be it the light coined by "the minting shade of the trees" that shines on clinking glasses and laughing eyes, or one of a wintrier brightness. They shiver and sway happily with the sound of winds and waters. Yet they are apt to close upon a somber chord, to admit an intrusive shadow.

The lyric called "Part of a Letter," with its luminous evocation of a golden moment, confronts "The Pardon," which gravely contrasts the boy's and the man's attitude toward the death of a dog. Similarly, upon so slight an incident as "The Death of a Toad," Mr. Wilbur builds a deeply felt, skillfully managed lyric. He has said that Herrick and Milton stand equally high in his Pantheon. He too can make enchanting music on a small theme, and he handles it with greater subtlety than was possible to the royalist vicar. If he cannot compass the grandeur of the republican poet, his lyrics show a finer moral fiber. The pleased twinkle with which he greets music-box tunes does not contradict his sense of the fact that

The New York Times Book Review, February 11, 1951, p. 12.

> No tinkling music-box can play
> The slow, deep-grounded masses of the year.

Presumably "Ceremony," far from the finest piece in the book, was chosen as the title poem because it states the poet's preference for form and design, for that which defines the limits of a work of art, declares its artificiality, and invites the ingenuity of the artist. As he observed in his preface to the poems recently anthologized in *Mid-Century American Poets*: ". . . the strength of the genie comes of his being confined in a bottle."[1]

Mr. Wilbur's bottles, whether clear or colored, are well wrought. Only elaborate analysis could show how admirable his workmanship is: the sweats of labor have been rubbed from the polished glass. The genie is a friendly one. In one or two poems, notably "Still, Citizen Sparrow," there are unaccountable shifts. Yet, with the fewest exceptions, matter and manner are on the right terms, texture and tenor knit as flesh and bone.

Mr. Wilbur manipulates his cadences, his consonants and vowels, his rhymes and assonances, with musicianly skill. His imagery is original without being offensively obtrusive. A happy instance is "A Simile for Her Smile." It is a tribute to this lyric, as to ampler ones, such as "Castles and Distances" or the memorable poem on a phrase of Traherne's, that they should not be paraphrased. Here is poetry to be read with the eye, the ear, the heart and the mind.

NOTE

1. John Ciardi, ed., *Mid-Century American Poets* (New York: Twayne, 1950).

JOSEPH BENNETT

From "Five Books, Four Poets"

Richard Wilbur's book *Ceremony* must be criticized with reference to the highest and most exacting standards. His work is
rounded and mature, and to deal with it merely by compliment
and compromise while reserving more difficult judgments,
would be to render the poet an injustice. Mr. Wilbur has stature.

But he does not have enough ambition. The work is graceful,
golden-tongued, sweet, even, and smooth. But much of it lacks
vigor and force, is loose and merely cordial. There are a dozen
very fine poems in this book. The rest suffer from facility and
most of all from *flaccidity*. Mr. Wilbur writes too much and he
writes too rapidly; one has the feeling that everything he writes
'gets printed'; that he has many topics and poems about all of
them. There is much talent here, much native instinctive grace
with language; and much laziness.

Mr. Wilbur allows himself to be precious, "the too amenable
sea"; to be sloppy, "receding fingers terribly tell"; to be meaningless, "on the brink / Of absence" "absence mopes"; to be
insipid, "from a gunmetal bay / No one would dream of
drowning in." He has a 'conversational tone' that is lifeless,
"And I've known / The sea so rich and black / It gave the
starlight back / Brighter." His rhetoric is often gassy and 'put-
on'; it is often an 'added touch,' not arising spontaneous from
the exuberance of the occasion, "To shake our gravity up.
Whee, in the air" "O false gemmation! Flashy fall!" He allows
himself to be sentimental, with a stilted, off-key pathos ("The
Pardon"), with a mushy, screechy 'moral,' as when he ruins the

The Hudson Review 4 (Spring 1951):131–45. Other poets reviewed in the article:
Carl Sandburg, *Complete Poems* (Harcourt Brace); Wallace Stevens, *The Auroras
of Autumn* (Knopf); Delmore Schwartz, *Vaudeville for a Princess* (New Directions); James Merrill, *First Poems* (Knopf).

delicate Persian decoration of "Marché aux Oiseaux." 'Important subject matter' becomes, as always, an excuse for slipshod workmanship and technical mediocrities. He can let his ear go flat from time to time ("Conjuration," "Part Of A Letter") and his epigrams and parables are labored and cute. He can be very unfunny ("Museum Piece").

There is no excuse for this. Mr. Wilbur has the ear, the technique, and the intelligence to be satisfied with nothing less than perfection. In one of lesser gifts one would be content merely to praise the praisable and pass over the rest. If Mr. Wilbur had left out two-thirds of this book and published a pamphlet instead, we would have a work of sustained brilliance, verve, and sophistication:

> Here luxury's the common lot. The light
> Lies on the rain-pocked rocks like yellow wool
> And around the rocks the soil is rusty bright
> From too much wealth of water, so that the grass
> Mashes under the foot, and all is full
> Of heat and juice and a heavy jammed excess.
>
> Whatever moves moves with the slow complete
> Gestures of statuary. Flower smells
> Are set in the golden day, and shelled in heat,
> Pine and columnar cypress stand. The palm
> Sinks its combs in the sky. This whole South swells
> To a soft rigor, a rich and crowded calm. . . .
>
> Even when seen from near, the olive shows
> A hue of far away. Perhaps for this
> The dove brought olive back, a tree which grows
> Unearthly pale, which ever dims and dries,
> And whose great thirst, exceeding all excess,
> Teaches the South it is not paradise.

These are the first two and the last stanzas of "Grasse: The Olive Trees," a poem which is without flaw. There is no flaccidity here. The rhythms are exact, the timing faultless; the language vivid, profuse and carefully disciplined; it is very full-throated and moves with measured ease and amplitude. The imagery is sharp-edged, of remarkable clarity; the mind moves with the tongue; and the poem is allowed to end itself in a blaze of dramatic utterance of the first magnitude.

"Year's End" with its "great mammoths" is a precise and brilliant thing, marred by a forced conclusion, a stanza which tries to point up an 'important statement,' when all that is needed is to let the poem exfoliate from the lines of progression already established. "The Avowal" is deft and elegant. "Five Women Bathing" is an unblemished complex of modulated, serene and subtle observation:

> The bathers whitely come and stand.
> Water diffuses them, their hair
> Like seaweed slurs the shoulders, and
> Their voices in the moonstrung air
>
> Go plucked of words.

In "The Terrace," a Monet piece, the purest, most unblushing strains of impressionism are marred with another forced conclusion. "A Glance from the Bridge" is an exactly observed quiddity, tight, true, and clean, authoritatively executed, as are "A Simile for Her Smile," equally brilliant, and "The Death of a Toad"—all three miraculously phrased and *constructed* down to the last syllable. If we overlook the word "poignancy," the poem entitled "Clearness" must also be ranked with Wilbur's best:

> when the snow for all its softness
> Tumbles in adamant forms, turning and turning
> Its perfect faces, littering on our sight
> The heirs and types of timeless dynasties.

This is language that, for all its delicacy, is durable, as Mr. Stevens' is durable. The poem ends with a curious and disturbing vision which partakes of the nature of a poetic charm.[1] "Beowulf" is so good that it compares with the *Poèmes Barbares* of Leconte de Lisle—the same sort of massive, rapt and thudding, yet rigorous, detachment:

> He died in his own country, a kinless king,
> A name heavy with deeds, and mourned as one
> Will mourn for the frozen year when it is done.
> They buried him next the sea on a thrust of land:
> Twelve men rode round his barrow all in a ring,
> Singing of him what they could understand.

Wilbur's is the strongest poetic talent I can see in America below the generation now in their fifties.

NOTE

1. This "fabulous town" is also in the north. The influence of Crane's "The Harbor Dawn" can be discerned in stanza four of Mr. Wilbur's poem.

REED WHITTEMORE

Verse

This is our animal issue (why shouldn't it be our animal issue?).
It is therefore fitting that I begin by mentioning Richard Wilbur's stake in the animal kingdom. In *Ceremony* appear crabs,
camels, dogs, cows, walrus, deer, toads, canaries, sparrows,
vultures, gulls, horses, mammoths, bees, larks and several unspecified birds and beasts. Dogs and sparrows have, I think, a
slight edge in numbers over the others, but morally the vulture's
strength is as the strength of ten. Camels err most; canaries
suffer most; toads and deer and walrus die best.

But I do not wish to give the impression that these poems are
about animals. And, though roses, olive trees, acacia trees, honeysuckle vines, pine trees and other trees and flowers appear, the
poems are not about trees and flowers. And, though the seasons
are mentioned a great deal, the poems are not about seasons. The
poems are not about people either. What are they about?

Ceremony? The title poem is about ceremony; Mr. Wilbur is
in favor of it and believes that Nature is still natural when it is to
advantage dressed. But the title poem is thematically misleading, since the rest of the poems are not—or at least not primarily—about ceremony.

They are about two or three of the world's familiar dilemmas

Furioso (Northfield, Minnesota) 6 (Spring 1951):80–82.

Reviewer's Note: "My complaint in the review—that the tradition had become a
profession—was a mild ironic dig at the traces of academia I found in Mr.
Wilbur's metaphysics back in 1951, and I confess that in 1982 I would be happy
to see traces of almost any metaphysics in contemporary poetry. Also, thirty
years incline me to wish to alter the tone of the review a bit. After thirty years
Ceremony still looks firm and elegant to me—a *successful* ceremony—and could I
live the review o'er I'd give that side of the book more credit" (Reed Whittemore, 1982).

which, as Howard Nemerov once suggested in an essay in this magazine,[1] may possibly be reduced to one:

> Now there is, I conceive, one duality that underlies a great deal of poetry, especially the kind of poetry that is called (aptly, I think) 'metaphysical': it is, in largest terms, the duality of the One and the Many. Metaphysical poetry is a poetry of the dilemma, and the dilemma which paradoxes and antitheses continually seek to display is the famous one at which all philosophies falter, the relation of the One with the Many, the leap by which infinity becomes finite, essence becomes existence; the commingling of the spirit with matter, the working of God in the world.

But I do not choose to make the great reduction here. Rather, let me very briefly summarize the dilemmas presented in a few of Mr. Wilbur's poems.

"La Rose des Vents." A poet and a lady argue, the former looking for immortality, the latter begging him to "Forsake those roses / Of the mind / And tend the true, / The mortal flower."

"Conjuration." The sea's double nature ("My double deep") is described: a place of pearls, a place of "muck and shell." When the tide goes out "dreams / Drain into morning shine, and the cheat is ended," but the poet, not satisfied with merely Wordsworth's light of common day, would have his pearl "rise, rise and brighten, wear clear air," or, in other words, become 'real' too.

"'A World Without Objects Is a Sensible Emptiness.'" The world of the mind or spirit is opposed to the material world, the former being like a desert and therefore full of heavenly mirages, the latter being no cheat but heaven indeed, "the spirit's right oasis."

"Castles and Distances." Those distant places of the mind "where harmlessly the hidden heart / Might hold creation whole," are opposed to the nearnesses of living where, paradoxically, in the midst of evil good emerges, in the act of cruelty mercy is found. Thus hunters "regret the beastly pain" while moviegoers watching a killing do not; and kingdoms fall "the deeper into tyranny" as their kings steal "through Ardens out to Eden isles apart."

Obviously in these poems Mr. Wilbur is saying that the ideal is to be found in the real, the essence in experience, God in the world; he is proposing an immanent, as opposed to a transcendental, principle of Being. He is, furthermore, similarly disposed toward the problem of the perpetuation of this Being, inclining toward immortalities of an earthly kind. Thus the gardener who dies in "He Was" is immortalized by "having planted a young orchard with so great care" that "the found voice of his buried hands / Rose in the sparrowy air," after the manner of the young man in Shakespeare's sonnets who is encouraged to breed; and "The Death of a Toad" is as much an occasion for reflection upon the agelessness of the venerable class of Amphibia as upon the death of the individual toad in question—the king is dead, long live the king.

It seems to me that upon all this at least two observations can be made safely: first, that Mr. Wilbur is writing within the familiar metaphysical pattern Mr. Nemerov has described, since he is insistent upon the miraculous "leap by which infinity becomes finite, essence becomes existence"; and second, and more narrowly, that he is using the traditional "paradoxes and antitheses" to do so. Indeed the literary tradition seems to me to be more important to him than the metaphysical pattern which (Mr. Nemerov says) underlies it. Perhaps I am wrong about this. Perhaps I am influenced by having read on the book's jacket that Mr. Wilbur is a teacher of English and therefore obliged to run through the tradition like a well-trained sprinter at least once, and maybe many times a year. For I am a teacher too, and, while I am not against the tradition, my reaction to it, unlike his, is increasingly one of suspicion—not suspicion of the metaphysicals who are safely in the tradition but of the writers in my own time who think that they are. It is in the sense that the tradition has become a profession that I am suspicious of it; and, suspicious as I am, I perhaps wrongly suspect Mr. Wilbur of being more attached to the forms and ceremonies of the metaphysical tradition than to the metaphysics of the tradition, of writing a book about Ceremony after all, and of writing it without regard for the problem of the validity of traditional ceremony in these here modern times.

But having said this I must at least partly retract it right away, for my suspicions are readily soothed by his book's special excellences, which have been described by the critics on the back jacket as "this ease of pace, this seemingly effortless advance to a resolute conclusion" (Louise Bogan), as "his freshening of the sense of life within a rigid metrical frame" (Robert Fitzgerald), as his extraordinary cleverness "in the handling of vocables" (Babette Deutsch), and so on. I am not up to another such statement, but I agree that the cleverness, the ease is there and I am genuinely impressed. Also, to contradict my previous position, I do not believe that the rhetorical qualities of which these critics speak can be separated from the metaphysical patterns of which I am suspicious:

> Sometimes, as one can see
> Carved at Amboise in a high relief, on the lintel stone
> Of the castle chapel, hunters have strangely come
> To a mild close of the chase, bending the knee
> Instead of the bow, struck sweetly dumb
> To see from the brow bone
>
> Of the hounded stag a cross
> Grown, and the eyes clear with grace. . . .

Clearly the firmness of this verse is largely attributable to the matter, to the order inherent in the neat antithesis between knee and bow. And if I were to say, as I might, that the antithesis is too neat, is too much a neatness of another age, and could not therefore serve as a description of 'real' hunters, the author could with great justice reply that after all it is *not* a description of 'real' hunters but of hunters "carved at Amboise in a high relief."

NOTE

1. "The Current of the Frozen Stream: An Essay on the Poetry of Allen Tate," *Furioso* (Fall 1948).

RANDALL JARRELL

From "A View of Three Poets"

Richard Wilbur is a delicate, charming, and skillful poet—his poems not only make you use, but make you eager to use, words like *attractive* and *appealing* and *engaging*. His poems are often gay and often elegiac—almost professionally elegiac, sometimes; funny or witty; individual; beautiful or at least pretty; accomplished in their rhymes and rhythms and language. Somebody said about Christopher Fry—and almost anybody must have felt it—"I don't think real poetry is ever as *poetic* as this." One feels this way about some of Mr. Wilbur's language (and about some of what he says, too; what poets say is often just part of their language); but generally his language has a slight incongruity or "offness," a skillful use of verbs and kinesthetic words, a relishable relishing texture, a sugar-coated-slap-in-the-face rhetoric, that produce a real though rather mild pleasure. The reader notices that the poet never gets so lost either in his subject or in his emotions that he forgets to mix in his usual judicious proportion of all these things; his manners and manner never fail.

Mr. Wilbur seems to be a naturally lyric or descriptive poet. His book is rather like a picture gallery—he often mentions painters—and his people are usually not much more than portions of landscapes or still-lifes. The poems are all Scenes, none of them dramatic; and if the reader is someone who feels that you can't look at the best sunset for more than a few minutes (but that people sometimes last for centuries), he is sure to start

Partisan Review 18 (November–December 1951):691–700. Later reprinted as "Three Books" in *Poetry and the Age* (New York: Knopf, 1953), pp. 250–65. Other poets reviewed in the article: Robert Lowell, *The Mills of The Kavanaughs* (Harcourt Brace); William Carlos Williams, *Paterson, Books I–IV* (New Directions).

longing for a murder or a Character—after thirty or forty pages he would pay dollars for one dramatic monologue, some blessed graceless human voice that has not yet learned to express itself so composedly as poets do.

When you read "The Death of a Toad," a poem that begins "A toad the power mower caught, / Chewed and clipped of a leg, with a hobbling hop has got / To the garden verge," you stop to shudder at the raw being of the world, at all that "*a hobbling hop*" has brought to life—*that* toad is real, all right. But when you read on, when Mr. Wilbur says that the toad "dies / Toward some deep monotone, / Toward misted and ebullient seas / And cooling shores, toward lost Amphibia's emperies," you think with a surge of irritation and dismay, "So it was all only an excuse for some Poetry." And when you read Mr. Wilbur's "Beowulf," the poem seems about as convincing and appropriate as Marie Laurencin illustrations to the *Iliad*. Yet the same poet can say to a sycamore,

> Sycamore, trawled by the tilt sun,
> Still scrawl your trunk with tattered lights, and keep
> The spotted toad upon your patchy bark,
> Baffle the sight to sleep,
> Be such a deep
> Rapids of lacing light and dark . . .

and can say about olive trees in the "heavy jammed excess" of southern France,

> Even when seen from near, the olive shows
> A hue of far away. Perhaps for this
> The dove brought olive back, a tree which grows
> Unearthly pale, which ever dims and dries,
> And whose great thirst, exceeding all excess,
> Teaches the South it is not paradise.

These quotations seem to me to have an easy and graceful beauty; and one is delighted with the wit and delicacy of a passage like

> Who worked at none but wit's expense,
> Putting dirigibles together
> Out in the yard, in the quiet weather,
> Whistling beyond Tom Sawyer's fence.

When someone apostrophizes an eggplant: "Natural pomp! Excessive Nightshade's Prince! Polished potato," or says about a bird's nest fallen from a tree, "Oh risk hallowed eggs, oh / Triumph of lightness! Legerity begs no / Quarter: my Aunt Virginia, when"—when anybody speaks so, you say to him: "Good old Marianne Moore! Isn't she *wonderful?*" But Mr. Wilbur is not influenced by her anymore; I wish he were. His second book seems more affected by general Victorian poetic practice than by any live poet; the reader sometimes thinks in surprise, "Why would anybody *want* to write like that?" An ambitious and felt and thoughtful poem like his first book's "Water Walker" (an animal-morality poem about St. Paul; it, like Elizabeth Bishop's beautiful animal-morality poem about St. Peter, is a member of a genre that Miss Moore discovered and perfected) is a partial failure, but surely anybody would rather have written it than some of Mr. Wilbur's slight and conventional successes.

Most of his poetry consents too easily, with innocent complacence, to its own unnecessary limitations. Once an unusually reflective halfback told me that as a run develops there will sometimes be a moment when you can "settle for six or eight yards, or else take a chance and get stopped cold or, if you're lucky, go the whole way." Mr. Wilbur almost always settles for six or eight yards; and so many reviewers have praised him for this that in his second book he takes fewer risks than in his first. (He is one of those Southern girls to whom everybody north of Baltimore has said, "Whatever you do, *don't* lose that lovely Southern accent of yours"; after a few years they sound like Amos and Andy.) If I were those reviewers I would quote to Mr. Wilbur something queer and true that Blake said on the same subject: "You never know what is enough unless you know what is more than enough." Mr. Wilbur never goes too far, but he never goes far enough. In the most serious sense of the word he is not a very satisfactory poet. And yet he seems the best of the quite young poets writing in this country, poets considerably younger than Lowell and Bishop and Shapiro and Schwartz; I want to finish by admiring his best poems, not by complaining about their limitations. But I can't blame his readers if they say to him in encouraging impatient voices: "Come on, *take a chance*!" If you never look *just* wrong to your contemporaries you will never look just right to posterity—every writer has to be, to some extent, sometimes, a law unto himself.

PETER VIERECK

From "Technique and Inspiration— A Year of Poetry"

Richard Wilbur, born in 1921, is the youngest of America's leading contemporary poets. He is also their outstanding perfectionist. Few surpass him in sensitivity of simile and in delicacy of rhythmic modulation. He has all the qualities of a great artist except vulgarity. By that I mean: he seems often to lack the human-all-too-human quality that gives a poet universal earthy humanity. That is the price he paid in his first book, *The Beautiful Changes,* for too serene a poise. But his second book, despite its characteristic title of *Ceremony* (Harcourt Brace), advances beyond the impasse of what seemed a sterile glass-flower perfection. At its best, *Ceremony* adds the terror of an under-ground Dionysus to the decorum of the above-ground Apollo.

Wilbur's new capacity for a lurking ferocity will save him from his greatest esthetic danger: blandness. This compelling tension between surface sunniness and subsurface storms makes his deceptively bland title an ironic "double-take." The subsurface Dionysian storm is most typically suggested by the closing lines of *Ceremony*:

> What's lightly hid is deepest understood,
> And when with social smile and formal dress
> She teaches leaves to curtsey and quadrille,
> I think there are most tigers in the wood.

In "Books and Men," *The Atlantic Monthly,* January, 1952, pp. 81–83. Other poets reviewed in the article: W. B. Yeats, *Collected Poems* (Macmillan); Theodore Roethke, *Praise to the End* (Doubleday); W. H. Auden, *Nones* (Random House); Robert Lowell, *The Mills of the Kavanaughs* (Harcourt Brace); Randall Jarrell, *The Seven-League Crutches* (Harcourt Brace); John Ciardi, *Mid-Century American Poets* (Twayne); Adrienne Rich, *A Change of World* (Yale University Press); Rolfe Humphries, translator, *The Aeneid of Virgil* (Scribners); Roy Campbell, translator, *Poems of St. John of the Cross* (Pantheon Books).

THINGS OF THIS WORLD
1956

JOHN CIARDI

Our Most Melodic Poet

These have been busy times for Richard Wilbur. Within a month
or two of one another he has just published a new translation
of *The Misanthrope,* a bestiary anthology, and a new book
of poems. An unusual burst of energy surely, and certainly occasion enough for some sort of interim evaluation of one of
our most interesting poets of what Don Hall once called "The
Before-Second-Chin School."

Wilbur's first book, *The Beautiful Changes* (1947), marked
him immediately as something special. A trace of indebtedness
to Yeats and a clear line of descent from Marianne Moore were
visible as signs that his talent was still emergent, but of the
existence of that talent there could be no doubt. The poems,
richly worded and strictly formal, nevertheless moved within
their strictures with an ease and assurance that marked Wilbur as
the possessor of as fine an ear for the smooth-flowing line and
the self-rounding stanza rhythm as could be claimed by any man
now writing in English. He had, moreover, achieved a metaphoric sense undeniably his own. Consider for example this
description of a ballet dancer fresh from the formal perfections
of her dance and now slumped into the shapelessness of human
fatigue:

> So she will turn and walk through metal halls
> To where some ancient woman will unmesh
> Her small strict shape and yawns will turn her face
> Into a little wilderness of flesh.

The Saturday Review, August 18, 1956, pp. 18–19. Review of Wilbur's *Things of
This World* (Harcourt Brace); Molière's *The Misanthrope,* translated by Richard
Wilbur (Harcourt Brace); and *A Bestiary,* compiled by Richard Wilbur and illus-
trated by Alexander Calder (Pantheon Books).

And rich as are the immediate physical sensations of such a description, it is the nature of Wilbur's talent that these physical punctualities are precisely *that which is thought with*. As William Carlos Williams once cried: "No ideas but in things." The true mark of the poet is that his "things" are ideas and his ideas things. The passage is not only a description of a particular tired dancer, but of the boundary between life and artifice, a boundary crossed and recrossed in Wilbur's poems, always with the central driving intention of finding that artifice which will most include the most of life. For Wilbur is a poet at mortal play, an artificer. Even the title of his first book ("changes" must be read both as a noun and as a verb) attests how carefully he plans his double meanings.

This theme of artifice—I am tempted almost to call it the theology and humanism of artifice—rose free of the earlier indebtednesses and emerged deepened and enriched in *Ceremony and Other Poems* (1950). And here, too, it became apparent both immediately and by hindsight that Wilbur was emerging as a master of a subtle, urbane, and self-convincing diction that was peculiarly his own, the mark of his own way of seeing and saying. No one example will characterize a good poet's diction, but consider these first two lines from a poem called "Year's End":

> Now winter downs the dying of the year,
> And night is all a settlement of snow.

"Settlement" is the fascinating word here. "Descent" is, of course, the obvious first meaning. But a "settlement" is also a colonization, a "taking possession of"; and it is also the resolution of a dispute, a "quietus." Several other functional meanings are also adducible, but these will do. Even more remarkably, it would be simple to show in a detailed analysis of the poem that all of these happily concurring ambiguities are not only clearly intended but that they establish the very structure and development of the poem. A musical analogy will illustrate: it is as if "settlement" were the first, most condensed statement of the themes which expand and interact to become the structure of meaning. More specifically, the themes we may label "descent," "taking possession of," and "dispute-and-resolution" are the three interplays that give the poem its structure and its performance of a meaning. Perhaps *Ceremony* was kept more charming than ultimately persuasive by a kind of near-frivolous exuberance in playing what Wilbur calls "games," but no capable reader could miss the authenticity and richness of Wilbur's gift.

Now with *Things of This World* his enormous gifts grown into their mature assurance, Wilbur certainly emerges as our serenest, urbanest, and most melodic poet. To say Wilbur has matured is not to imply that he will not accomplish finer things yet, and I would suggest for instance that in his search for a serene diction he might place less reliance on such adjectives as "clear," "pure," "calm," and "graceful." It is exactly the qualities labeled by these adjectives that best describe the best Wilbur poems, but it is very much to the point, I believe, that in those best poems the clarity, purity, calm, and grace emerge thing-wise and self-living, not by adjectival assertion. Minor qualifications aside (and Wilbur's successes would sustain far greater flaws than these) there is a kind of unmistakable inevitability in a typical Wilbur passage. There is nothing flashy about; in fact, Wilbur makes it look so easy that one might almost overlook how good it really is. Consider these lines for example, a passage following a reference to children at play:

> Above their heads the maples with a stiff
>
> > Compliance entertain the air
> > In abrupt gusts, losing the look of trees
> > In rushed and cloudy metamorphoses,
> > Their shadows all a brilliant disrepair.

The self-rounding of the total stanza rhythm is one Wilbur signature. The quality of the metaphor, physically suggestive yet alive with idea, is another. So are the play and paradox of "stiff compliance." And there is a fourth, to me even more impressive quality, and that is exactly the one most readers would most likely overlook, and that is the Latin root-sense that shines through so much of Wilbur's diction. "Compliance" means in current usage "to yield to" but at root it means either (the derivation may be disputed either way) "to fold up" or "to be filled up with." And whether one hears the root as *plicare* or *plere* the root does function. So, even more clearly in "entertain" (from the roots *inter* and *tenir,* "to hold between"). The aptness of those root suggestions when applied to windblown trees and when juxtaposed to "stiff" (itself—and this joyously derived from Latin *stipes* meaning "a tree trunk or vegetable stalk") will illustrate how richly Wilbur works his diction in depth. One may slide over the surfaces paying no attention to these riches and find reward enough. Wilbur certainly is not the man to slug the reader into noticing his excellences. But they are there to be found. Nor is there any more valuable function the poet can perform than to reawaken the root sense of the language, to keep it a living instrument in the mouth of his people. As Valéry (I believe it was he) put it: "To purify the language of his tribe."

To these gifts one must now add Wilbur's attainments as a translator. This is not an occasion for a line-by-line comparison of the French and English texts, and since Wilbur has not intended a word-for-word translation such a comparison is not immediately apt. Rather, Wilbur has gone for what Dudley Fitts called "faithfulness" as distinguished from "strictness." Instead of cognate-snapping, as the academic dullards invariably do, Wilbur has found English equivalents for the turn and nuance of the French, and the fact that he has managed to do so in rhymed couplets that not only respect themselves as English poetry but that allow the play to be staged (as it has been by the Poets' Theatre of Cambridge) with great success is testament enough. Wilbur has brought *The Misanthrope* alive into English. Now let us hope that the publishers will allow it to be anthologized or reprinted in a cheap edition.

There are also to consider Wilbur's stunning translations of lyrics by Baudelaire, Valéry, Jammes, and Philippe de Thaun, the last two of which are included in both *Things of This World* and *A Bestiary.* Let his good fairy be left to say how he does it, but Wilbur has managed to take four sweetly tuned lyrics and to convey them, despite a heavy freight of rhyme, into English lyrics as sweetly tuned as the originals in a serene and urbane act of imagination and devotion. A rare miracle, Wilbur has caught it four times in these renderings.

Finally, of *A Bestiary* there is little enough to say. Wilbur has played a happy game of hunting out poems and prose passages dealing with animals and has caught nicely the flavor, perhaps one should say the "mystique," of the medieval bestiary, and Alexander Calder has contributed some of his zany but accomplished line drawings which would have struck me as much zanier and much more accomplished had they been less indebted to James Thurber.

DONALD HALL

Claims on the Poet

It is nearly nine years since the publication of Richard Wilbur's first book, *The Beautiful Changes. Ceremony* came in 1950, his translation of Molière's *The Misanthrope* last fall, and now his third book of poems, *Things of This World*. If it seems silly to review the oeuvre of a man of thirty-five, I hope it will prove useful; I think Wilbur's position has been typical of the newest generation of poets, a position which has not been understood. It should be obvious that the serious consideration of a young poet is not equivalent to calling him a great poet.

Things of This World is perhaps less of a book than the first two volumes of poems. I mean that it is smaller (forty-seven pages of poems, of which seven pages are translations) and that even its slight weight cannot be called pure gold. Some small poems add up to nothing, and others are flawed by an easy use of modifiers which has cropped up in Wilbur before. Because there is less density to this book, and because the reader will not find the unadulterated elegance he probably expects, it may disappoint the casual critic. But the sum of the parts is not the whole point; a book of poems as a book disappears in a collection. It is very much to the point that the best poems Wilbur has yet written are in this volume, and point out a new direction of his mind.

Before we describe the new original poems, a word should be said about the translations, which in this volume do excellent justice to Baudelaire, Valéry, Jammes and Philippe de Thaun. Wilbur's delicacy of feeling, his poetical tact, is never more apparent than in his translations. They all sound a bit like Wilbur, which is a good thing, for if a man changes his accent whenever

Poetry 88 (September 1956):398–403. Review of Wilbur's *Things of This World;* Molière's *The Misanthrope,* translated by Richard Wilbur.

57

he changes his subject, you don't trust him. *The Misanthrope* is Wilbur's chef d'oeuvre as a translator; it contains passages which do not curl up and die at the mention of Dryden:

> However high the praise, there's nothing worse
> Than sharing honors with the universe.
> Esteem is founded on comparison:
> To honor all men is to honor none.
> Since you embrace this indiscriminate vice,
> Your friendship comes at far too cheap a price;
> I spurn the easy tribute of a heart
> Which will not set the worthy man apart:
> I choose, Sir, to be chosen; and in fine,
> The friend of mankind is no friend of mine.

The language varies from the archaic to the colloquial, being no actual speech, yet consistently achieves a right tone. Though there are a few bad couplets, and some awkwardness, the proportion of virtues to vices is a thousand to one.

The Beautiful Changes, like most first books, contains many poems which are responses to events. Wilbur sees something—"First Snow in Alsace," "On The Eyes of an SS Officer"—and is moved to write about it. The result is a description, followed or not by a decision. "Tywater" ends as a young man may often have to end such a poem, in a quandary, "And what to say of him, God knows. / Such violence. And such repose." Besides the poems out of events, there are many which are carefully constructed to contain and exemplify ideas. A situation is stated and argued, sometimes resolved and sometimes only displayed. The process is perhaps more cerebral than emotional; verse is a device of accuracy, balancing tone to achieve a whole precision of meaning, on all levels, which prose can never imitate. In *Ceremony,* most of the poems follow this pattern; "A Problem from Milton" announces the method in its title. Wilbur has also continued, though more rarely after *The Beautiful Changes,* to write the simple lyric of direct emotional statement—the kind of poem which happens to a poet—and the descriptive meditation on events; but the made, considered, argued poem remains the center of his work, and his best poems are these.

The thoughts in Wilbur's poems have varied, but until *Things of This World,* one set of ideas has dominated. It has been an attitude whose godfathers were Mallarmé and Wallace Stevens, an epistemology which approaches aesthetic nihilism. Objects, in *The Beautiful Changes* and *Ceremony,* are truer when imagined than when sensed. "Caught Summer is always an imagined time." "Absence" confers upon things a greater reality than presence. There is a kind of asceticism here, an avoidance of the world of the senses, which is expressed in the most gorgeous imagery. Wilbur is conscious of the paradox, and in a part of *Ceremony* sets about arguing himself out of the position. His couplet,

> We milk the cow of the world, and as we do
> We whisper in her ear, "You are not true."

is a highly successful self-critique. In "'A World Without Objects Is a Sensible Emptiness,'" he admonishes his "tall camels of the spirit" (who are so proud of their ability not to drink water for long periods) to seek "the spirit's right / Oasis, light incarnate."

So Wilbur has been negating as well as professing his interior gorgeosity and exterior asceticism, but the negations of *Ceremony* make no solution to the problem, only satirizing the contrary belief. Wilbur is more consistent when, in the poem "Ceremony," ("What's lightly hid is deepest understood, . . .") and in "In the Elegy Season," he affirms the original propositions. He is more consistent because it is undoubtedly true, that even when he is attacking the love for illusion, his style contradicts him; the very fanciness of the image of the "camels of the spirit" seems to say, "I am only spoofing; they are much pleasanter than real camels; light incarnate hurts the eyes, but what a fine turn it makes with which to end a poem." I don't mean that these poems are insincere; if poems were people, if poetry were life, they might be insincere, but since they are poems and about life, they are ironical: interior contradiction affirms negation! But irony can become a reflex, and it can limit a poet's subject matter.

A language which seems first of all to delight in itself is not the greatest language in poetry. We can delight in sheer skill, and it can survive for generations if it is *that* good, but it is not the best poetry. In the very greatest, in Shakespeare, Donne, Pope, and some of Yeats, the language is extraordinarily clever, yet the language as language disappears in the very urgency with which it points at its subject matter. Wilbur has been a particularly accomplished poet of delight; I think that "Museum Piece," "Epistemology," "La Rose des Vents," "Juggler," "Year's End," "Still, Citizen Sparrow" and several others have a secure place among the anthologies of the future by their cleverness, by the joy they give anyone who can appreciate the handling of language in verse at its most intricate. We might characterize the success of most of these poems as the kind of achievement that gets a long, low whistle of admiration. But Wilbur has, it seems to me, tried in his newest book to escape from the circle of words delighting in themselves, and though he has not yet written a great poem, he has taken a necessary step in that direction.

We can start to see a difference in two changed habits of thought. He has moved from the mental play of ". . . the soul bathes in warm conceptual lakes," to involvement with the present and physical. And with this, Wilbur has moved in his descriptions from the witty and formalistic imagery of nature to a consideration of human works. A change in what the poems were about would be only superficial were it not accompanied by a change in the implicit meaning of the style. The best poems in *Things of This World* are not looking at themselves, but are looking at their subject matter. Wilbur can still be clever, but the cleverness seems more than self-delighting, and it seems to point outwards. The last poem in the book praises the new railway station in Rome over the ruins of the ancient city, and ends,

> "What is our praise or pride
> But to imagine excellence, and try to make it?
> What does it say over the door of Heaven
> But *homo fecit?*"

Perhaps this last rhyme will seem to disprove what I am claiming, but I choose it deliberately to show that in my opinion the change need be only small on the surface to be large in essence.

Here the cleverness may elicit a whistle, but it should have a deeper response as well. The rhyming of Latin and English, of the two words with the one, is brilliant but is more than decorative. The rhyme is of synonyms, and the concept of "making excellence" is the key to the whole poem. The rhyme is no mere decoration, it creates the meaning. In "Beasts," the "suitors of excellence" are men working alone at night in the city—making. Their works may be devastating, but their human labor, their effort toward excellence, is itself beautiful. In *Ceremony,* it was the "Juggler" whose skill was celebrated, for by his skill he ". . . has won for once over the world's weight." One feels, in this later book, that Wilbur now subscribes to a hierarchy by which the dexterity of the juggler would be accounted less than the excellence of the architect. By extension, the intelligent poem is better than the brilliant one.

I said that along with his new concern for man's works, Wilbur involves himself in the "things of this world" as he has never done before. Appetite links the two themes. The best poem Wilbur has yet written, and a good modern poem, is "A Voice from under the Table." Its subject is the pursuit of sensual pleasure, its inevitable defeat, and its unaltered persistence. "How shall the wine be drunk, or the woman known?" it begins. Appetite is more immense than the possibilities of its enjoyment. The "horizontal monument," who ends the poem "O sweet frustrations, I shall be back for more," discloses:

> Helen was no such high discarnate thought
> As men in dry symposia pursue,
> But was as bitterly fugitive, not to be caught
> By what men's arms in love or fight could do.
> Groan in your cell; rape Troy with sword and flame;
> The end of thirst exceeds experience.
> A devil told me it was all the same
> Whether to fail by spirit or by sense.

And truly, it is the same; though here it is entirely sense which informs the appetite, it is an appetite, hugely indulged, which drives the "suitors of excellence." The latter metaphor is, after all, sexual; it is pursuit of human satisfaction which is consistently Wilbur's subject. The poem which gives the book its title, "Love Calls Us to the Things of This World," presents Wilbur's change dramatically. Waking, the poet sees a world of laundry outside his window, and day-dreams "The morning air is all awash with angels." Impressed with this angelic purity,

> The soul shrinks

> From all that it is about to remember,
> From the punctual rape of every blessed day,
> And cries,
> > "Oh, let there be nothing on earth but laundry, . . .

Yet, when the sun picks out colors in the world, "The soul descends once more in bitter love / To accept the waking body . . ." and to exult in it, reminded still of the purity potential in the laundry. In another of his best poems, "A Baroque Wall-Fountain in the Villa Sciarra," a marvel of description, Wilbur compares the ornate fountain of the title with the more classical plainness of a jet before St. Peter's, and decides in favor of the humane and intricate over the austere.

> Francis, perhaps, who lay in sister snow

> > Before the wealthy gate
> > Freezing and praising, might have seen in this
> > > No trifle, but a shade of bliss—
> > That land of tolerable flowers, that state

> > As near and far as grass
> > Where eyes become the sunlight, and the hand
> > > Is worthy of water: the dreamt land
> > Toward which all hungers leap, all pleasures pass.

The parallels between this poem and the soliloquy of the drunkard under the table demonstrate the extent of Wilbur's position.

Imagination as a word has tended to associate with the bodiless. "Imaginary" and "fictional" are synonyms. In Wilbur's previous work, the attempt is to divest objects of being or relevance, and create a world of the imagination independent of objects. Here we find imagination in another function, applied to things not to uncover an inner reality superior to the outer, but to present their gaudiness and to celebrate sensuous enjoyment of them. If we "imagine excellence" it is in order to "try to *make* it."

Things of This World as a whole is no violent change; the reader looking for total novelty is likely to overlook the change that does occur. There are old-time Wilbur pieces here, a few among them the best of his elegant set-pieces; "Merlin Enthralled" is a particular delight. There are poems in which elegance is not the point, and which fail in a way Wilbur has seldom failed before, through lack of control over the medium. There is at least one poem which sets forth his old ideas in full flower. It is not necessary to list the many fine poems, like his best short lyric, "Mind," which are unmentioned because they do not fit into my perhaps over-neat exposition. Also, it should be said that there are hints of the less formalistic Wilbur, and the Wilbur of the newer ideas, in *Ceremony* and even, a little, as far back as *The Beautiful Changes*. A poet writes best about one set of problems when he is through with it, when he has moved on, tentatively and without full understanding, to a different attitude. Wilbur could not have written *Ceremony* if he had not been moving toward *Things of This World*.

All qualifications made, something has happened in these three books. There has been a steady intellectual growth, and a movement away from the destitution of formalism into the beginnings of something else; from a self-delighting loveliness (and the poems, let it be insisted, really *are* lovely) not to any "affirmation" as *Life* editors would have it, but toward the discovery of some "things of this world." In "A Voice from under the Table," it is possible to foresee a poetry which might be major without being systematic.

M. L. ROSENTHAL

From "Tradition and Transition"

To liberate oneself from "influences" that not only guide but bully, it is sometimes necessary to reach back behind them, to their own sources. Many contemporary poets, in their several ways and with varying clearsightedness, are now making this effort—an effort to get in touch anew with the root-motivations animating the Romantics, the French Symbolists, the experimentalists of thirty *and* of sixty or seventy years ago, and their other literary ancestors. The currently renewed fascination with sacred and mythological themes indicates even more the effort at self-rediscovery.

The transitions are not easy, especially when there is only dim consciousness of what is happening and the distress signals are everywhere, and everywhere different. Thus, in *Things of This World* Richard Wilbur seems beset by a sort of ennui, the result of a conceptual dependence which bedevils him with an especially treasonous subtlety. Though he is still one of our better poets, the things his poetry says and lives by are so much of the essence of the modern Anglo-American heritage that others have already pre-empted the original and audacious modes of expression he might otherwise use. Compare his "An Event" with Stevens' "Thirteen Ways of Looking at a Blackbird," for instance. The younger poet has been almost forced into a blander, more discursive tack, for which even his highly developed grace and skill of rhetoric cannot fully compensate. Rhetoric, incidentally, is put to sharper use in the one political piece here: "Speech for the Repeal of the McCarran Act." Genuine

The Nation, November 3, 1956, pp. 372–74. Other poets reviewed in the article: Stephen Stephanchev, *Three Priests in April* (Contemporary Poetry); Edwin Muir, *One Foot in Eden* (Grove Press).

poetic energy and concreteness quicken the effect of this piece, which augurs the revival of a genre recently much neglected. But this poet's main chance does not lie in a political direction.

Wilbur's own medicine for his disease is, for him, a good one: translation, and a turn of emphasis toward French sources that goes with it. His dominating vision has always been the aesthetic-secular one of the post-Romantic tradition:

> I take this world for better or for worse,
> But seeing rose carafes conceive the sun
> My thirst conceives a fierier universe.

Still, Wilbur finds it difficult, in his usual voice, to present this vision as truth; he rather argues for it as an ideal. Everything changes, however, when he takes on a different voice or mask by translating from the French. Then, particularly in rendering Baudelaire's "L'Invitation au Voyage" and Valéry's "Helen," he is at once far within the vision. Again, with Jammes' "A Prayer to Go to Paradise with the Donkeys," he is from the start at a pitch of pure elation for which he strives in vain elsewhere. Moreover, of the successful poems here that are *not* translations, the best are those most closely approaching the dream-atmosphere of the French Symbolist tradition (as opposed to the Emersonian or morally melioristic streak in contemporary American poetry, which has at times overborne Wilbur's sense of himself). Such poems are "Merlin Enthralled" and "Marginalia," the latter of which tells us that

> Descending into sleep (as when the night-lift
> Falls past a brilliant floor), we glimpse a sublime
> Décor and hear, perhaps, a complete music. . . .

Recent Poetry

Each poet has a prevalent mood which drives him to the writing of poetry. Some men write their poems in response to their agonies; some, to their delights. Joy is a rare bird under any circumstances, but in our days, if our poets are to bear witness, it is as elusive as a lunar rainbow. Thus it is that we are always meeting and fighting with devils, whether they be in the mind, in the memory, in the workaday or political world, or on the stair behind us as we struggle unhappily up the Purgatorial Mount.

And this brings us to the extraordinary Mr. Wilbur. He walks among the devils that his fellow poets keep pointing out to him, but he doesn't see them. Instead, he persists in seeing angels. Other poets would see angels if they could. They peer, they squint, they turn about quickly sometimes to catch an unwary angel that may be wandering about.

Meanwhile Richard Wilbur—as in the first poem in this collection—goes walking, finds himself in a church, looks up into its dome and imagines the splendid race of creatures there. They are not solitary, glum, Miltonic angels; they remind us more of medieval knights and ladies:

> They chat no doubt of love,
> The pleasant burden of their courtesy. . . .

In brief, they are married (or courting) angels. And why not? Prayer creates them and holds them up, but they are angels of a world where there is giving and taking in marriage.

This attitude of Wilbur's is seen most significantly in both the

The Yale Review 46 (December 1956):295–96.

title and content of his second poem, "Love Calls Us to the Things of This World." Here we are told directly that

> The morning air is all awash with angels.
>
> Some are in bed-sheets, some are in blouses,
> Some are in smocks. . . .

We discover soon that the poem is, on its literal level, a praise of wash hung out on the line. But the soul of the poet, in approving of this phenomenon, finds larger meanings:

> "Oh, let there be nothing on earth but laundry,
> Nothing but rosy hands in the rising steam
> And clear dances done in the light of heaven."

And as the laundry is transformed into something strange, so too are other humble things. In the poem on Bruna Sandoval, who tends the church at San Ysidro, it is said that

> the early sun
> Shines as she flings the scrubwater out, with a crash
> Of grimy rainbows, and the stained suds flash
> Like angel-feathers.

But the angelic element in Wilbur is not always revealed in such explicit terms. Usually it shows itself more subtly: in a gaiety, graciousness, or ease of tone, in a glint or luminescence that surrounds and rises from the objects described. Sometimes, as in the amusing "A Voice from under the Table," he reminds us a little of Wallace Stevens; at other times Marianne Moore comes to mind. Echoes come to us too of his studies in French literature, and of his reading in the medieval period. But all this is usually absorbed: he is almost always himself.

It is astonishing how rarely Wilbur writes in the bleak, bitter or inconsolable mood. His visions of evil are muted, temporary, tentative. John Chrysostom, who, we are told, had in times past crawled on his hands and knees like a beast, is caught here at the moment when "a gust of grace" touches him, and when his voice rings forth "like a great choir." The lonely night scene in

"After the Last Bulletins" resolves itself at the end into a picture of "saintlike men" picking up yesterday's newspapers in the park, while the songbirds are in the "public boughs."

Brought up, as we have been, to a literature of violence, one sometimes misses in Wilbur's work the extremes we find elsewhere: the exaltations and depressions, the corrosions of the spirit, the distortions of the psyche, the tumultuous passions, the animal griefs—in brief, our old friends the devils and trolls. Is this the reader's fault for having his taste corrupted by the apostles of violence? Or is this a fault (if it *is* a fault) of Wilbur's poetry? For here is one of the finest of our young poets, and of the older poets who go under the name of young poets. And this latest book is his most successful one. But what about his angels? How does he come by them? Those who stretch forth their hands like Tantalus might well ask upon what nectar he nourishes himself. What charm or exorcism does he use? How can he be so damnably good-natured in an abominable world?

ADVICE TO A PROPHET
AND OTHER POEMS
  1961

THOM GUNN

From "Imitations and Originals"

The reputation of Richard Wilbur has gone into a slight decline since the time when it stood equal to Lowell's. The public prefers a wild and changeable poet to one who has pursued a single end consistently and quietly. It has been widely acknowledged that Wilbur possesses considerable technical skill, but the acknowledgment has often been without enthusiasm, suggesting as it does in isolation that he lacks more important qualities. And it is true that there are plenty of reservations to be made about his earlier work, which was at times too smart and facile. But such reservations cannot be made about his latest book, which I find his best. It is a short collection, but besides the translations and light verse which make up about a third of its bulk, there is a group of poems in which the famous skill has become an instrument of deepening precision, or rather an element inseparable from the statement of the poetry.

> Even when first her face
> Younger than any spring,
> Older than Pharaoh's grain
> And fresh as Phoenix-ashes,
> Shadowed under its lashes
> Every earthly thing,
> There was another place
> I saw in a flash of pain:

The Yale Review 51 (March 1962):480–89. Other poets reviewed in the article: Robert Lowell, *Imitations* (Farrar, Straus and Giroux); Louis MacNeice, *Solstices* (Oxford University Press); Maxine Kumin, *Halfway* (Holt, Rinehart & Winston); William Stafford, *West of Your City* (Talisman Press); Thomas Kinsella, *Poems and Translations* (Atheneum); Ruthven Todd, *Garland for the Winter Solstice* (Atlantic-Little, Brown).

Off in the fathomless dark
Beyond the verge of love
I saw blind fishes move,
And under a stone shelf
Rode the recusant shark—
Cold, waiting, himself.

The tone of the passage is one of controlled melancholy, very characteristic of this new book. But so subtly managed is the technique that the mere substitution of a monosyllabic foot at the start of the final line is sufficient to turn it to one of barely submerged terror.

Wilbur's progress has been in exactly the opposite direction to that of Lowell, who has tended to particularize more and more closely. In *Advice to a Prophet* symbol and perception have started to take on a general force. The shark in the quoted lines is not a merely personal symbol: it is a symbol in which particularities are implied, acting in relationship to one another, even though it is an image fully realized in itself.

The generalizing power is most successfully in evidence at the start of "The Aspen and the Stream" where the Aspen says:

Beholding element, in whose pure eye
My boughs upon a ground of heaven lie—
O deep surrendered mind, where cloud and stone
Compose their beings and efface your own,
Teach me, like you, to drink creation whole
And, casting out my self, become a soul.

The dialogue of which this is a part is obviously suggested by the seventeenth-century dialogue between inanimate objects, but it is not pastiche. It is writing both nourished by and nourishing a tradition.

THEODORE HOLMES

Wilbur's New Book—Two Views
I. A Prophet Without a Prophecy

Mr. Wilbur sees man's life as the spoof which the real world
plays on his understanding of his destiny; but his poems fall into
the error of taking this vision of things as the inner principle by
which they proceed to embody it. They are for the most part a
spoof played on the reader's legitimate concern for something to
put in place of the old attachments which they wipe away. As
admirable as this view of human experience may be, the poems
supply no deeper resource in understanding by which life may
be led with dignity and compassion for our frailties,—they are
like a ceremony gotten up by the mind to distract us from the
truth they represent. One comes away from them with the feeling of a diversion, by which we can entertain this vision and be
reconciled to it without having to come to terms with the implications it bears for our lives. This arises especially from the
texture of style, manner, polish, wit, and decoration of vocabulary and learning out of which the poems are constructed. Nine-
tenths of each poem is absorbed with the world that dupes us,
and only at the end are we given some sibylline apostrophe of
the life that eludes us. In poems like "Marginalia," "Ceremony," "The Terrace," "The Beacon," "For the New Railway
Station at Rome," and "Mind," such a procedure is hypos-
tasized into the terms of an answer; it is offered simply as the
only possibility open to human providence. "Looking into History" exhorts the mind's capacities to "some fervent fraud."

As close as Mr. Wilbur ever comes to providing us something
to put in place of the substance of human cognition which his
poems call into question is an adoption of our personal attach-

Poetry 100 (April 1962):37–39.

ment to the things themselves. It is the hopelessness of the mind caught in this virtual tautology that takes refuge for an answer in the despair of style. Holding up the things of this world in their own ultimate status in ontology as a solution to the dilemmas of human existence can only be satisfactory for the privileged and unthinking, for to the others of us who must bear their weight they contain within them the very problems which these poems take them as solving. It is the purview of things seen from the Parnassian heights of wealth, privilege, ease, refinement, and education, looking down on the permanent sufferings of humankind without being part of them. The poems seem almost at times a dance or a ritual enacted in the face of a mystery they don't understand; an obeisance performed to the divine agony of our lives out of all the pageantry and pomp its world can muster: rhyme, meter, myth, history, reference, obscurity, and precious intellection, that would reconcile us to our trouble without comprehending it. The style is of exceptional grace and often beautiful, the manner perfect, and the mind tuned, but such a period glamor of the human mind can never fill those needs which rise to it from its deepest resources.

This latest book of Mr. Wilbur's is chiefly the kind of thing that is so often the end of an essentially formal attachment to thought; the deep disaffiliation with the springs of truth that eventuates in a waning of interest. There results an overt weakening of mastery, the loss of force, and being caught up with trivia and mannerism. It is the ritual that once shone with the light of belief now fallen to the motions of a code no longer adhered to. At his best Mr. Wilbur's work, by the very act of his miming, shines with the truth he brings to it—as often ceremony does, but all that had been his skill, his precision, his sense of grace, the *élan* of his mind, here becomes tired of itself and caves in to a mere posturing.

In *Advice to a Prophet* the poems are for the most part dialogues, song, tricks, and small situations—the skill of the ritual left after it has become perfunctory. Gone is the force of spirit and verve in accomplishment that made them, if not profound, one of the delights of the passing scene in present-day letters. And yet the opening poems are strangely out of keeping with the rest of the performance in the book; about them there are intimations of something that looks beyond any of the work that has preceded them. There is an openness, a straightforwardness, a giving voice to his own heart, a compassion out of involvement that almost makes recourse to device superfluous, to the title poem that sets it apart from anything else Mr. Wilbur has done. He feels a little strange in this new freedom he has granted himself, is not able to fill all this space with the dimensions of thought it demands, but all the same it is a direction that beckons hopefully and with good omen. In the poem called "Junk" Mr. Wilbur achieves more of a philosophic ordinance over his essential vision of things than I am able to find anywhere else in his work; it is a movingly honest and compassionate confrontation by the mind of the implications of its despair, and would be a total poem did it not, as these poems so often do, take refuge in myth and allusion at the end. The first poem in the book portrays a touch with renunciation, self-effacement, and humility that are quite foreign to the ordinary prosecution of the sensibility that produced it:

TWO VOICES IN A MEADOW

A Milkweed

Anonymous as cherubs
Over the crib of God,
White seeds are floating
Out of my burst pod.
What power had I
Before I learned to yield?
Shatter me, great wind:
I shall possess the field.

A Stone

As casual as cow-dung
Under the crib of God,
I lie where chance would have me,
Up to the ears in sod.
Why should I move? To move

Befits a light desire.
The sill of Heaven would founder,
Did such as I aspire.

If Mr. Wilbur would fashion his poems from such stuff of the heart as a lived-in experience, and not simply the virtuosity of an intellectual mastery attained over it, then they would afford the reader a basis for giving a permanent meaning to life. Possibly why the author chose these poems to open the book is that he felt them endowed with a certain preeminence of aspiration and augury.

WILLIAM MEREDITH

Wilbur's New Book—Two Views
II. A Note on Richard Wilbur

There are states of closed-mindedness—for and against—which ought to disqualify a man from reviewing particular books, and I suppose I am as badly qualified to review Richard Wilbur's *Advice to a Prophet* as, say, Jack Kerouac would be. We get committed to certain positions to the point where we aren't even interesting, let alone objective. But having said this, here are some words of caution I put in a letter recently. If a poem can say, as poems do, *pay attention to life,* a poet must sometimes say of the work he admires, *pay attention to these poems.*

It seems to me that for people who know and care about Wilbur's work, this is just the excellent book they had hoped for and expected. For other readers it is something of a booby-trap. It invites careless reading: how genteel this all is, they think, how cheerful and Episcopalian, how very damned elegant. But these accusations, the ones that are actually derogatory anyhow, are self-generated. The poems will not support them.

Wilbur's poetry, like a lot of good poetry, has always been about order in the universe. Nowadays perceptions of disorder, even the most casually observed ones, are somehow taken to be more *serious.* Wilbur's poetry (like most good art, could you say?) explores the human capacity for happiness. The human capacity for despair (not to be confused with tragedy) is very big now with a lot of artists, and even novelists and poets who are not gifted in despair sometimes feel impelled to fake it.

But grace of form, a sweet accuracy of speech, a passionate sense of purpose still comprise most of what we know about poetry. *Advice to a Prophet* strikes me as the strongest assertion

Poetry 100 (April 1962):40.

yet, by this poet, that the universe is *decent,* in the lovely derivative sense of that word. Like that word, the book is unfashionably quiet in what it asserts, and subject to misuse.

These poems are the kind of booby-trap that life itself mines our path with. A reticence is part of the riddle. We all ignore the world somewhat, each in his own dull way, but never except to our cost. These poems are the observations of a man who has a sharp eye and ear for moral order. You ask yourself whether some of the poets whose work proclaims that the universe has lately become unseemly are as observant as Wilbur, whether they have as much regard for the riddle itself, the subject of our song.

RALPH J. MILLS, JR.

The Lyricism of Richard Wilbur

Twenty years ago, in an essay entitled "The End of the Line," Randall Jarrell—who has proven to be the best poetry critic as well as one of the best poets of his generation—traced briefly but shrewdly the history of "modernist" poetry from its origins to its decline. Jarrell was quite advanced in his views, and it is only recently that other critics and scholars have agreed that the revolution carried out by Eliot, Pound, Yeats, Rilke, and Valéry was in effect finished by 1930. But we must remember that Jarrell had the advantage of speaking as a practicing poet faced with the problems of forming a style, discovering a language and a poetic identity in the confusion of the 1940s. So what he has to say on this matter is relevant to the other young poets who then shared his predicament; and surely we must assume that he was, in some sense, speaking for many of them, such as Karl Shapiro, Theodore Roethke, Richard Wilbur, John Nims, Delmore Schwartz, and Robert Lowell, when he wrote,

> Among modernist poets from 1910 to 1925, there was the same feeling of confident excitement, of an individual but irregularly cooperative experimentalism, of revolutionary discoveries just around the corner, that one regularly sees at certain stages in the development of a science; they had ahead of them the same Manifest Destiny that poets have behind them today. Today, for the poet, there is an embarrassment of choices: young poets can choose—do choose—to write anything from surrealism to imitations of Robert Bridges; the only thing they have no choice about is making their own

Modern Age 6 (Fall 1962):436–40.

choice. The Muse, forsaking her sterner laws, says to everyone: "Do what you will."

Jarrell's remarks were brilliantly accurate in 1942, and remain
so now; it is for this reason that I have used them to preface a
short discussion of Richard Wilbur's poems. When Wilbur, Jarrell, and the other poets who are roughly their contemporaries,
began to write, they found themselves on a shore littered with
the residue of a great and powerful wave of literary experimen-
tation that had rushed poets and novelists forward on its crest,
frequently with magnificent results. With the movement finally
spent, however, all that a new poet could see was a bewildering
variety of innovations and revivals and fresh influences in
rhythm, diction, and form from which he might select what
suited his purposes; the contagious spirit of adventure which had
spread through the arts in England, America, and Europe before
World War I and continued for more than a decade afterwards
was dead. Of course, I cannot tell how much this situation affected Richard Wilbur, whose first book appeared in 1947, but I
like to think, having reread most of his poems recently and with
his fourth volume before me, that he has never really missed
being a part of the post-Symbolist movement in modern poetry
because his instincts as a writer led him elsewhere to begin with.

Looking back over Wilbur's poems, the reader will find little
alteration in general aim, manner, or voice: poems from his first
book mix very comfortably with those from his latest. And I say
this without malice, without any intention of devaluating his
considerable accomplishment. Let me explain myself. It is clear
that, from the outset of his poetic career, Wilbur was tempted
neither to write surrealist poems nor to imitate Robert
Bridges—or if he was, these temptations were overcome in secret—but that, instead, his gifts and inclinations drew him toward the tradition of English lyricism which maintains its center
in formalism and wit and musical grace. Thus his natural prede-
cessors can be located most easily among the Elizabethan, Metaphysical, and Cavalier poets, but also in Emily Dickinson and A.
E. Housman. Yet I do not want to mislead the reader into believing that Wilbur lacks his own voice, or that his voice is

merely a tissue of other voices from the past; that is just not so, and I offer here some substantial proof:

> The tall camels of the spirit
> Steer for their deserts, passing the last groves loud
> With the sawmill shrill of the locust, to the whole honey
>   of the arid
> Sun. They are slow, proud,

> And move with a stilted stride
> To the land of sheer horizon, hunting Traherne's
> *Sensible emptiness,* there where the brain's lantern-slide
>   Revels in vast returns.

★ ★ ★

> Things concentrate at the edges; the pond-surface
> Is bourne to fish and man and it is spread
> In textile scum and damask light, on which
> The lily-pads are set; and there are also
>   Inlaid ruddy twigs, becalmed pine-leaves,
>   Air-baubles, and the chain mail of froth.

★ ★ ★

> In a dry world more huge than rhyming or dreaming
> We hear the sentences of straws and stones,
> Stand in the wind and, bowing to this time,
> Practise the candor of our bones.

These passages are taken from poems in three separate volumes by Wilbur, the last from *Advice to a Prophet.* I think the language and its movements, the preoccupations and the ways of treating a theme, are distinctive. Wilbur is a poet of endless celebrations; even when, as in the first of the quotations above, he moves onto the plane of the spiritual, he does so with a rich profusion of language and imagery that fills out the supposedly remote zones of the spirit with mass and weight and color. While it would be an exaggeration to call him a religious poet in any strict or doctrinal sense of the word, it is equally false not to recognize the fact that he is often concerned with an experience of life which can only be named religious. That experience, and the spiritual threads deep within it, usually comes to Wilbur through his amazing sensitivity to the phenomenal world, to every fluctuation of nuance in his surroundings, and to the incredible beauty he perceives there. I choose an example, "October Maples, Portland," from his new book.

The leaves, though little time they have to live,
Were never so unfallen as today,
And seem to yield us through a rustled sieve
The very light from which time fell away.

A showered fire we thought forever lost
Redeems the air. Where friends in passing meet,
They parley in the tongues of Pentecost.
Gold ranks of temples flank the dazzled street.

It is a light of maples, and will go;
But not before it washes eye and brain
With such a tincture, such a sanguine glow
As cannot fail to leave a lasting stain.

So Mary's laundered mantle (in the tale
Which, like all pretty tales, may still be true),
Spread on the rosemary-bush, so drenched the pale
Slight blooms in its irradiated hue,

They could not choose but to return in blue.

The natural world in its particular mood and season becomes, through the poet's eye, through a wealth of analogy and allusion, sacramental; though with Wilbur this awareness of the spiritual possibilities inherent in the physical order never reaches to the level of visionary or mystical intuition. Like Robert Herrick, whom he resembles somewhat in the ease and perfection with which he writes, employs forms, captures the right tone and phrase, Wilbur is essentially a poet of sensible realities—and of their implications. But one ought to add that he is not so attracted to the composition of erotic and amatory verse as Herrick was. At the same time, we should observe that he is not, either, the sort of poet who will ultimately provide us with a systematic view of things after the fashion of Eliot or Yeats, or many another modern poet. Wilbur is an occasional poet of the finest kind. "What is in a poem is essentially the same as that which is in one's own life," Erich Heller quotes Goethe as saying; I should like to add the word "good" before "poem" and say that Goethe's dictum describes Wilbur's art. Take the poem called "A Hole in the Floor," which is dedicated to the surrealist artist René Magritte, who painted precise images of dream and the subconscious:

> The carpenter's made a hole
> In the parlor floor, and I'm standing
> Staring down into it now
> At four o'clock in the evening,
> As Schliemann stood when his shovel
> Knocked on the crowns of Troy.
>
> A clean-cut sawdust sparkles
> On the grey, shaggy laths,
> And here is a cluster of shavings
> From the time when the floor was laid.
> They are silvery-gold, the color
> Of Hesperian apple-parings.
>
> Kneeling, I look in under
> Where the joists go into hiding.
> A pure street, faintly littered
> With bits and strokes of light,
> Enters the long darkness
> Where its parallels will meet.
>
> The radiator-pipe
> Rises in middle distance
> Like a shuttered kiosk, standing
> Where the only news is night.
> Here it's not painted green,
> As it is in the visible world.

For God's sake, what am I after?
Some treasure, or tiny garden?
Or that untrodden place,
The house's very soul,
Where time has stored our footbeats
And the long skein of our voices?

Not these, but the buried strangeness
Which nourishes the known:
That spring from which the floor-lamp
Drinks now a wilder bloom,
Inflaming the damask love-seat
And the whole dangerous room.

Wilbur makes his poem very like a surrealist painting (but not like a surrealist poem): the objects of ordinary reality, in this case, parts of a house, are transformed into counters for the unseen psychic world. Characteristically, he does not linger in subterranean places, but offers the reader, in the final stanza, what amounts to a commentary on the value of this descent below the surface of the quotidian. Such a conclusion brings us to one further thought about Wilbur, one that is perhaps seldom entertained because of the urbanity and intelligence of his poetic manner; I mean the moral element which informs so much of his writing. Obviously, I do not imply that he is addicted to the platitude or to easy moralizing; rather he tends to handle the poetic events he creates in a way that involves his own deepest instincts and considered judgment. Sometimes his judgment inheres in a disarming lightness of touch; sometimes, as in the book's title poem, it is expanded into a more comprehensive imaginative vision. In that poem—one of Wilbur's best—he advises a prophet how he may convince men of their folly by an appropriate illustration of the kind of penalty they can expect to force upon themselves. The poem is again an occasional one, arising from the hostility and terror of the world's present condition, but its meaning might be felt under any such circumstances. As we read through the opening stanzas, we find the poet enumerating, then discarding, various threats to the con-

tinued existence of man as insufficient to make the necessary
impression:

> Spare us all word of the weapons, their force and range,
> The long numbers that rocket the mind;
> Our slow, unreckoning hearts will be left behind,
> Unable to fear what is too strange.

> Nor shall you scare us with talk of the death of the race.
> How should we dream of this place without us?

Alternatively, the poet tells the prophet, "Speak of the
world's own change"; and in the stanzas that follow Wilbur
proceeds to demonstrate, through a fullness of image and metaphor, how the natural world—trees and rivers, birds and
beasts—could alienate itself, voluntarily, from man, leaving him
alone in a universe that has robbed him of the meanings for
himself he had once found reflected there:

> Ask us, prophet, how we shall call
> Our natures forth when that live tongue is all
> Dispelled, that glass obscured or broken

> In which we have said the rose of our love and the clean
> Horse of our courage, in which beheld
> The singing locust of the soul unshelled,
> And all we mean or wish to mean.

> Ask us, ask us whether with the worldless rose
> Our hearts shall fail us; come demanding
> Whether there shall be lofty or long standing
> When the bronze annals of the oak-tree close.

If Richard Wilbur seems now, after four volumes, to have
undertaken no radical changes in his poetry, to have sought no
new and different forms simply for the sake of novelty, we
should hardly discredit him for that. From the very start, his art
has exhibited the finest lyrical qualities, the highest standards of
craftsmanship, a compassionate and reverential attitude towards
life. One cannot ask for much more.

RANDALL JARRELL

From "Fifty Years of American Poetry"

Petronius spoke of the "studied felicity" of Horace's poetry, and I can never read one of Richard Wilbur's books without thinking of this phrase. His impersonal, exactly accomplished, faintly sententious skill produces poems that, ordinarily, compose themselves into a little too regular a beauty—there is no eminent beauty without a certain strangeness in the proportion; and yet "A Baroque Wall-Fountain in the Villa Sciarra" is one of the most marvellously beautiful, one of the most nearly perfect, poems any American has written, and poems like "A Black November Turkey" and "A Hole in the Floor" are the little differentiated, complete-in-themselves universes that true works of art are. Wilbur's lyric calling-to-life of the things of this world—the things, rather than the processes or the people—specializes in both true and false happy endings, not by choice but by necessity; he obsessively sees, and shows, the bright underside of every dark thing. What he says about his childhood is true of his maturity: "In my kind world the dead were out of range / And I could not forgive the sad or strange / In beast or man." This compulsion limits his poems; and yet it is this compulsion, and not merely his greater talent and skill, that differentiates him so favorably from the controlled, accomplished, correct poets who are common nowadays.

Prairie Schooner 37 (Spring 1963):1–27. Later reprinted in *Third Book of Criticism* (New York: Farrar, Straus and Giroux, 1969), pp. 295–334.

WALKING TO SLEEP—
NEW POEMS AND TRANSLATIONS
   1969

HENRY TAYLOR

Two Worlds Taken as They Come
Richard Wilbur's *Walking to Sleep*

Since 1947, when Richard Wilbur published *The Beautiful Changes,* he has been widely recognized as one of the finest poets who began their careers after World War II. By 1956, with the publication of *Things of This World,* he had established himself as a poet of the first rank. In the spring of 1961, Robert Frost told an audience at the University of Virginia that Wilbur, because of the natural beauty of his language and craft, was one of the younger poets who, without any conscious effort to "write down," could reach the wider audience which poets (and audiences too) have dreamed of for a long time.

What Frost said is still true, though changes in literary fashion have obscured the issue. Wilbur's technical brilliance was gradually taken for granted, and then became for some readers an object of suspicion. When his fourth collection, *Advice to a Prophet,* appeared in 1961, it met with a variety of critical reactions. Among those readers who had previously been suspicious of Wilbur's technical mastery, and who had in some cases looked too hard for evidence of bold and obvious development, there were some who congratulated him for having tried, finally, to come to grips with the Problems of Contemporary Life, while others attacked him for having treated grave matters with what they had become accustomed to calling his characteristic lightness. Even among the critics who had steadily praised Wilbur's work since it had begun to appear, there were those who expressed disappointment in *Advice to a Prophet,* because they thought that Wilbur's technical virtuosity had been lavished

The Hollins Critic 6 (July 1969):1–12.

on "slight" poems, while others, more "major" perhaps, seemed looser and farther flung.

One reason for these mixed reactions was that *Advice to a Prophet* had been preceded by *Things of This World* (1956), which had won the Edna St. Vincent Millay Memorial Award, the National Book Award, and the Pulitzer Prize. In that collection, Wilbur had brought to its culmination the style which had developed through *The Beautiful Changes* (1947) and *Ceremony* (1950); *Advice to a Prophet* gave some indication that he was now beginning to move away from the "pleasure, flash, and waterfall" of his earlier work. However, he did not entirely abandon the earlier style, and this may have something to do with some of the dissatisfaction; it is fun to imagine the enthusiasm which might have resulted if Wilbur had dispensed altogether with the formal complexity for which he is so well known. As it was, *Advice to a Prophet* was sufficiently different from *Things of This World* to arouse dissatisfaction in those who admired the earlier style, but it was not different enough to please those who had been searching Wilbur's work for more evidence of what Oscar Cargill called "virility."

Wilbur's new collection, *Walking to Sleep,* seems to indicate even more clearly than *Advice to a Prophet* the direction he had begun to take in the earlier book. *Walking to Sleep* contains twenty-two new poems and eleven translations; in these, Wilbur continues to work with certain themes and techniques with which he has always been occupied, but he also develops a number of the concerns which had previously been most evident in *Advice to a Prophet.* The breadth of his vision has increased; though most of these poems, like the earlier ones, take rise from the sharp perception of minute particulars, they more often move from these starting points toward broader and deeper conclusions. Wilbur is more consistently and effortlessly involved in the upheaval of our times, in poems which are less oratorical than "Speech for the Repeal of the McCarran Act" or "Advice to a Prophet"; and the translations, all of them touched by Wilbur's usual excellence, are more various in voice and manner than those in the earlier books. Wilbur's development has not been characterized by the radical shifts which other poets of his generation have gone through; unlike the victims of what

George Garrett has called "The General Motors Aesthetic," he has not "obsolesced" his earlier work; he has instead extended it, in the process of moving into deeper and broader areas of experience and vision.

II

If *Advice to a Prophet* had detractors as well as admirers, there was no one who failed to recognize that Wilbur remains one of the most knowledgeable masters of verse technique now writing; and he continues to exercise this mastery in the poems in *Walking to Sleep*. No one familiar with his earlier work could mistake the authorship of this passage, for example, from "In the Field":

> Black in her glinting chains,
> Andromeda feared nothing from the seas,
> Preserved as by no hero's pains,
> Or hushed Euripides',
>
> And there the dolphin glowed,
> Still flailing through a diamond froth of stars,
> Flawless as when Arion rode
> One of its avatars.

It is the diction, of course, as much as the metrical precision, which marks this passage as Wilbur's, and the diction results in the ease with which the erudition is carried. In his note on this poem, Wilbur says, in part, "Some think that Euripides' lost play *Andromeda* told of the transformation of Andromeda . . . into the constellation bearing [her name]." Reading this, I am struck with the rightness, for example, of the adjective *hushed* in the fourth line above.

That Wilbur is a master of form means not only that he is able to work within traditional forms, but also that he can revise metrical patterns to his own ends, as he does in "Advice to a Prophet":

> Speak of the world's own change. Though we cannot conceive
> Of an undreamt thing, we know to our cost

How the dreamt cloud crumbles, the vines are blackened
    by frost,
How the view alters. We could believe,

If you told us so, that the white-tailed deer will slip
Into perfect shade, grown perfectly shy . . .

I once heard Wilbur answer a student who had asked him
about the meter of this poem; Wilbur began by saying that there
was a pattern, but backed off after having counted on his fingers
through the first stanza; he concluded by saying that he rarely
counted syllables and stresses, but worked instead for what he
called a rhythmical rightness which would coincide with a rightness he also wished to achieve in the tone and diction of each
line, each poem. This is a broader notion of the usefulness of
form than is often inferred from Wilbur's familiar remark, "The
strength of the genie comes of his being confined in a bottle."
(People also forget that Robert Frost was aware of the interesting things that can sometimes happen when one plays tennis
with the net down.) Richard Wilbur's genie inhabits a bottle that
sometimes reminds me of Snoopy's doghouse: it may seem
barely large enough for the genie, but there are many modern
conveniences arranged spaciously within it.

Most of the poems in *Walking to Sleep* are formal in the traditional sense, but there are several in which such variations as I
have mentioned are used to advantage; and there are also several
which make contemporary music of forms which do not often
show up in today's poetry. The first poem in the book, "The
Lilacs," is composed in the Anglo-Saxon alliterative form which
Wilbur used for the first time ("Junk") in *Advice to a Prophet;*
another, "Thyme Flowering among Rocks," is composed of
rhymed stanzas which maintain the 5-7-5 syllable-count of the
English *haiku:*

This, if Japanese,
Would represent grey boulders
Walloped by rough seas

> So that, here or there,
> The balked water tossed its froth
> Straight into the air.

As the poem continues, it exemplifies the delicate balance called for in a statement Wilbur made in his essay, "The Genie in the Bottle": "I think it is a great vice to convey everything by imagery. . . . There ought to be areas of statement. But the statement should not equal and abolish the 'objects' in the poem. . . ." The description in "Thyme Flowering Among Rocks" continues for several stanzas, until "You / Are lost now in dense / Fact, fact which one might have thought / Hidden from the sense." But then the poem concludes with a statement, a movement from the facts to their implications:

> It makes the craned head
> Spin. Unfathomed thyme! The world's
> A dream, Basho said,
>
> Not because that dream's
> A falsehood, but because it's
> Truer than it seems.

Perhaps the finest example of this movement from image to statement is "In the Field," which also best exemplifies the broadening vision I have mentioned. The poem begins with a recollection of the previous night, a walk in a field which led to a conversation about what the universe was doing as the speaker and his companion watched it. Following the two stanzas I have already quoted, in which the speaker points out constellations, comes the realization of the changes that are taking place before their eyes; remembering that "Egypt's north was in the Dragon's tail," they imagine the ultimate expansion of the universe, the stars moving away forever, "not coming back

> Unless they should at last,
> Like hard-flung dice that ramble out the throw,
> Be gathered for another cast.

Finally, "the nip of fear" takes hold of the speaker and his companion, as they imagine "a scan of space / Blown black and hollow by our spent grenade"; but the following day, the present of the poem, they are in the field again, unable to see the universe beyond the flowers about their knees:

> White daisy-drifts where you
> Sink down to pick an armload as we pass,
> Sighting the heal-all's minor blue
> In chasms of the grass,
>
> And strews of hawkweed where,
> Amongst the reds or yellows as they burn,
> A few dead polls commit to air
> The seeds of their return.

It is the soul's wish for survival, the hope that the "flung dice" of the universe might "Be gathered for another cast," that leads to the comparison between the movement of the stars and the movement of the hawkweed seeds; but, as is indicated below in the unobtrusive word *mistake,* the comparison is misleading:

> We could no doubt mistake
> These flowers for some answer to that fright
> We felt for all creation's sake
> In our dark talk last night,
>
> Taking to heart what came
> Of the heart's wish for life, which, staking here
> In the least field an endless claim,
> Beats on from sphere to sphere
>
> And pounds beyond the sun,
> Where nothing less peremptory can go,
> And is ourselves, and is the one
> Unbounded thing we know.

The passage abounds with paradoxes, the tensions of which are deceptively slackened by the rhetorical pitch and graceful flow of the language. The "heart's wish for life" is peremptory, yet unbounded; the claim it stakes out is endless, yet it is a mistake to take that wish to heart, at least to the extent that we are blinded to grim possibilities. Yet, that wish, which is one with ourselves, is boundless as the universe, but somehow knowable. How deeply we know ourselves is one of the abiding concerns of Wilbur's poetry; if there are countless mysteries to be sounded, we have to begin where we stand the best chance; from there, with luck, we can turn to face the others once again.

I have given so much space to this poem partly because I cannot shake the suspicion that it is Wilbur's finest poem so far, but mainly because I think it provides answers to some of the questions which Wilbur's poetry has always raised. Some readers have feared that his well-wrought surfaces contain little more than themselves, and, in the broadest sense, this is true, for his forms and their content are finally inseparable. But his forms are made of words, words whose meanings have been carefully considered; thus the forms themselves become the ideas in Wilbur's poetry.

That much of Wilbur's poetry amounts to celebration does not mean that he is oblivious to those areas of experience which inspire less "amiable" poems; his willingness to celebrate the things of this world, the "heart's wish for life," arises out of a strong moral sense, sometimes amounting to a religious vision, which prompts him to take account of the discrepancy between this world and another, variously seen as the world of dreams and imagination, or the world beyond bodily death. The tension caused by this discrepancy is created, in different poems, by juxtaposing various versions of the actual and the ideal; but the moral sense and the religious vision prevent him from trying to reconcile, by means of forms or figures, the tensions with which he is occupied; as he has said in "A Christmas Hymn" (*Advice to a Prophet*), the resolution of these tensions requires a miracle:

> And every stone shall cry
> In praises of the child
> By whose descent among us
> The worlds are reconciled.

Wilbur's vision of the things of this world, informed by his moral sense, has sometimes led him toward satire and public indignation, as in "Marché aux Oiseaux" (*Ceremony*) and "Advice to a Prophet," respectively. Both modes appear in *Walking to Sleep;* "Playboy," for instance, is a wicked study of a young stockroom clerk, occupied during his lunch hour with a photograph in a magazine: "Nothing escapes him of her body's grace / Or of her floodlit skin, so sleek and warm / And yet so strangely like a uniform . . ." And "Matthew VIII, 28 ff." takes off from the story in those verses of Christ's having exorcised evil spirits from two men of the Gadarenes. When the devils left the men, they went into a herd of swine and led them over a cliff into the sea; when Christ came to the city, he was enjoined to depart. Wilbur has modern America speak through the Gadarenes:

> It is true that we go insane;
> That for no good reason we are possessed by devils;
> That we suffer, despite the amenities which obtain
> At all but the lowest levels.
>
> We shall not, however, resign
> Our trust in the high-heaped table and the full trough.
> If you cannot cure us without destroying our swine,
> We had rather you shoved off.

Less subtle and witty, but considerably more indignant, is "A Miltonic Sonnet for Mr. Johnson on His Refusal of Peter Hurd's Official Portrait":

> Heir to the office of a man not dead
> Who drew our Declaration up, who planned
> Range and Rotunda with his drawing-hand
> And harbored Palestrina in his head,
> Who would have wept to see small nations dread
> The imposition of our cattle-brand,

With public truth at home mistold or banned,
And in whose term no army's blood was shed,

Rightly you say the picture is too large
Which Peter Hurd by your appointment drew,
And justly call that Capitol too bright
Which signifies our people in your charge;
Wait, Sir, and see how time will render you,
Who talk of vision but are weak of sight.

6 January 1967

This is the only poem to which Wilbur has ever appended a date, designed to remind us of the time he is writing about, but also, I think, intended to tell us that the poem was written in a single day. For my money, it shows, which may be one of the reasons Wilbur has let us know; the slight awkwardness with which the seventh line fits the syntax of the poem's single sentence, and the easy punning of the last line, are not characteristic of Wilbur's best work. And so my reactions to its inclusion in this book are mixed; I admire the sentiment, but I have seen too many poems of Wilbur's which are too superior to this one for me to be comfortable with it. On the other hand, that he has included it, especially in a collection which often touches on the sickness of our times, indicates his willingness to show his personality more directly than he has before.

Until recently, Wilbur has avoided the intrusion of his personality; he has let it speak through poems in which it is as subtly interwoven with the forms as his meanings are. But in *Walking to Sleep* a first-person speaker, not readily distinguishable from the poet, appears and is at ease in a number of poems. Unlike the Messrs. Confessional, he has not directly treated his own mind and spirit in many of his poems; but in "Running," one of the finest poems in this collection, the self is the subject.

The poem consists of three parts; the first is a brief recollection of the joy of running during a childhood game; the second is a magnificent account of having stood along the road in Wellesley, Massachusetts, waiting for the Marathon runners to pass through on their way to Boston. The final section, "Dodwells Road," is not a recollection, but a meditation arising from the present moment. The speaker is walking through the woods, jogging occasionally, regarding his ability to do so with a pride that indicates his age:

> What is the thing which men will not surrender?
> It is what they have never had, I think,
> Or missed in its true season,
>
> So that their thoughts turn in
> At the same roadhouse nightly, the same cloister,
> The wild mouth of the same brave river
> Never now to be charted.
>
> You, whoever you are,
> If you want to walk with me you must step lively.
> I run, too, when the mood offers,
> Though the god of that has left me.

"But why in the hell spoil it?" he asks, for his two sons burst into view, and he makes them "a clean gift of his young running." It is an old theme, but Wilbur has made it his own, and his success is partly a result of his having spoken so personally.

The speaker of the title poem takes a more austere stance than does the speaker of "Running," but the poem is one of Wilbur's most personal. The speaker's attitude is that of a lecturer; he addresses a "you," asserts his authority from time to time, and with great patience and at some length (about 140 lines of blank verse) he lays out a tactic by which his listener may fall asleep. The first part of the poem is devoted to the importance of imagining a landscape free of suggestions which could lead to dread and insomnia: "above all, put a stop / To the known stranger up ahead, whose face / Half turns to mark you with a creased expression." There follows a virtuoso description of the mutable and transitionless journey one takes on his way to sleep—into a house, through the cellar, up a mineshaft which becomes the route to Cheops' burial chamber, and so on to the point at which "The kind assassin Sleep will draw a bead / And blow your brains out."

At this point, the poem turns: "What, are you still awake? /

Then you must risk another tack and footing." This time the journey no longer requires the wilful rejection of disturbing images; if one is led past a gallows, for instance, he is to look up and "Stare [his] brother down." Even under these circumstances, one may find, with luck,

> A moment's perfect carelessness, in which
> To stumble a few steps and sink to sleep
> In the same clearing where, in the old story,
> A holy man discovered Vishnu sleeping,
> Wrapped in his maya, dreaming by a pool
> On whose calm face all images whatever
> Lay clear, unfathomed, taken as they came.

It is clear from the movement of this poem that, of the two "methods" of falling asleep, the second, though risky, is somehow preferable. I do not wish to turn this poem into an allegory, but something of Wilbur's tendency as a poet is revealed in his preference for the second journey; the wilful rejection of images may be safer, but to take them as they come requires a great imaginative strength and serenity. The poem leads again to considerations of the tensions between the actual and the ideal; here, I think, the world of dreams, as described in the second part of the poem, becomes almost inseparable from the waking world. It is through intimate acquaintance with the things of this world that one may reach "that state

> As near and far as grass
> Where eyes become the sunlight, and the hand
> Is worthy of water: the dreamt land
> Toward which all hungers leap, all pleasures pass."
> > "A Baroque Wall-Fountain in the Villa Sciarra,"
> > from *Things of This World*

A brief look at the eleven translations in this book provides a clue to Wilbur's expanding scope and technique. Until now, his verse translations have seemed barely distinguishable from his own poems; of course, all good translators do best with poems they might reasonably wish to have written, but in many of Wilbur's translations, his own voice has all but swallowed the voice of the original. The translations in this collection are as expertly wrought as any he has done, but there are several in which a voice different from Wilbur's is clearly distinguishable. I have in mind especially the three sonnets from the Spanish of Jorge Luís Borges and the three poems from the Russian of Andrei Voznesensky. The Borges poems move, in a tough, dense verse, through vast considerations of an explicitly "cosmic" nature; here is the sestet from "Everness":

> And everything is part of that diverse
> Crystalline memory, the universe;
> Whoever through its endless mazes wanders
> Hears door on door click shut behind his stride,
> And only from the sunset's farther side
> Shall view at last the Archetypes and Splendors.

And here, in violent contrast, are the opening lines from Voznesensky's "Antiworlds":

> The clerk Bukashkin is our neighbor:
> His face is grey as blotting-paper.
>
> But like balloons of blue or red,
> Bright Antiworlds
>   float over his head!
> On them reposes, prestidigitous,
> Ruling the cosmos, a demon-magician,
> Anti-Bukashkin the academician,
> Lapped in the arms of Lollobrigidas.

Not even in "Water Walker" or "Juggler" do we find anything quite as flashy as this. I lack the tongues to compare these to their originals, but they are remarkable passages in English. I feel confident that they are faithful, since I have been able to compare the French translations to their originals, and they are astounding for their fidelity and for the ease with which they speak their adopted language. But it is to the Spanish and Russian translations that I return, because the expanding sympathies they demonstrate seem to be reflected in the variety of manners I find in Wilbur's own new poems.

In *Walking to Sleep* Wilbur moves farther and deeper from each of his many points of departure; he moves in more various directions. Even after five books of poems, which have gained him a reputation as solid as that of any living poet, he remains a vital and developing talent whose future it is exciting to anticipate.

MICHAEL BENEDIKT

Witty and Eerie

The title alone suggests it; and what comes after fulfills it. For all the continuities with the previous four collections, Richard Wilbur's new book involves a considerable shift of emphasis. The poet is now much less devout a servant of that late-Symbolist literary faith which sees artifice as the sole God redeeming man from nature. Wilbur has always been friendly to the New England landscape, and it seems to me that he is the very best equipped, wittiest traveler in that land of indigenous artifice in which Wallace Stevens is certainly the Columbus, at least for New England writers. Now, from a concern for keeping a "difficult balance" (to quote from the title poem of his book before last, *Things of This World*), Wilbur has moved to a specific interest in inspecting the "inertness" of nature. In the first poem of *Walking to Sleep*, entitled "The Lilacs," he says of those flowers:

> Out of present pain
> > and from past terror
> Their bullet-shaped buds
> > came quick and bursting,
> As if they aimed
> > to be open with us!

The exclamation point is justified! This is no mere extension, in the manner of the Impressionist painters of whom Stevens also approved, of the assertion that "Sunlight Is Imagination" (a title from Wilbur's first book, *The Beautiful Changes*); but an announcement that the poet is now looking through and beneath *at,* and finally *into,* the life of nature. It seems to me that this

---

Poetry 115 (March 1970):422–25. Revision © 1982 by Michael Benedikt.

involves a crucial shift for any poet (or poetry): one from a visual mode of approach to the world, to a visionary one. Put another way, one might say that there is a de-emphasis on picture-making, and the methodology of the great post-Eliotic mode of "objective correlative"; and a fresh stress on a kind of subjective correlative, with the poet starting out with the assumption that anything he might read into nature says something not only about himself, but also about it. A radical shift! Still, the objective must be attended to. It is after looking clearly *at,* that we may look *into,* Wilbur seems to insist in these poems. Most begin with clear-headed, more or less "objective" description. Some "Fern-Beds in Hampshire County," for example, are described with great intensity—indeed, this scrupulousness is almost hallucinatory—before Wilbur's astonishing summing-up regarding what is called, often all too casually, "plant life":

> Whatever at the heart
> Of creatures makes them branch and burst apart,
> Or at the core of star or tree may burn
> At last to turn
> To make an end of time,
> These airy plants, tenacious of their prime,
> Dwell in the swept recurrence of
> An ancient conquest, shaken by first love
> As when they answered to the boomed command
> That the sea's green rise up and take the land.

Who booms this command? *Walking to Sleep* is full not only of crisp visual description, but of the kind of music that ensues when a poet pulls all the stops out of a technically perfect instrument. The sounds are grand, yet inclusively allusive. In another poem which strikes me as outstanding for both easefulness and ambitiousness, "Seed Leaves," plant life is meticulously beheld; and yet there is surely something epically embryonic about these seeds which grow from "the oval form of sleep," "toothless and fat"; finally sprouting "resigned / To being self-defined / Before it can commerce / With the great universe." Finally, like man inside some new space vehicle, or perhaps like man within one of his old religions, the seed "takes aim at all the sky / and starts to ramify."

That a concern for the ramifications of man should proliferate from this concern for modest things like plants, first, should not surprise. "A Late Aubade" is an exquisite love lyric with extraordinary resonance. The tradition of the Provençal *aubade* or dawn-song notwithstanding, the poem carries the suggestion that the poet is reluctant to leave his lady not only because he really likes her, but because leaving a lady's bed (filled, significantly I think, with fruit that the lovers have been consuming from time to time), also denotes departure from all the good things of the ground, and of earth itself. The ramifications of "Running," a tryptych, are equally intimate, and stem, similarly, from informed—even haunted—observations of the literal. "1933," Part One, pictures the poet participating in chasing games as a child; Part Two, about a race on "Patriot's Day," pictures the poet admiring a champion American runner, one "rocked in his will, at rest within his run." Ramification—if only on the personal level—seems the subject of Part Three, "Dodwell's Road." The poet implies that it is impossible to live by standing still, and that a personal ramification is required. But when the poet pictures himself running again for ". . . the two boys who break into view . . . flushing a pheasant / Who lifts now from the blustery grass / Flying full tilt already," one feels that the poet is referring here, too, to a desire to run altogether from the earth. This strange, sad theme is also invoked in "The Agent," a haunting (as well as hauntingly Audenesque) poem about a spy who starts liking the people he is spying on, and who thus becomes homeless on earth; and in "For Dudley," a lovely elegy most appropriately present since, in my reading at least, the thrust of this book is oddly elegiac. "Under Cygnus" is also, in its way, an elegy, offering the curious consolation that, although the poet is a "dying swan," the solar system itself is drifting off toward the constellation of Cygnus the Swan, so that all finally remains in balance. If this poem seems metaphorically and metaphysically rather forced, yet effective (and if two other poems, "Complaint" and "In a Churchyard," seem forced and *in*effective), it is probably because, though all these poems tend to use the old idea of metaphysical "wit" and of multiple levels of meaning, the best of the poems explore something else: an uncanny fusion of the witty and the eerie which, in the long run, may be wiser than irony.

The long title poem, "Walking to Sleep," combines all these issues. One feels here that Wilbur is not ending something, but beginning it. The poem not only exemplifies an altered standpoint, but is about it. It opens with an image which appears to be plucked from the air ("As a queen sits down, knowing that a chair will be there, / Or a general raises his hand and is given the field-glasses, / Step off assuredly into the blank of your mind. / Something will come to you"), and continues with phantasmagoric compilations of collars, meadows, skies, taxidermies, hieroglyphics, fire-inspectors, cloaca, ships, St. Elmo's fires, hooded men, cathedrals, rookeries, and boudoirs. Once Wilbur alludes in passing to "an old film jump[ing] in the projector"; but it seems to me that cinematic qualities are more common in our poetry than what Wilbur is after. There is a strange, almost automatist, dreamlike offhandedness about this procession of disparates; but the celebrated gracefulness of technique continues, and it would be forcing things to call this poem Surrealist, although "Walking to Sleep" is surely the most surrealistic poem the poet has published to date. Wilbur represents Jorge Luís Borges generously in the book's selection of translations, but that isn't it either. The key to both poem and book seems to me the poet's recommendation that we "answer to our suppler self"—with all that implies, in earthly as well as extraearthly terms. In an interview last year (with Joan Hutton, published in *Transatlantic Review*[1]), Wilbur says enthusiastic things about Emerson; and it is indeed as if, reversing the usual procedure, he had moved from a late-Symbolist concern for redemption through artifice, to an early-Symbolist concern for transcendental details, for intimate "correspondences" between human life and earthly life, more or less in the manner of Swedenborg—whom Emerson, in one essay, introduced to these shores. Or perhaps more exotic influences still are implied in the remarkable closing lines, which recommend:

> A moment's perfect carelessness, in which
> To stumble a few steps and sink to sleep

In the same clearing where, in the old story,
A holy man discovered Vishnu sleeping,
Wrapped in his maya, dreaming by a pool
On whose calm face all images whatever
Lay clear, unfathomed, taken as they came.

NOTE

1. Joan Hutton, ed., "Richard Wilbur Talking to Joan Hutton," *Transatlantic Review* 29 (Summer 1968):58–67.

CLIVE JAMES

When the Gloves Are Off

In 1962 a brace of small but influential Penguins waddled into prominence: *Contemporary American Poetry*, selected and edited by Donald Hall, and *The New Poetry*, selected and edited by A. Alvarez. Hall picked on two immediately postwar books as marking the culmination of "past poetries" and the beginning of a new poetry: these were Lowell's *Lord Weary's Castle* and Richard Wilbur's *The Beautiful Changes*. For tremendous power under tremendous pressure, Lowell was your only man. For skilful elegance—but not for passion—Wilbur was likewise nonpareil. As Hall went on to point out, it was Wilbur who had the most plausible imitators, and the typical duff poem of the fifties was the *poème bien fait* that was not *bien fait*—the Wilbur poem not written by Wilbur. By 1962, Wilbur, in addition to *The Beautiful Changes*, had published *Ceremony* (1950), *Things of This World* (1956) and had brought out a large selection in England, *Poems 1943–1956*. *Advice to a Prophet* (1961) was also out here by 1962, having been brought straight across by Faber with a haste wellnigh unseemly. Wilbur's stock was high on both sides of the pond.

Turning to *The New Poetry* though, we see that the two American poets Alvarez put forward as exemplary were not Lowell and Wilbur but Lowell and Berryman. Hanging by one wellmuscled arm from an ice-axe lodged firmly in the north face of the Future, Alvarez wasn't interested in grace under pressure so much as in the registration of pressure itself. For the New Seriousness, "gentility, decency and all the other social totems" were not in themselves sufficient for the task of responding to

The Review (London), no. 26 (Summer 1971):35–44.

the unique contemporary evils: if skill got in the road of urgency, then skill was out. Not much room for Wilbur there. (Not
much room for Larkin, either: it was in his introduction to this
volume that Alvarez discovered Larkin's horses to be less violent, less brutish and consequently somehow less acceptably
horsey than Hughes's horses. It looked like Larkin wasn't wor-
ried enough about Buchenwald.)

Getting on for ten years later, Wilbur has in fact faded right
out: it's doubtful if he is now thought of, on either side of the
water, as any kind of force at all. Earlier this year a further
volume came out, *Walking to Sleep*. A disproportionate amount
of it consists of translations and although the original poems
retain his customary technical perfection they hold no surprises
beyond the usual polite sparkle of his aerated language—it's the
same old *acqua minerale* and either it or our liver has lost tone.
The book was greeted with muted satisfaction by the squarer
critics but otherwise it was correctly thought to be a bit tired.

As it happens, I saw Wilbur in action at the American Embassy
in that very Year of the Penguins, 1962. His reading was pref-
aced by a short expository routine from John Wain, who, while
preparing us for Wilbur's qualities, unaccountably chose to im-
personate one of his own characters, Charles Froulish from
Hurry On Down. (I think particularly of the moment when the
rumpled and wildly gesticulating Froulish, getting set to read his
magnum opus aloud, rips off his tie and throws it in the fire.)
Into the pocket of high pressure created by this performance
strode Wilbur, the epitome of cool. It was all there: the Ivy
League hair-cut, the candy-stripe jacket, the full burnished image of the Amherst phi bete. Riding his audience like the Silver
Surfer, he took European Culture out of his pocket and laid it
right on us. We were stoned. It was the Kennedy era and somehow it seemed plausible that the traditional high culture of Europe should be represented in a super-refined form by an American who looked like a jet-jockey and that the State Department
should pay the hotel bills. As the world well knows, the dream
couldn't last. It got ambushed in Dallas the following year. But
it's sometimes difficult to remember now just how solid-sound-
ing a civilized front the U. S. was putting up in that period: it all

clicked and it was all official. The internationalism of a mind like Wilbur's, its seemingly relaxed roaming in the European tradition, fitted the picture perfectly.

Of that picture there is now nothing left, not even fragments, and looking back on it with what benefits accrue to a blighted hindsight we see that it was always false in the main—arrogant, insidious and self-serving. Better Johnson's or Nixon's instincts than Kennedy's pretensions. Yet within the Kennedy era's delusive atmosphere of distinction, Wilbur's own distinction was real. He could not, in the ensuing years, respond to his country's altered situation in the way that Lowell did, but I would be surprised if this meagreness of reactive energy turned out to be determined by complacency; up to 1956 at any rate, there is plenty in his poetry to show that he was deeply troubled by the huge dislocations that Alvarez saw as a characteristic, even exclusive, twentieth-century evil. But the point, I think, is that Wilbur's intricately coherent art is suited to the long allaying of an old mental wound, and not to the sudden coping with a new one. The evidence of his work is that he was able to employ the decade or so after the war as a time of tranquility in which his experience of wartime Europe could be assimilated and in a way *given back:* his images of order, his virtuosities of symmetry, are particularly orderly and symmetrical when he is dealing with Italy and France, the two countries in which he served. In a sentimentalized but still powerful form, we can see the same spirit at work in the J. D. Salinger story "For Esmé, With Love and Squalor," and with the same emphasis on fluent, formal speech as the instrument of recuperation. In the strict senses of both parts of the word, it is recollection: the healing wisdom comes after the event. Wilbur's comparative silence in the face of the new (and this time American-inspired) disintegration of the world-picture is less likely to be a failure of response than a need for time. There is no doubt, incidentally, about what he thinks of it all—in 1967 he wrote a shattering occasional poem against Johnson's philistinism, comparing him with Jefferson "who would have wept to see small nations dread / The imposition of our cattle-brand." But otherwise in this decade he has mainly written mechanically in his own manner, giving the impression that an early challenge to his equilibrium had long been met and that a new one has not yet been faced. For the time being, at any rate, his poetry has lost its relevance. What I want to do now is to indicate what that relevance was when his poetry still had it.

The Beautiful Changes set the level for Wilbur's technical bravura and he has never since dropped very far below it: if the recent products look ordinary, it's worth remembering that they are ordinary in a way that Wilbur himself established. If there were no more going on in his early poems than the dextrous flourishes of the dab hand that put them together, they would still be of permanent interest. Suggestions that Wilbur is fundamentally a punster in his diction are misleading. He is fundamentally a precisionist—he will make a word divert to a parallel, or revert to an antecedent, etymological stage, not to pun with it but to refurbish it.

> Easy as cove-water rustles its pebbles and shells
> In the slosh, spread, seethe, and the backsliding
> Wallop and tuck of the wave . . .

The restoration of "backsliding" to pristine condition is characteristic of his handling of language, and the enforced transfer of the reader's eye-line back and down to the next starting-point ("backsliding"—pause—"Wallop and tuck") is an elementary example of his mastery of mimesis. These lines are actually from a poem in *Ceremony:* I choose them because they contain instances of his two main technical preoccupations handily demonstrated in the one spot. But each trick was already everywhere employed in *The Beautiful Changes* and working to perfection. This, for example, is from "Cicadas":

> You know those windless summer evenings, swollen to stasis
> by too-substantial melodies, rich as a
> running-down record, ground round
> to full quiet.

Sound thickens when a disc slows down. Wilbur has noticed the too-muchness of the noise and neatly picked the word "rich" as appropriate: the connotations, partly established by the preceding use of "swollen" and "too-substantial," are of a superabundance of nutrition rather than of pelf. As for the kinetic copycatting, it's so neatly done he makes it look easy: that two-ton spondee "ground round" slows the line to a crawl and the enforced pause of the enjambement kills the action stone dead. Sheer class. This point-for-point matching of form to action reached one kind of excellence (I say one kind because I think that elsewhere there is another) in "My Father Paints the Summer":

> They talk by the lobby fire but no one hears
> For the thrum of the rain. In the dim and sounding halls,
> Din at the ears,
> Dark at the eyes well in the head, and the ping-pong balls
> Scatter their hollow knocks
> Like crazy clocks.

Just how it goes: ping/pong; SKAT! (could be a backhand smash); k/k/kk/k. Less easily noticed, but still contributory, is the preceding Din/Dark, a duller pair of consonants. What we are given is a kind of Doppler effect as the writer leaves the hotel lobby and walks towards the source of the noises. Copycat equivalence has here reached one kind of limit (not that Wilbur didn't go on exploiting it in later volumes) but in his superb poem "Grace" it reached another kind—immediately more fruitful and eventually more troublesome. In these two stanzas from the poem, the first shows the first kind, the second the second:

> One is tickled, again, by the dining-car waiter's absurd
> Acrobacy—tipfingered tray like a wind-besting bird
> Plumblines his swinging shoes, the sole things sure
> In the shaken train; but this is all done for food,
> Is habitude, if not pure
>
> Hebetude. It is a graph of a theme that flings
> The dancer kneeling on nothing into the wings,
> And Nijinsky hadn't the words to make the laws
> For learning to loiter in air; he "merely" said,
> "I merely leap and pause."

The first stanza is Wilbur's customary five or so under par for the course, and one surfaces from the dictionary convinced that the transition from stanza to stanza by way of those two near-homophones is neat and just. What "a graph of a theme" is I don't quite grasp, and can only deduce that it is the opposite of whatever motivates a dining-car waiter. But "The dancer kneeling on nothing into the wings" is a genuinely amazing stroke, probably the best early instance in Wilbur of the mighty, or killer-diller, line. Here the mechanical principles of the mimetic effect are not fully open to inspection as they are in the earlier examples: the feeling, the "art-emotion" that Eliot said could be created out of ordinary emotions, is not reducible to technicalities. Unprogrammed instead of programmed, perhaps even irrational instead of rational, the effect has been snatched out of the air by Wilbur during a temporary holiday from his usual punishing round of meticulous fidelity. When he showed he was capable of effects like this, he showed that the bulk of his poetry—his craftsmanship—was slightly stiff by his own best standards. As a rule of thumb, it can be said that the really glaring moments of falsity throughout Wilbur's poetry are brought about when, in pursuit of such an effect, he snatches and misses. An early example is the last couplet of "The Peace of Cities," which like a good many of his poems has the form of a two-part contention. Cities in peacetime are characterized first, and found to be more dreadful, because more inconsequential, than cities in wartime, which are characterized thus:

> . . . there was a louder and deeper
>
> Peace in those other cities, when silver fear
> Drove the people to fields, and there they heard
>
> The Luftwaffe waft what let the sunshine in
> And blew the bolt from everybody's door.

This clinching couplet sounds transcendentally silly, like some polished and perfumed banality dropped by Oscar Wilde on an off night. But the reasons for its emptiness go beyond a mere lapse of taste: they follow from what Wilbur is trying to do with his subject matter. He is trying to absorb the war's evil into a continuous, self-regulating process—a process in which a subdued Manichaean principle is balanced against an aesthetic Grace. The material resists that absorption. The war is a mental hot-spot Wilbur tries to cool out, make sense of, reduce to order: trying to do that, he tends to devalue the experience, and his wealth of language becomes merely expensive-looking. All his poems on wartime subjects are flawed in their handling of language—his best gift goes against him. To take another example from *The Beautiful Changes,* "First Snow in Alsace" holds a delicate balance for most of its length as the snowfall softens the deadly starkness:

> The ration stacks are milky domes;
> Across the ammunition pile
> The snow has climbed in sparkling combs.
>
> You think: beyond this town a mile
> Or two, this snowfall fills the eyes
> Of soldiers dead a little while.

But he rounds the poem out with an orgy of consolation, providing the exact verbal equivalent of a Norman Rockwell cover-painting:

> The night guard coming from his post,
> Ten first-snows back in thought, walks slow
> And warms him with a boyish boast:
>
> He was the first to see the snow.

With the possible exception of "Mined Country" (and even that one is rounded out with a tough-tender metaphysical bromide) the poems in *The Beautiful Changes* that treat the war theme directly are failures in total form as well as local detail. But they cast light on the poems that treat the war indirectly or leave it out altogether—they demonstrate what kind of pressure it is that makes the successful poems such convincing examples of formal order attained with technical assurance but against great spiritual stress. "Lightness," the best poem in the book and one of the finest things Wilbur ever wrote, is a two-part contention—and equation—about a falling birds-nest and a dying old American lady. It ends like this ("he" being her husband):

> He called her "Birdie," which was good for him.
> And he and the others, the strong, the involved, in-the-swim,
> Seeing her there in the garden, in her gay shroud
> As vague and as self-possessed as a cloud,
> Requiring nothing of them any more,
> And one hand lightly laid on a fatal door,
> Thought of the health of the sick, and, what mocked their sighing,
> Of the strange intactness of the gladly dying.

Aware of the countless European people whom death had found by no means intact and the reverse of glad, Wilbur picked his words here with an authority that has nothing to do with glibness. Strange, now, to think of a time when America could mean peace.

In all the elements I have so far dealt with, Wilbur's first volume set the course for the subsequent ones—except that the overt treatment of war was for the most part dropped, and any concern for current, well-defined political crises was dropped along with it. He subsumed such things in a general concept of disorderly force, operative throughout history: they were the subjects his poem would redeem, rather than deal with. Each poem was to be a model of limpidity and no disturbance would be admitted which could not be deftly counterbalanced in the quest for equipoise. From *Ceremony* onwards, successes and failures accumulated in about equal number; but what *guaranteed* failure was when the disturbing force, the element of awkwardness, was smoothly denatured before being introduced as a component. It sometimes seemed possible that Wilbur was working in a dream-factory. Here is the second half of "A Plain Song for Comadre," from *Things of This World:*

> It is seventeen years
> Come tomorrow
>
> That Bruna Sandoval has kept the church
> Of San Ysidro, sweeping

And scrubbing the aisles, keeping
The candlesticks and the plaster faces bright,
And seen no visions but the thing done right
From the clay porch

To the white altar. For love and in all weathers
This is what she has done.
Sometimes the early sun
Shines as she flings the scrubwater out, with a crash
Of grimy rainbows, and the stained suds flash
Like angel-feathers.

In poems like this the images of order came too easily: out-of-the-way hamlets were stiff with peasants who knew their place, and every bucket of slops could be depended upon to house an angel's ailerons. But the successes, when they happened, were of high quality. "A Baroque Wall-Fountain in the Villa Sciarra" is the stand-out poem in *Things of This World*. Again a two-part contention, it compares an elaborate fountain with a simple one, and without the slightest sense of strain draws a subtle conclusion that doubles back through its own argument. In describing the plain fountains in front of St. Peter's Wilbur took his copy-catting to dizzy new heights:

Are we not

More intricately expressed
In the plain fountains that Maderna set
Before St. Peter's—the main jet
Struggling aloft until it seems at rest

In the act of rising, until
The very wish of water is reversed,
That heaviness borne up to burst
In a clear, high, cavorting head, to fill

With blaze, and then in gauze
Delays, in a gnatlike shimmering, in a fine
Illumined version of itself, decline,
And patter on the stones its own applause?

Virtuose almost beyond belief, this is *perizia* taken to the limit. The way the vocabulary deflates as the water collapses, the way "patter" and "applause," already connected in the common speech, are separated and exploited mimetically—well, it'll do till something cleverer comes along.

Of the killer-diller line there were a few instances, most notably in "Loves of the Puppets" from *Advice to a Prophet*. It's symptomatic, although not necessarily sad, that the lovers in Wilbur's finest love poem should be made of papier mâché. The desperation of the last stanza, and the plangency of the tremendous final line, are prepared for not only by the rest of the poem but by our knowledge of Wilbur's whole attitude: to ensure order in the real world, the disorder of unbridled passion must be transferred to Toy-land.

> Then maladroitly they embraced once more,
> And hollow rang to hollow with a sound
> That tuned the brooks more sweetly than before,
> And made the birds explode for miles around.

But not many attempts at the art-thrill were as startling as that one. As Wilbur solidified his position, the general run of his poetry slipped past limpidity and got close to torpor. By the time of *Advice to a Prophet* self-parody was creeping in.

> In a dry world more huge than rhyme or dreaming
> We hear the sentences of straws and stones,
> Stand in the wind and, bowing to this time,
> Practise the candor of our bones.

Here the pendulum has stopped oscillating or even shivering: it's just a softly glowing, static blob.

Ten years have gone by since *Advice to a Prophet* and for most of that time the major American poets have been sweatily engaged in doing all the things Wilbur was intent on avoiding. Instead of ordering disorder, they have revealed the disorder in order; instead of cherishing a personal equilibrium they have explored their own disintegration; where he clammed up or elegantly hinted, they have clamorously confessed. To be doubtful about the course American poetry (and a lot of British poetry along with it) has taken, you do not have to be in entire agreement with Hannah Arendt's warning that those men are making a mistake who identify their own personalities with the battlefield of history. You need only to be suspicious about artists playing an apocalyptic role. Nevertheless it is true that there is something sadly hermetic about Wilbur's recent work.

> Though, high above the shore
> On someone's porch, spread wings of newsprint flap
> The tidings of some dirty war,
> It is a perfect day:

Here Wilbur seems to be trying to get at something specific, but once again he can only generalize—which is not the same as being specific in an oblique way. Apart from the powerful but localized hit at Johnson mentioned earlier, the serenity of previous volumes continues untroubled by any hint of altered circumstances. A solitary war poem, "The Agent" consists entirely of formula situations sketched in flat language: the hardware is World War II surplus and the setting is a backlot assemblage of instant Europe. It reads like a worn-out answer to a new challenge. The opening lines of the long title poem guilelessly reveal the strain of a metaphysical essay being flogged into existence:

> As a queen sits down, knowing that a chair will be there,
> Or a general raises his hand and is given the field-glasses,
> Step off assuredly into the blank of your mind.
> Something will come to you.

Something does—nearly two hundred lines of wheezing exhortation. ("Avoid the pleasant room / Where someone, smiling to herself, has placed / A bowl of yellow freesias.") Wilbur's judicious retreat from raw experience has turned into mere insularity. It's a relief to get to the collection of translations at the back of the book, and the back goes more than a third of the way towards the front.

Yet with all this taken into account, there is still no reason to think that Wilbur will not eventually come up with something. At present he is off balance, a condition he is constitutionally unfitted to exploit. While he was on balance, though, he wrote a good number of poised, civilized and very beautiful poems. They'll be worth remembering when some of the rough, tough, gloves-off stuff we're lately supposed to admire starts looking thin. The beautiful changes—nobody denies that—but it doesn't change that much. I don't think it changes into *Crow*.

THE MIND-READER
1976

HERBERT LEIBOWITZ

Review of *The Mind-Reader*

Among those middle-aged poets who speak in a moderate voice, Richard Wilbur has won his share of awards and plaudits, but his virtues leave us somewhat uneasy. While we acknowledge his erudition and urbanity, we regretfully liken his mildness to the amiable normality of the bourgeois citizen. Emergencies are absent in his poems; he is unseduced by the romantic equation of knowledge and power; he seldom rails at the world. Suspicious of grandiose gestures, of parading the ego, he mediates experience through reason.

Technically, Wilbur's verse displays considerable skill. He rhymes adroitly, fashions polished epigrams, commands a suave syntax, and he entertains with an edifying wit. De Tocqueville would have judged him more an aristocratic writer than a democratic one, for Wilbur strives to please more than to astonish, to charm taste rather than to stir passion.

For nearly thirty years, Wilbur has written poems of a playful decorum in which one hears "the tempered consonants of discipline." In his latest volume, *The Mind-Reader*, Wilbur continues his Apollonian pursuit of "joining world and mind" with a sociable clarity. The eye is the privileged sense, composing phenomena "within the sudden premise of a frame." The dark rumblings of passion are contained in a diffident formality of manner, a conceptual modesty, "the language of the mended soul."

The pleasures of *The Mind-Reader* are those of an old friend whose talk is genial but familiar—and occasionally dull. The poems move easily from family to history, from books to movies, riddles, jests; such figures as Ulysses S. Grant, Linnaeus, Johnny Appleseed, Lewis Carroll, and St. Teresa make

The New York Times Book Review, June 13, 1976, pp. 11, 13.

cameo appearances and then leave the stage. There are a few deft translations, and best of all, since Wilbur is a fine amateur natural historian, careful observations of mushrooms, a black birch in winter, or a March storm:

> From the edge of the woods, in gusts,
> The leaves are scuttled forth
> Onto a pasture drifted
> Like tundras of the north,
>
> To migrate there in dry
> Skitter or fluttered brawl,
> Then flock into some hollow
> Like this, below the wall,
>
> With veins swept back like feathers
> To our prophetic sight,
> And bodies of gold shadow
> Pecking at sparks of light.

"March" exhibits the refined music of Wilbur's neoclassical style. What the eye records with chaste exactitude is balanced by the ear's subtle attention to pulse and enjambment in this uneven collection. No clangorous syllables disturb the muted dynamics of Wilbur's best lyrics: "In Limbo," "Children of Darkness," "Teresa" and most of "The Fourth of July."

But the penalty of shunning rhetoric so assiduously is that *The Mind-Reader* induces a certain affable blandness. Eloquence slides into elocution, talk into "genteel chat" and platitude: "It is always a matter, my darling, / Of life and death, as I had forgotten." "There is nothing to do with a day except to live it." "Which is to say that what love sees is true." One wishes that Wilbur would sometimes risk his mellifluous order and regularity for some of Plath's "brilliant negative / In poems free and helpless and unjust." His too legible poems threaten to become a tepid formula.

The rougher texture of the title poem, a dramatic monologue, offers welcome variety. The speaker, an aging, seedy Italian, sits at a cafe and cadges drinks, recounting his career as a mind-reader. A self-mocking performer, yet proud of his trade as a bogus oracle, he caters to respectable clients in search of clues from the unknown, guidance in business and love affairs, and retrieval of lost objects. "The Mind-Reader" explores the burdens and gifts of memory, that borderland between fraud and truth "where the soul mopes in private."

Wilbur's fascination with this mental trickster leads him to set aside his fluency. The poem is the better for it, as would have been the collection.

ANTHONY HECHT

The Motions of the Mind

Let me try to list some of the virtues that distinguish the poetry of Richard Wilbur. First of all, a superb ear (unequalled, I think, in the work of any poet now writing in English) for stately measure, cadences of a slow, processional grandeur, and a rich, ceremonial orchestration. A philosophic bent and a religious temper, which are by no means the same thing, but which here consort comfortably together. Wit, polish, a formal elegance that is never haughty or condescending, though certain free-wheeling poets take it for a chilling frigidity. And an unfeigned gusto, a naturally happy and grateful response to the physical beauty of life, of women, of works of art, landscapes, weather, and the perceiving, constructing mind that tries to know them. But in a way I think most characteristic of all, his is the most kinetic poetry I know: verbs are among his conspicuously important tools, and his poetry is everywhere a vision of *action,* of motion and performance.

That this is no mere casual habit but instead deliberate policy can be shown, I think, by the fact that pivotal and energetic verbs so often are placed in a rhyming position, and by that slight but potent musical device call some attention to themselves.

We could believe,

If you told us so, that the white-tailed deer will slip
Into perfect shade, grown perfectly shy,
The lark avoid the reaches of our eye,
The jack-pine lose its knuckled grip

The Times Literary Supplement, no. 3923 (May 20, 1977):602.

On the cold ledge, and every torrent burn
As Xanthus once. . . .
                              "Advice to a Prophet"

Or brewed in gulleys, steeped in wells, they spend
In chilly steam their last aromas, yield
From shallow hells a revenance of field
And orchard air. . . .
                              "In the Elegy Season"

For all they cannot share,
All that the world cannot in fact afford,
Their lofty premises are floored
With the massed voices of continual prayer.
                              "Altitudes"

Sweet water brims a cockle and braids down

Past spattered mosses, breaks
On the tipped edge of a second shell, and fills
The massive third below. It spills
In threads then from the scalloped rim, and makes

A scrim or summery tent. . . .
          "A Baroque Wall-Fountain in the Villa Sciarra"

          . . . remembering how the bed
Of layered rock two miles above my head

Hove ages up and broke
Soundless asunder, when the shrinking skin
Of Earth, blacked out by steam and smoke,
Gave passage to the muddled fire within,
Its crannies flooding with a sweat of quartz,
And lathered magmas out of deep retorts

Welled up, as here, to fill
With tumbled rockmeal, stone-fume, lithic spray,
The dike's brief chasm and the sill.

> Weathered until the sixth and human day
> By sanding winds and water, scuffed and brayed
> By the slow glacier's heel, these forms were made
> "On the Marginal Way"

There may be those, viewing the whole enterprise of formal poetry with suspicion or derision, who may suppose that this richness of inflections, this abundance of verbs, has been forced upon the poet by the ruthless exigencies of stanzaic form: the necessity, one way or another, of digging up a rhyme. For those to whom formal poetry is in itself unnatural, an embarrassed or twisted parlance of one who is self-consciously ill-at-ease holding the floor, any unusual feature of poetry, even its most towering graces, can be thought of as no more than the by-products, the industrial waste, entailed by meter and rhyme; and therefore (in the name of directness, of authenticity, of courage, of any number of Rousseauian virtues that belong exclusively to the noble savage) to be deplored as a victimization, as no grace at all but a crippled response to life and language. This sort of argument is marvellously self-serving, and based utterly on ignorance. In any case, there are far too many poets who employ strict formal devices (e.g., Housman, Auden, Graves, Ransom) and in whose work verb-forms play an almost unnoticed part, to make it plausible to explain this distinctive quality of Wilbur's as no more than an inadvertence over which he has neither choice nor control.

The truth is, if anything, just the opposite. Wilbur has been from the first a poet with a gymnastic sense of bodily agility and control, a delight in the fluencies we all admire in a trained athlete, in the vitality and importance of stamina and focused energy. We are not to be surprised that the poet who can praise

> the dining-car waiter's absurd
> Acrobacy—tipfingered tray like a wind-besting bird
> Plumblines his swinging shoes, the sole things sure
> In the shaken train. . . .

should also take it into his head to celebrate the skills of a juggler and the leap of Nijinsky, a Degas dancer, the sinuous and angelic floatings of laundry on a line, the scamper and swirl of blown newspaper, the convening in the air "like a drunken fingerprint" of a flock of birds, even, in the realm of the purely mechanical, a fire-truck "blurring to sheer verb." Or that he should write poems called "Running" and "Walking to Sleep."

This delight in nimbleness, this lively sense of coordinated and practiced skill is, first of all, a clear extension of the dexterity the verse itself performs. If it were no more than this it might be suspected for an exercise in that self-approval which, like one of the poet's fountains, patters "its own applause." But it is more. For again and again in Wilbur's poems this admirable grace or strength of body is a sign of or symbol for the inward motions of the mind or condition of the soul. Most obviously in "Mind," the very executive operations of the mind correspond to the speed, the passage, the radar intelligence of a bat. But think also of how the two contrasted fountains (in the Baroque Fountain poem) represent two alternative postures of the spirit, one of relaxed and worldly grace, and the other of strenuous, earth-denying effort. Think, too, of these opening lines:

> As a queen sits down, knowing that a chair will be there,
> Or a general raises his hand and is given the field-glasses,
> Step off assuredly into the blank of your mind.
> Something will come to you. . . .

This poet's recurrent subject is not only the motion of change and transition but how that motion ("In the Elegy Season," "Marginalia," "On the Marginal Way," "'A World Without Objects Is a Sensible Emptiness,'" "Year's End," "Merlin Enthralled," and "Digging for China" are only random examples) is the very motion of the mind itself.

It is, I think, remarkable that this double fluency, of style and of subject, should be so singularly Wilbur's own, and that his poetry should exhibit so often the most important and best aspects of cinematic film: the observation of things in motion from a viewpoint that can, if it cares to, move with an equal and astonishing grace. But what these poems can do so magnificently that is probably beyond the range of motion pictures is, specifically, a transition, or, rather, a translation, of outward physical action (the heave of a weight, the bounce of a ball, the spring of a runner) into a condition of the imagination; a dissolving of one realm of reality into another, for which the poem "Merlin Enthralled" might serve as an example. As perhaps these stanzas might also:

> And once my arm was lifted to hew down
>   A cavalier from off his saddle-bow,
> That bore a lady from a leaguer'd town,
>   And then, I know not how,
> All those sharp fancies, by down-lapsing thought
>   Stream'd onward, lost their edges, and did creep
> Roll'd on each other, rounded, smooth'd and brought
>   Into the gulfs of sleep.

As it happens, these stanzas are by Tennyson, and I suggest that they supply a far more likely source for some of Wilbur's techniques than Hollywood could come up with. The two poets share an unparalleled musical ear and an enormous sense of physical vitality. But I think these eight lines worth a little examination, since I hope to show that they may indicate as much about Wilbur as about his great Victorian predecessor. First, the immense variety, ferocity, and activity compressed within the first three of these eight lines. The speaker, armed, in a transitional posture of combat, presumably on foot, courageously prepared to challenge a well-seated and, presumably, armed horseman—who is either rescuing or, more likely, abducting a lady from a town under military siege—as if the whole vast enterprise of war and the fate of thousands were painted small in the background of a picture whose main foreground features were the lady and her abductor on horseback, and the challenging hero. Part of the huge Delacroix energy of these lines (which could plausibly remind one of that painter's "The Massacre of Chios") comes from the indeterminate antecedent of "That," the first word of the third line, which can be read as referring either to "saddle-bow" or "cavalier." But then, after the coiled springs of those three lines, there follow five of soft intoxicated swoon. But they are more than that. As opposed to the compressed action, alarms and dangers of the first three lines, the swoon here involves a process of glacial patience and geological refinement, a vast secular effort of withdrawal, leaving in its wake a moraine of verbs, like a scatter of polished boulders come to rest. It would be easy to believe that these lines and those of "On the Marginal Way" came out of the same imagination.

Publishers are not always judicious about their dust-jacket claims, but Wilbur's American publishers have been wise to quote the following from Theodore Roethke's posthumously published notebooks: "Wilbur: can look at a thing, and talk about it beautifully, can turn it over in his mind, and draw truths from a scene, easily and effortlessly (it would seem)—though this kind of writing requires the hardest kind of discipline, it must be remembered. Not a graceful mind—that's a mistake—but a mind of grace, an altogether different and higher thing."

That mind of grace is brilliantly at work in *The Mind-Reader,* Wilbur's latest book, and nowhere more than in the title poem, a dramatic monologue of immense poignancy and mastery, which opens with these lines:

> Some things are truly lost. Think of a sun-hat
> Laid for the moment on a parapet
> While three young women—one, perhaps, in mourning—
> Talk in the crenellate shade. A slight wind plucks
> And budges it; it scuffs to the edge and cartwheels
> Into a giant view of some description:
> Haggard escarpments, if you like, plunge down
> Through mica shimmer to a moss of pines
> Amidst which, here or there, a half-seen river
> Lobs up a blink of light. The sun-hat falls,
> With what free flirts and stoops you can imagine,
> Down through that reeling vista or another,
> Unseen by any, even by you or me.
> It is as when a pipe-wrench, catapulted
> From the jounced back of a pick-up truck, dives headlong
> Into a bushy culvert; or a book
> Whose reader is asleep, garbling the story,
> Glides from beneath a steamer chair and yields
> Its flurried pages to the printless sea.

This deserves to be savoured carefully and at length. There is the superb visualization of motion, of diminution into irretrievable distances; but for all the specificity of imagery, the event is all conjectural, hypothetical, the work and motion of the mind itself. The sun-hat is merely proposed as a subject for thought, everything it moves through is contingent ("a giant view of some description: / Haggard escarpments, if you like, . .") as is its own motion ("With what free flirts and stoops can you imagine . . ."). And so, initially, this floating, limpid descent becomes a metaphor for the imagination, the graceful motions of the mind. In this sense, it is part of that important vein of modern poetry, of which Wallace Stevens is one of the grand practitioners, a poetry about poetry. But this is only the beginning. The ease, the smoothness, the very "grace" described in these lines is a grace, a humanity, of their speaker, an old Italian "dipso" who cadges drinks, at a cafe that is all but his "office," from transient patrons in exchange for his mind-reading act. And he manages with infinitely graceful tact to remind us how merciful is that Greek myth which tells us that the dead drink of the waters of Lethe, and are immediately blessed with forgetfulness. For, indeed, who could bear, even in life, to be afflicted with total and perfect recall of all his own failures, his acts of clumsiness and unkindness, his foolish errors and stupidities? Yet it appears that this old man has been singled out for this especial torment. Given the exquisite, interminable anguish of his life it is not surprising he should seek oblivion in drink, but it is absolutely astonishing that he should be able to address us, his chance patrons, with such affecting civility, such perfect "grace." He is, we recognize quickly, close kin to that tormented insomniac who speaks to himself in Wilbur's earlier poem, "Walking to Sleep."

Splendid as this poem is, it represents only one aspect of a remarkable versatility. A reviewer can scarcely hope to do justice to all the skills and graces here exhibited, so I must resort, weakly, to a sort of list. Few other poets could render so faithfully both the slum-bred, vulgar vitality of a Villon ballade and the fastidious, well-bred wit of La Fontaine and Voltaire. And there are the poet's utterly comfortable, colloquial translations from the modern Russian of Brodsky, Voznesensky and

Nikolai Morshen. There is a little group of truly funny poems of which one in particular, "The Prisoner of Zenda," I earnestly commend to the editorial attention of Kingsley Amis who is, I understand, at work on an Oxford Book of Light Verse. And there is, finally (though first in the volume) a group of twenty-two new lyric poems, some of them as brilliant as anything Wilbur has done. "The Fourth of July," for example, bids fair to be the best thing to come out of the American Bicentennial. But in this poetic era of arrogant solipsism and limp narcissism—when great, shaggy herds of poets write only about themselves, or about the casual workings of their rather tedious minds—it is essential to our sanity, salutary to our humility, and a minimal obeisance to the truth to acknowledge, with Wilbur, in poem after poem, but here especially in one called "The Eye," the vast alterity, the "otherness" of the world, that huge corrective to our self-sufficiency. The poem is about the pleasures, the dangers, the temptations merely of "looking," and it ends with a prayer addressed to St. Lucy that concludes,

> Forbid my vision
> To take itself for a curious angel.
> Remind me that I am here in body,
> A passenger, and rumpled.
>
> Charge me to see
> In all bodies the beat of spirit,
> Not merely in the *tout en l'air*
> Or double pike with layout
>
> But in the strong,
> Shouldering gait of the legless man,
> The calm walk of the blind young woman
> Whose cane touches the curbstone.
>
> Correct my view
> That the far mountain is much diminished,
> That the fovea is prime composer,
> That the lid's closure frees me.

Let me be touched
By the alien hands of love forever,
That this eye not be folly's loophole
But giver of due regard.

BRUCE MICHELSON

Richard Wilbur's *The Mind-Reader*

When it came out in 1976, *The Mind-Reader* didn't change any minds. As Richard Wilbur's latest collection of poems, the book was reviewed about eighteen times in predictable ways: people who had understood and liked his work before had more nice things to say (William Pritchard, for example, in the *Hudson Review*), and people who were stuck on the old idea that Wilbur is a safe soul, somebody to be arch about, did their usual dance. Wilbur has spent thirty years sharpening our sense of irony and showing us that wit and passionate intensity can have everything to do with each other. That is the kind of cause that divides people for good—and so it is no surprise that some of *The Mind-Reader*'s readers found there the same old Wilbur they expected.

There are, however, some new sides to the Wilbur who shows himself here. One thing that is new is the book's defiant surfaces. The poems are as witty and elegant and deadly serious as ever, but the collection, taken altogether, seems to stand up against every kind of poet-chic, as if Wilbur meant to strut around for a moment, with an angry glint in his eye, wearing the "bourgeois" mask which his detractors hang on him. The defiance runs cover to cover, literally; the jacket front shows a silhouette of somebody sitting with legs crossed at a café table, evidently recollecting in too much tranquility; the back is a photograph of The Poet in the Parlor, looking tweedy and comfy and sane—looking all wrong. Inside, there is a poem about politics (the first since his crack about President Johnson ten years ago), telling the student strikers of 1970 to do more talking and thinking than rock throwing (still an unfashionable idea, given all the effort now to romanticize those hard years). There are

The Southern Review 15 (July 1979):763–68.

some lines called "What's Good for the Soul Is Good for Sales," a punch at the morose confessionalism which gets so much play:

> If fictive music fails your lyre, confess—
> Though not, of course, to any happiness.
> So be it tristful, tell us what you choose:
> Hangover, Nixon on the TV news,
> God's death, the memory of your rocking-horse,
> Entropy, housework, Buchenwald, divorce,
> Those damned flamingoes in your neighbor's yard. . .
> All hangs together if you take it hard.

We get a marriage toast that celebrates marriage, we get riddles and jokes, tour de force translations of Villon, Du Bellay, Voznesensky, and others, poems about Johnny Appleseed and his apples, the Fourth of July, milkweed, mushrooms, shallots, all of them graceful, well-mannered, and outwardly tranquil celebrations of love, light, life. But the readers who are usually irked by that sort of thing will be especially upset with "Cottage Street, 1953," which seems to have irreverent things to say about Sylvia Plath.

"Cottage Street" is, according to Wilbur, a "composite" recollection of the young woman Wilbur actually knew. The setting is the Wellesley home of Edna Ward, Wilbur's mother-in-law and a friend of "frightened Mrs. Plath," who is here for tea with her "pale, slumped daughter" recovering from a suicide attempt. But there is nothing snide about the poem. It is meant to recall the powerlessness that Wilbur felt (and must still feel), with his hard-won faith in the order of things, to speak of that faith to such abject despair:

> It is my office to exemplify
> The published poet in his happiness,
> Thus cheering Sylvia, who has wished to die;
> But half-ashamed, and impotent to bless,
>
> I am a stupid life-guard who has found,
> Swept to his shallows by the tide, a girl
> Who, far from shore, has been immensely drowned, . . .

How large is her refusal; and how slight
The genteel chat whereby we recommend
Life, of a summer afternoon, despite
The brewing dusk which hints that it may end.

Wilbur has been in that brewing dusk before, knows the breadth and intensity of Sylvia's night—but what can he do? The poem ends by contrasting the death of Edna Ward, at eighty-eight, with Sylvia's suicide; and these are the lines which anger people. Mrs. Ward dies,

The thin hand reaching out, the last word *love,*

Outliving Sylvia who, condemned to live,
Shall study for a decade, as she must,
To state at last her brilliant negative
In poems free and helpless and unjust.

The bluntness is surprising, but no poet writing in this language has ever chosen his words more carefully than Wilbur, and "unjust" is exactly what he means. His sympathy for the desperate, brilliant young woman runs deep, but finally he states his positive, as *he* must, his faith in an obscure but fundamental goodness in life. He turns away from a vision which is ontologically "unjust," meaning faithless as well as unfair. This is the first occasion when Wilbur in any of his poems has spoken directly about a fellow poet, and it seems to me as gentle and just an observation as anyone who believes can make about anyone who doesn't. But in these touchy times a small noise like that is enough to stampede Ms. Plath's wild hierophants. Perhaps the poem had to be written; perhaps Wilbur had to orient himself in public under the shadow that she currently casts. Yet "Cottage Street" has surely put off people who might otherwise read Wilbur with more care.

Close reading is what Wilbur still requires, not because his poems have grown more obscure and idiosyncratic. The rich surfaces have grown rougher and wilder, the resolutions are down deeper and take a steadier gaze to find. But the poems still work like Wyeth's paintings: we enter into familiar worlds full of light and fresh air—and then we find that there are tigers aprowl in the tall grass and that the safe artist who dreams these safe landscapes has been farther out on the edge than most of the sword-dancers we have heard about. The life-and-death business is still the struggle of the imagination to make sense of the world's turbulence, the difference is that the turbulence is more intense. The Johnny Appleseed poem, "John Chapman," is about the sexuality and wildness that can be neither repressed nor let go. They have to be understood, praised, and at the same time, transformed. These are the last two stanzas:

> Out of your grave, John Chapman, in Fort Wayne,
> May you arise, and flower, and come true.
> We meanwhile, being of a spotted strain
> And born into a wilder land than you,
>
> Expecting less of natural tree or man
> And dubious of working out the brute,
> Affix such hopeful scions as we can
> To the rude, forked, and ever savage root.

"The Shallot" is likewise about a refined beauty rising somehow from savage roots, and it too seems (fittingly) earthier than usual, as Wilbur's botany poems go:

> The full cloves
> Of your buttocks, the convex
> Curve of your belly, the curved
> Cleft of your sex—
>
> Out of this corm
> That's planted in strong thighs
> The slender stem and radiant
> Flower rise.

The best use of this new roughness turns up in the mushroom poem, "Children of Darkness," a lyric about those rootless, nasty-looking things that grow in the deep shade, feeding on death and rot. Wilbur has written about ugly things before, dead dogs and vultures; but he has never been this lurid before:

> An elm-bole cocks a bloody ear;
> In the oak's shadow lies a strew of brains.
> Wherever, after the deep rains,
>
> The woodlands are morose and reek of punk,
> These gobbets grow—
> Tongue, lobe, hand, hoof or butchered toe
> Amassing on the fallen branch half-sunk
> In leaf-mold, or the riddled trunk.

And so on, through "shameless phalloi," "to whose slimed heads come carrion flies." The beauty in all this horror is that these ugly things break death down so that life can rise up again; they keep nature new and fresh, and a steady, serious look at them can do the same thing for us:

> Gargoyles is what they are at worst, and should
> They preen themselves
> On being demons, ghouls, or elves,
> The holy chiaroscuro of the wood
> Still would embrace them. They are good.

There is one perfect, classic haiku in the book, "Sleepless at Crown Point," which catches Wilbur's whole struggle in twelve words:

> All night, this headland
> Lunges into the rumpling
> Capework of the wind.

For three decades Wilbur's head-land, that wakeful, witty sensibility of his, has been lunging into dark, vaporous, disheveled places. Everything takes place on the border between light and shadow; it is no good if you go to sleep at your crown point and never go sleepless into the dark; it is no good if you go out there and never come back again. Sometimes the escape from the darkness is a narrow one. The collection's title poem is a dramatic monologue (the first long one that Wilbur has published), from the kind of sensibility that Wilbur's almost is—that is, one that hasn't found its way back. The speaker is a heavy-drinking Italian with a powerful intuition; he is a charlatan and a desperate man because he has lost the battle with that intuition and it has swept him off into solipsism, obsession, confusion:

> What can be wiped from memory? Not the least
> Meanness, obscenity, humiliation,
> Terror which made you clench your eyes, or pulse
> Of happiness which quickened your despair.
> Nothing can be forgotten, as I am not
> Permitted to forget.
>
> It was not far
> From that to this—this corner café table
> Where, with my lank grey hair and vatic gaze,
> I sit and drink at the receipt of custom.
> They come here, day and night, so many people:
> Sad women of the quarter, dressed in black,
> As to a black confession; blinking clerks
> Who half-suppose that Taurus ruminates
> Upon their destinies; men of affairs
> Down from Milan to clear it with the magus
> Before they buy or sell some stock or other;
> My fellow drunkards; . . .

That man on the front of the dust jacket, the silhouette at the café table, has Wilbur's shape, as he should; for this mind worn down with detail and misfortune and all those perceptions which can break anyone who seeks the "resonance in all their fretting" *is* Wilbur, the other side of the man—not simply the visionary that he struggles against becoming, but the visionary that, for all controlled surfaces, he always is.

The story goes that Randall Jarrell "discovered" Frost for himself while Jarrell was soaking in a New Jersey swimming pool, daydreaming about the New England woods, and coming back again and again to the rightness of Frost's lines. *The Mind-*

Reader is the same kind of mind-grower, for there are poems here which, unfolding as they do with each new reading, are going to be hard to get rid of. If I am a little uneasy it is for one unfair reason: I find myself wishing that this astounding poet would put out something big or flashy enough to turn more heads and absolutely stop all this talk about safety and propriety. The biggest surprise in the book is that dramatic monologue, and if it turns out to be a direction that Wilbur will follow, I may get my foolish wish. But what we have from him already is poetry to be very grateful for, poetry that we cannot be permitted to forget.

OPPOSITES
1973

MYRA COHN LIVINGSTON

Review of *Opposites*

It's enchanting to think of a dinner table, such as Richard Wilbur's, where a game called Opposites is played; but a great deal more fortunate for all of us that this game has been winnowed, culled and preserved in a book called *Opposites,* complete with the poet's amusing drawings.

Some months ago I read a verse by a child who stated, dully, that the opposite of fat was thin, tall of short, ad nauseum. Wilbur's new book ought to begin a whole new thing with children, as well as adults, for it starts the imagination whirling. Would any of us, before reading *Opposites* be able to leap to Wilbur's observation that

> There's more than one way to be right
> About the opposite of *white,*
> And those who merely answer *black*
> Are very, very single-track.
> They make one want to scream, "I beg
> Your pardon, but within an egg
> (A fact known to the simplest folk)
> The opposite of white is *yolk!*"

Richard Wilbur is in tune with young people, their language, idiomatic expressions and guffaws;

> What is the opposite of *nuts?*
> It's *soup!* Let's have no ifs or buts.
> In any suitable repast
> The soup comes first, the nuts come last.

The New York Times Book Review, July 1, 1973, p. 8.

> Or that is what *sane* folk advise;
> You're nuts if you think otherwise.

The poet injects himself into his Opposites, with asides which bring nothing but delight to such as fourth-grade boys:

> The opposite of *spit*, I'd say,
> Would be *a narrow cove or bay*.
>
> (There is another sense of *spit*,
> But I refuse to think of it.
> It stands opposed to *all refined*
> *And decent instincts of mankind!*)

These witty asides, reminiscent of Hilaire Belloc (and occasionally W. S. Gilbert) punctuate the poems written in iambic tetrameter couplets; ever the master of meter, rhyme and form, Wilbur's poems are a reminder that an adherence to form in poetry yields its own rich rewards for the poet as well as the reader. "I said that just because it rhymes, / As lazy poets do at times."

There are thirty-nine amusingly illustrated Opposites in this book; every reader will find his favorites, but two of my own choice hinge on the neat disposition and beautiful brevity of Opposites numbers 8 and 12:

> What is the opposite of *riot?*
> It's *lots of people keeping quiet*.
>
> What is the opposite of *two?*
> *A lonely me, a lonely you*.

It takes a Pulitzer Prize winner to do *that!*

RESPONSES—
PROSE PIECES: 1953–1976
1976

CLIVE JAMES

As a Matter of Tact

There is nothing surprising in the fact that the most intelligent, fastidious and refined of contemporary American poets should produce intelligent, fastidious and refined prose, but it does no harm to have the likelihood confirmed. This collection of Richard Wilbur's critical writings is an immediate pleasure to read. Beyond that, the book provides an absorbing tour of Wilbur's preoccupations, which admirers of his poetry had already guessed to be of high interest. Beyond that again, there is the harsh matter, steadily becoming more urgent, of whether or not the study of literature is killing literature.

In America, the place where crises burst first, it has long been apparent that the output of critical works from the universities, most of them uttered by student teachers fatally combining intellectual mediocrity and wetness behind the ears, has reached the proportions of an ecological disaster. Yet here is one book, written by a professor of English at Wesleyan University, which would have to be saved from the holocaust if President Carter were to take the sensible step of rationalising his energy programme by ordering all academic writings on the subject of English literature to be fed directly to the flames, thereby ensuring that useless books, inflated from only slightly less useless doctoral theses, would find at least a semblance of creative life by providing enough electric power to light a pig-sty, if only for a few seconds.

But then Wilbur is no ordinary professor. His university career has really been a kind of monastic hideaway, where he has been able to hole up and contemplate his principal early experience, which was the Second World War in Europe. Military

New Statesman, June 17, 1977, pp. 815–16.

service was Wilbur's first university. If forever afterwards he was a writer in residence, at least he was writing about something that he had seen in the outside world. In the deceptively elegant symmetries of Wilbur's early poetry could be detected a pressure of awareness which amply warranted his retreat to the cloisters.

While his contemporaries held the mirror up to chaos, Wilbur took the opposite line: the more extreme the thing contained, the more finely wrought the container had to be. Berryman and Lowell went in for stringy hair, open-necked shirts, nonrhyming sonnets that multiplied like bacilli, and nervous breakdowns. Wilbur, on the other hand, looked like an advertisement for Ivy League tailoring and turned out poems built like Fabergé toy trains. I think there is a case for arguing that by the time the sixties rolled around Wilbur had cherished his early experience too long for the good of his work, which in his later volumes is simply indecisive. But earlier on he was not indecisive at all— just indirect, which is a different thing. The poems in *The Beautiful Changes, Ceremony* and *Things of This World* sound better and better as time goes on. Where his coevals looked fecund, they now look slovenly; where he once seemed merely exquisite, he now seems a model of judicious strength; as was bound to happen, it was the artful contrivance which retained its spontaneity and the avowedly spontaneous which ended up looking contrived. There is no reason to be ashamed at feeling charmed by Wilbur's poetry. The sanity of his level voice is a hard-won triumph of the contemplative intelligence.

Selected from twenty years of occasional prose, the essays and addresses collected in *Responses* combine conciseness with resonance, each of them wrapping up its nominal subject while simultaneously raising all the relevant general issues—the best kind of criticism for a student to read. A lecture like "Round About a Poem of Housman's" could be put into a beginner's hands with some confidence that it would leave him wiser than before, instead of merely cockier. Previously available only in that useful anthology *The Moment of Poetry,*[1] the piece gains from being set among others from the same pen. It is an excellent instance of close reading wedded to hard thinking. The general statements are as tightly focused as the specific observations, which from so sensitive a reader are very specific indeed. By attending patiently to Housman's delicately judged tones of voice in "Epitaph on an Army of Mercenaries," Wilbur is able to show that the contempt superficially evinced for the hired soldiers is meant to imply an underlying respect. The casual reader might miss this not just through being deaf to poetry, but through being deaf to meaning in general. "A tactful person is one who understands not merely what is said, but also what is meant." But meaning is not confined to statements: in fact the sure way to miss the point of Housman's poem is to do a practical criticism that confines itself to paraphrase. A song like "It's Only a Paper Moon" and a poem like "Dover Beach" can be paraphrased in exactly the same way. (This seemingly off-hand illustration is typical of Wilbur's knack for the perfect example.) It follows that meaning embraces not just statement but sound, pacing, diction. Thus the subject expands to include questions of why poetry is written the way it is. How much can the poet legitimately expect the reader to take in?

Yeats, for example, overdoes his allusions in "King and No King." It is one thing for Milton to expect you to spot the reference to the *Aeneid* when Satan wakes in Hell, but another for Yeats to expect you to know a bad play by Beaumont and Fletcher. For one thing, you can see what Milton means even if you have never read Virgil, whereas Yeats' point seems not to be particularly well made even when you have Beaumont and Fletcher at your fingertips—in fact pride at being in possession of such information is likely to colour your judgment. (Says Wilbur, who *did* possess such information, and whose judgment *was* coloured.)

It is worth pausing at this juncture to say that in a few paragraphs Wilbur has not only raised, but to a large extent settled, theoretical points which more famous critical savants have pursued to the extent of whole essays. In *Lectures in America* Dr. Leavis argues, with crushing intransigence, that Yeats' poetry needs too much ancillary apparatus to explain it, so that when you get right down to it there are only two poems in Yeats' entire *oeuvre* which earn the status of a "fully achieved thing." Wilbur takes the same point exactly as far as it should be taken, which is nowhere near as far. Possessing tact himself, he can see

Yeats' lack of it, but correctly supposes this to be a local fault, not a typical one. If Dr. Leavis is unable to consider such a possibility, perhaps it might be of interest to Professor Donoghue, who in a recent issue of the *New York Review of Books* was to be heard complaining about Yeats' limitations at some length. It is a bit steep when an academic who devotes half his life to a dead poet starts doubting the poet's merits instead of questioning the effects of his own bookishness.

As for Wilbur's reference to Milton, well, it is very relevant to some of the positions adopted by Dr. Steiner, whose important gift of transmitting his enthusiasm for the culture of the past seriously overstepped itself in Milton's case. Perhaps goaded by the misplaced self-confidence of a student generation who not only knew nothing about the history of civilisation but had erected their doltishness into an ideology, Dr. Steiner declared that you couldn't tell what was going on in *Paradise Lost* unless you were intimate with the classical literature to which Milton was alluding. Wilbur's fleeting look at this very topic helps remind us that Dr. Steiner got it wrong two ways at once. If you *did* have to know about those things, then Milton would not deserve his reputation. But you *don't* have to know, since the allusions merely reinforce what Milton is tactful enough to make plain.

Such matters are important to criticism and crucial to pedagogy. For all Dr. Steiner's good intentions, it is easy to imagine students being scared off if they are told that they can't hope to read an English poet without first mastering classical literature. Wilbur's approach, while being no less concerned about the universality of culture, at least offers the ignoramus some hope. Anyway, Wilbur simply happens to be right: poets allude to the past (his essay "Poetry's Debt to Poetry" shows that all revolutions in art are palace revolutions) but if they are original at all then they will make their first appeal on a level which demands of the reader no more than an ability to understand the language. Which nowadays is demanding a lot, but let that pass.

"Poetry and Happiness" is another richly suggestive piece of work. Wilbur talks of a primitive desire that is radical to poetry, "the desire to lay claim to as much of the world as possible through uttering the names of things." Employing the same gift for metaphysical precision which he demonstrates elsewhere in his essay on Emily Dickinson, Wilbur is able to show what forms this desire usually takes and how it affects the poet's proverbial necessity to "find himself." I don't think it is too facetious to suggest that this might be a particularly touchy subject for Wilbur. Complaining about the lack of unity in American culture, he seems really to be talking about his own difficulties in writing about the American present with the same unforced originality—finding yourself—which marked his earlier poems about Europe.

In the following essay, a fascinating piece (indispensable for the student of his poems) called "On My Own Work," he rephrases the complaint as a challenge. "Yet the incoherence of America need not enforce a stance of alienation on the poet: rather, it may be seen as placing on him a peculiar imaginative burden." It is a nice point whether Wilbur has ever really taken that burden up. I am inclined to think that he has not, and that the too-typical quietness of his later work ("characteristic," in the sense Randall Jarrell meant when he decided that Wallace Stevens had fallen to copying himself) represents a great loss to all of us. But we ought to learn to be appropriately grateful for what we have been given, before we start complaining about what has been taken away.

"It is one mark of the good critic," Wilbur observes, "that he abstains from busywork." Except for the essays on Poe, which tend to the repetitive, this whole collection has scarcely a superfluous sentence. When Wilbur's critical sense lapses, it is usually through kindness. He makes as good a case as can be made for Theodore Roethke's openness to influence, calling admirable what he should see to be crippling. But even full-time critics can be excused for an occasional disinclination to tell the cruel truth, and on the whole this is a better book of criticism than we can logically expect a poet to come up with. If there is a gulf between English and American literature in modern times, at least there are some interesting bridges over it. The critical writings produced by some of the best American poets form one of those bridges. Tate, Berryman, Jarrell, John Peale Bishop, Edmund Wilson—those among them who were primarily critics were still considerable poets, and those among them who were primarily poets have yet managed to produce some of the most humane criticism we possess. With this superlative book, Richard Wilbur takes a leading place among their number.

NOTE

1. Don Cameron Allen, ed., *The Moment of Poetry* (Baltimore: Johns Hopkins University Press, 1962). Later published as *Four Poets on Poetry* (1959) and *A Celebration of Poets* (1967) by the same publisher.

PART TWO   *Under Discussion*

ROBERT F. SAYRE

A Case for Richard Wilbur as Nature Poet

The standard view of the poetry of Richard Wilbur is still essentially the one taken by Randall Jarrell over ten years ago in a review of *Ceremony* and then repeated in *Poetry and the Age*. Jarrell praised Wilbur's delicacy and skill but regretted that so much talent should be so timid. "Mr. Wilbur never goes too far, but he never goes far enough." He then urged Wilbur to run a few risks, show a little nerve, as if he might be a Whitman hiding in the skin of a Longfellow. The passage of time, however, has not seen Wilbur become a literatus, and Jarrell's criticism was later seconded yet again by Leslie Fiedler in the twenty-fifth anniversary issue of *The Kenyon Review*. In Fiedler's language, Wilbur was safely the "best" of "the male neo-Genteel Poets," who cater to a "liberal, culture-hungry, new bourgeoisie" which likes irony but still fears "madness and unrestraint."

I would like, just the same, to set aside this judgment, which is based almost entirely on the manner of Wilbur's poems, and to look instead at his most important subject. Wilbur, who was born in 1921, is clearly one of the leading American poets of his generation, and he has freely acknowledged belonging to the so-called New Formalists. But Fiedler is misleading in saying Wilbur "was born in the suburbs of New York" and in then supplying him with a middle-class background. A Harvard education and a college professorship, furthermore, need no more make Wilbur a neo-Genteel Poet than they make Fiedler (who also has these distinctions!) a neo-Genteel Critic. Wilbur's own statement, from Stanley Kunitz's *Twentieth Century Authors,* is corrective. "I spent the first two years of my life, or so I am told,

Moderna Spraak (Stockholm) 61 (1967):114–22.

in what was to be the shadow of the George Washington Bridge." He grew up, he goes on, in a "pocket of resistance to suburbia (since infiltrated)"—a farm in North Caldwell, New Jersey, where his father, the artist Lawrence Wilbur, had a pre-Revolutionary stone house in a corner of a rich man's country estate. "I grew up among woods, orchards, corn-fields, horses, hogs, cows, and hay-wagons." The correction should be made because Wilbur appears to have had to designate himself as a sort of predestined pastoralist. "A friend recently remarked that my poems are unfashionably favorable toward nature, and I must blame this warp on a rural, pleasant and somewhat solitary boyhood."

The phrase "nature poet" is so dated, somehow, that one hesitates to use it. Robert Frost was a "naturalist" in a far different sense of that word. Theodore Roethke, as the son of an owner of greenhouses, had the perceptions of a sort of Freudian botanist: "Scurry of warm over small plants. / Ordnung! ordnung! / Papa is coming!" It *is* possible, nevertheless, to point to the quintessential modern American nature *poem,* William Carlos Williams'

> so much depends
> upon
>
> a red wheel
> barrow
>
> glazed with rain
> water
>
> beside the white
> chickens

For here, as well as being "unfashionably favorable toward nature," the poet commits himself to nature for his knowledge of himself. Each image, to quote Roy Harvey Pearce, is "a way we have of taking possession of our world without destroying it." In a simple but profound way these images *are* Williams the man. Dr. Williams' effort, moreover, was made in the face of the gigantic effort of our age to remove such scenes or to block and destroy our relations with them—efforts as diverse as the "model farms" Thoreau long ago derided and the slick Kodachromes which represent nature by the remote splendors of National Parks. Williams' world, like Emerson's was "emblematic," nature was "the symbol of spirit," and a world without nature would have been a world without spirit. The two essentials of American nature poetry are the affection for nature and the Transcendentalist sense of correspondence between it and man.

Having called attention to these essentials, we might begin by seeing their powerful use in "Advice to a Prophet," a poem which is much more than simply an antiwar poem. The "prophet," of course, is the sayer of atomic doom, but Wilbur advises him to "Spare us all word of the weapons." They are dizzy facts given in "long numbers" which men cannot understand. They are nonnatural. To be understood, one must speak in terms of the natural world men have known. Therefore, Wilbur says, "Speak of the world's own change"—laying the stress on 'own' when reading to audiences. But the changes the poet then foresees are to the trees and animals which man has always drawn upon for metaphors of his own modesty, courage, or fidelity— "These things in which we have seen ourselves and spoken." Without subscribing to a Transcendentalist theory of one Spirit, Wilbur is still accepting Emerson's belief that "particular natural facts are symbols of particular spiritual facts," and that language itself is emblematic. Wilbur's basic point is that a "prophet" who does not by his language reconnect us with the natural world and thereby also recharge his language will not succeed. Although professedly just an advisor, he is strongest when making that connection himself.

> Ask us, ask us . . .
> Whether there shall be lofty or long standing
> When the bronze annals of the oak-tree close.

The oak-tree's endurance and strength have been man's own support and its "annals" man's annals. There are conventional prophets enough, we might add, because people of all persuasions cry about the weapons and the "long numbers." But the mad shrillness mostly proves the failure of communication. The audience is truly the "us" of the poem, and the poet is indeed a real prophet, showing that in this age ceasing to refresh our relation to nature can be more calamitous than ever before. By losing the means of talking sense, we will lose everything.

Refreshing our correspondence with nature is by no means easy, however. Wilbur sees it as having built-in pitfalls and tragedy. In "Beasts," for example, which was first published in his anthology *A Bestiary,* then republished in *Things of This World,* he shows the process of this kind of tragedy while also trying to revive the significance of the old legends of beasts. Logically enough, Wilbur sees our isolation from nature and the decline of bestiaries as very related. The poem opens with a somber description of animals sleeping and killing in their appointed and immemorial fashion, and, therefore, "in peace tonight." Even "the werewolf's painful change," though mysterious, is still tranquil and orderly. But elsewhere, "at high windows," a breed of very restless sort of super-werewolves called "suitors of excellence" are also moved by the night,

> Making such dreams for men
> As told will break their hearts as always, bringing
> Monsters into the city, crows on the public statues,
> Navies fed to the fish in the dark
> Unbridled waters.

These suitors' separation from nature does not insulate them from always having "to construe again the painful / Beauty of heaven," but they cannot seek their correspondence without heartbreak.

Wilbur is not a moralist about imagined testaments of nature, which he finds resolutely contradictory (see "Two Voices in a Meadow"), but about man's relations with nature. One is knowing and emblematic, the other detached and romantic. The "suitors of excellence," needless to say, are the archetypes of all midnight and weekend moon-watchers, who make dreams because they have so little real experience. Understandably, they are not "suitors of nature," not "suitors of women"! In

"Lamarck Elaborated" Wilbur sees this too lofty romancing as having come from the intellect rather than the senses, Lamarck's theory that "the environment creates the organ" inspiring the poet to a history of sensation and thought. The senses are products of the force of the physical world: "It was the song of doves begot the ear / And not the ear that first conceived of sound." But thought, that sense "most formidably dim," is a countercurrent.

> The shell of balance rolls in seas of thought.
> It was the mind that taught the head to swim.

Then "Newtonian numbers" introduced new "whirling worlds we could not know," changed our view of the physical world, and gave birth to romantic confusion. "And by the imagined floods of our desires / The voice of Sirens gave us vertigo." Wilbur might be called one of the most antisystematic of modern poets. He would much rather be drawn "to the things of this world" than come out, as he says of Emily Dickinson's neighbor in "Altitudes," "To pace about his garden, lost in thought." "The mind is like a bat," he says in "Mind"—both navigate dark caverns. The key exception is that "in the very happiest intellection / A graceful error may correct the cave." That is a cutting distinction.

Strange as it may sound to say so, I find the distrust of both romanticizing and intellectual systematizing stronger in Wilbur's poems than in the work of most "beat" poets, who are supposed to be the iconoclasts and rebels of contemporary America. Everything from Wilbur's personal appearance, which is as relaxed yet correct as a young count's, to his smoothly managed rhymes and meters make him emphatically nonbeat, but this isn't really the issue. His wit, his easy elegance, and his penchant for the eccentric or obscurely "learned" fact are all antisystematic. They are little gyroscopes of intelligence to steady and adjust wavering intellect, always directing him back to nature rather than away from it. His four-line "Epistemology," for example, first criticizes Samuel Johnson's crude stone-age rebuttal of Bishop Berkeley, then mocks Idealism in another way.

> We milk the cow of the world, and as we do
> We whisper in her ear, "You are not true."

This may be sheer play, but there is a kind of enlightened classicism about Wilbur. Learning and wit are aids in seeking a correspondence with nature, as they were to that superbly enlightened classicist Thoreau, and not antagonists, as they seemed to Wordsworth. Thoreau read Greek in his cabin, finding the morning hours conducive to study and study conducive to observation. Wilbur translates Molière, whose wit about manners complements Wilbur's wit about nature. But most important of all, man's creative spirit is as vital to the wholeness and richness of nature as nature is to man.

This last point seems to me especially evident in "Castles and Distances," from *Ceremony,* and "Looking into History," from *Things of This World.* And at the same time, these poems define the real value of the American "New Formalism," or what Wilbur exultantly calls a "live formality."

"Castles and Distances" deals with what the American, perhaps misguidedly, is likely to call European nature, that is, the beautiful harmony of gardens and wildness he finds at Renaissance chateaux and hunting parks. The visitor is drawn to them, I think, because they preserve a knowledge of nature and society that both European and American civilizations have lost, and our task at such places should be to understand what we so enjoy. With Wilbur, first the legend of the conversion of St. Hubert, as carved in the lintel stone of the chapel at Amboise, reveals the hunter's intimacy with nature and wilderness, as well as the religious mildness the animal's pain could inspire. Then the long avenues of trees between such castles and their forests reveal the aristocrat's and hunter's conscious sense of distance and difference between wilderness and court.

> Seen from a palace stair
> The wilderness was distance; difference; it spoke
> In the strong king's mind for mercy, while to the weak,
> To the weary of choice, it told of havens where
> The Sabbath stayed, and all were meek,
> And justice known a joke.

The recognized difference, we assume, is what kept the king from being the withdrawn suitor of excellence. At the same time, the very difference, the intimacy with both worlds, and the attraction of forest as seen from palace, and palace from forest also made possible the stories of Ardens and of kings going away to live in obscurity yet coming back renewed to find the "bounded empire good." But as the "tapered aisles of trees," the planned fountains and canals, and the embellished legends all demonstrate, the relation was gracefully formal. At the beginning of the poem Wilbur had described the mere cruelty of modern hunts as watched so informally on movie screens. The old relationship dignified both nature and society by the energy of human imagination.

"Looking into History" begins by noting the antique stillness of five soldiers in a Civil War photograph by Mathew Brady. Yet they are lifeless curiosities until forced into the poet's consciousness by a row of sycamores behind their tents. "The long-abated breeze // Flares in those boughs," forgotten battles begin again, and the poem suddenly turns to the connection between history, nature, and imagination. Wilbur compares history to the sea, for it buries but also preserves, and it *changes* in the senses of altering, of infinitely varying and repeating, and even of ringing and drowning out ("charging with a deathless cry"). What is constant or immortal, amazingly enough, is the Proteus of the poet's consciousness (related to the sea but purposeful in function) which, by entering into other objects and beings, can bring them back to life and penetrate the depths or slime in which the sea of history has held them. But the last analogy for imagination is not Proteus (who, it should be said, is never explicitly mentioned) but

> The self-established tree
> That draws all waters toward
> Its live formality.

The tree does not get inside other things but brings them inside itself, as Wilbur, by reviving the soldiers, brought them into himself. Appropriately, it defeats the "waters" of history by actually using them for its own sustenance. And it was the standing file of sycamores which awakened for Wilbur the moment of history, which had had a kind of sleeping life in the art of Brady. The photograph would have been ineffective for him without the familiar trees, the necessary natural symbol which literally sucked him in. Intelligence and imagination animate nature, and nature gives back spirit and power to art and self. In this ordered and alert meditation lies the real "live formality."

It is interesting, however, that in both these poems Wilbur has subjects which were already artistic forms. The castle parks and the soldiers and sycamores had been previously landscaped or recorded by other artists with ideas to unite with substance. Therefore, Wilbur's performance was in some ways less a work of new construction than of restoration. He found his form in breathing life into the forms of the past. This may explain, to a degree, why he is not a poet of really wild or "raw" nature and why he sometimes has trouble with subjects that have not had a strong, earlier organization. It may also account for his repeated references to paintings, to statues, or to the memorable gestures of other men. "After the Last Bulletins," for instance, incorporates a reference to paintings of Napoleon's retreat from Moscow—in the midst of a description of abandoned newspapers being blown about in a city park and shaking against a policeman's feet. The poem is not confusing, however, until morning comes and there are no other outside references to inform the new activity. For people to wake up to the next day's newscasts, buy their papers, and return to work is only ambiguous human habit, not a significant form, and Wilbur can't approve either the violence of news headlines, blown litter, and the night's dream world or the false stability of the working day.

All these poems, in any case, indicate that here "New Formalism" is much more than a matter of a return, after the experimentalism of the poets of the beginning of this century, to a more traditional verse. It is the poet's espousal of a formal relationship with his subject—particularly a formal relationship with nature. Indeed, the admiration of Wilbur's technique and "immaculate verbal choices" (to quote one widely circulated commendation) seems to me often disputable. His virtuosity frequently overpowers a weak subject or fabricates a poem out of thin air. See "Tywater," "Museum Piece," "Lightness," and

"Games." In "The Beacon," on the other hand, a potentially great poem has to struggle against distracting alliterations and self-conscious play with metaphors:

> A beacon blinks at its own brilliance,
> Over and over with cutless gaze
> Solving the Gordian waters, . . .

These are aspects of the dandyism Leslie Fiedler justly reminded Wilbur of. It may even be that dandyism—which in *The Human Condition* Hannah Arendt very cogently identified as one of the nineteenth century's responses to a world where one could create no enduring work—is Wilbur's worst defect. "As Wulfstan said on another occasion,"—this is not the way to begin a "Speech for the Repeal of the McCarran Act." But "live formality" is very, very different. It is a reviving of the consciousness dormant in old forms, the organic growth of new forms, and the use of formal relationships as a way of increasing one's powers of intelligence and observation. It ennobles sensation while it also enhances and protects the natural world. There is a fine moral, even, in the fact that Wilbur's own analogy for it is a sycamore tree. Wilbur is at present America's most profound moralist of man's relations with nature. We must not misread him because we must not neglect these relations. So much depends on them.

RAYMOND BENOIT

From "The New American Poetry"

The relative scarcity of critical estimations of contemporary American poetry stems from the problems that confront current critical approaches to the new poetry rather than from any want of admiration for it. More is involved than simply gaining distance in time. Often it will not explicate, and for good reasons, reasons in fact that take reason or intellectual judgments to task. This is not always so, as the following pages will make clear; but it happens enough to warrant the tentative generalization that the eye focusing on event has come to replace the mind building in metaphor. However, articles here and there and a few books, notably by M. L. Rosenthal and Ralph Mills, Jr., do begin to suggest an overall picture of this new and highly subjective mode that somehow constitutes a general and objective "poetry of experience," as Donald Hall cogently remarked in his introduction to the excellent Penguin anthology of contemporary American poetry. It is almost as though the dictum of T. S. Eliot had been turned around to read that in order to be impersonal the poet should be personal. Poets like John Logan, James Wright, and Edward Field do not retreat behind any mask. There is a disconcerting honesty about their poetry that has much to do with the tone of compassion and helplessness that seems dominant in so much work today. The voice is different, the mood has changed from the almost elegant anguish of Eliot or the ethical importunity of Pound. An epigraph for the new mood might be this line of Gary Snyder: "Against the ancient meaningless abstractions / Wet feet and the campfire out." But this line, while it charts new directions, makes clear at the same time a line of indebtedness to Pound and Eliot, two poets who

Thought 44 (July 1969):201–18. Excerpts: pp. 201–3, 208–12.

made abstraction their theme, Pound inveighing against it and Eliot offering something in its place, the symbolism of love of man and woman as that images man's relationship with God. What the concrete was for Pound the feminine was for Eliot: a recovery of something long lost to the modern masculine and technological consciousness.

More than any other person, if one excludes Plato for the moment, Descartes is responsible for the notion that truth is a matter of the mind, a mental formulation, a concept. But it will be a long while indeed before that attitude is changed, if it ever is changed. There are enough signs in our culture now, though, that truth is slowly but surely being redefined, being brought back into line with the whole human person. Vatican II is one of those signs; the poetry of William Stafford, if less broadcast, another. The philosophy of existentialism is a third. In his book, *What Is Existentialism?*, William Barrett constructs a dialogue between Alfred North Whitehead and Martin Heidegger in which they discuss the trend of philosophy in the last hundred years. Even the fact of their dialogue is significant; the form argues for the theme. The trend they agree to is: The Search for the Concrete. And that is also the trend, I believe, of contemporary American poetry. It is no accident that Sartre and Marcel write plays, that Heidegger is studying nineteenth-century German Romantic poetry. Very simply, literature is life and philosophy is not. Or less narrowly, truth is a matter of the whole person living his life at this time and in these circumstances, and it is not a matter of eternal mind. We hear the words "anxiety" and "care" and "death" in connection with Heidegger, and though he is concerned with these he is more concerned with truth; that is the real focus of his attention. His books, *Plato's Theory of Truth* (1942) and *On the Nature of Trust* (1943), state the line of questioning that culminated in his decision to study literature. In *Being and Time* as well, the nature of truth is a dominant concern. He argues that what we consider truth to be now, a matter of the mind, was not always the case, that actually our idea of truth is an aberration that begins with Plato from what the Greeks previously thought truth to consist in. His study takes note of the etymology of the Greek word for truth: "not to escape notice." The Greeks before Plato, Heidegger maintains, thought of truth as a matter of being: what is reveals itself and that revelation is truth. When things got detached from this ground for purposes of consideration, the nature of truth as well shifted from things in the whole context of their existence to the human mind judging correctly. It is my purpose here to show that contemporary poetry—particularly that of Gary Snyder, William Stafford, Richard Wilbur, and Howard Nemerov—is concerned also with letting things be, with letting things reveal themselves; that their poetry marks a significant change in the history of literature that is part of a larger shift in Western culture generally. . . .

Richard Wilbur is just as happy [as William Stafford] in the full dimensionality of the world. It is no springboard for him either; he relishes all its contours. One of his poems is titled, after Traherne, " 'A World Without Objects Is a Sensible Emptiness.' " Like Stafford, he wins us in this poem to dear detail; only here can ideal light be found. The ideal is the real for Wilbur, as it was for Coleridge. If Coleridge was right about a symbol being the translucence of the eternal through and in the temporal, then this poem is a symbol and contemporary American poetry is symbolic. Wilbur hangs on for dear life, and ours, to the temporal. The poem dramatizes the inadequacy of modern man's idea of truth as that misconception grows out of another—his idea of God as transcendent. Wilbur urges the Nativity upon us. Insight can only come from a plunge into the concrete. In the first four stanzas the "tall camels of the spirit," modern magi, "Steer for their deserts," but in the last three stanzas the poet directs these "connoisseurs of thirst" elsewhere:

> Turn, O turn
> From the fine sleights of the sand, from the long empty oven
> Where flames in flamings burn
>
> Back to the trees arrayed
> In bursts of glare, to the halo-dialing run
> Of the country creeks, and the hills' bracken tiaras made
> Gold in the sunken sun,
>
> Wisely watch for the sight
> Of the supernova burgeoning over the barn,

> Lampshine blurred in the steam of beasts, the spirit's right
> Oasis, light incarnate.

Sanctity is not a matter of otherworldliness; the poet anchors it in this world with a decisively powerful particularity. Wilbur advises himself in the poem to remember the early painters who capped the saints with merry-go-round rings (not halos) "jauntily worn." The advice is his own aesthetic, close to that of Coleridge and Browning. The parallel reminds us of the Romantic heritage of contemporary poetry, Romantic insofar as that term is associated with Coleridge's definition of the imagination that reveals itself in the reconciliation of the idea and the image, the general and abstract with the particular and concrete. That is the advice Wilbur gives the camels of the spirit when he directs them to the material. Christ, who reconciles heaven and earth, can be found where the idea is made flesh, where the star shines over the barn in the poem. William Whitla notices a similar connection between religious reconciliation and creative purpose in his book *The Central Truth: The Incarnation in Browning's Poetry*. We now understand that Browning, and Victorian poetry for that matter, does not break from Romantic poetry but continues it and bolsters it. Through Browning, Romanticism comes to Pound and Eliot and through them to Wilbur, to Nemerov, Stafford and Snyder. To put it simply, the line of evolution is toward a pure and purer reconciliation until the idea cannot be distinguished from the image. Just as the Incarnation is used by Browning (especially in "Fra Lippo Lippi" and in "Saul") and Eliot (in *Four Quartets,* especially "Dry Salvages") as the foundation of their themes, so Wilbur has used the Nativity in "'A World Without Objects Is a Sensible Emptiness.'" And all three apply their larger themes to art itself. Browning often used painters and musicians to give his poems this aesthetic dimension; Eliot continually asks in his poems whether the words used have been adequate to convey the Word; and Wilbur does both. Art should be whole, make manifest what it is about (Heidegger's definition of truth); art too should incarnate. What Ralph Mills noted of Wilbur's poem "October Maples, Portland" is true of his work generally: the natural world "is changed in the poet's eye, and through his deft use of analogy and allusion, into a sacramental reality: the zones of the spiritual and the material draw together momentarily in the poem, there to be experienced again and again." That is what the poem is about and that is what the poem does: shows the eternal through and in the temporal. In the poem, "A Prayer to Go to Paradise with the Donkeys" Francis Jammes imagines a heaven that is much like his own life on earth but in a finer tone. He would be lost without his donkeys and their "loads of feather-dusters and kitchen-wares." Like the painting of the Madonna and child Fra Lippo intends, the pleasures of time are set in timelessness:

> Dear God, let it be with these donkeys that I come,
> And let it be that angels lead us in peace
> To leafy streams where cherries tremble in air,
> Sleek as the laughing flesh of girls;

Francis Jammes can only think in images and that is precisely the point. His imagining is closest to the fact of the Incarnation—the same fact George Santayana overlooked in Browning's poetry when he called its sensual heavens barbaric. Wilbur also catches us up in irony if we admire the vision of Francis Jammes as touching or pleasant and poignant. Another phrase to describe contemporary American poetry, instead of a poetry of being, might be a poetry of the secular as sacred.

From the beginning Wilbur's poetry has had a religious intent that at first glance might not seem religious at all because we are not accustomed to thinking of religion in terms of the eternal-temporal. Santayana is an example. But religion implies a bond between God and time and Wilbur chooses to emphasize in that bond all that is involved in time: country creeks, kitchen-wares, junk, mountain fern, merry-go-rounds, everything. Having become man, it is in man and in time that Christ is to be found. He is a very religious poet in this sense. These lines are from his poem "Advice to a Prophet":

> Speak of the world's own change. Though we cannot conceive
> Of an undreamt thing, we know to our cost
> How the dreamt cloud crumbles, the vines are blackened by frost,
> How the view alters.

It is advice the poet must follow as well. The prophet's rhetoric, or the poet's, can itself be the stuff of prophecy. "A Christmas Hymn" celebrates the cardinal fact of history for Wilbur. The words, shifting between opposites, partake of the reality they render:

> But now, as at the ending,
> The low is lifted high;
> The stars shall bend their voices,
> And every stone shall cry,
> And every stone shall cry
> In praises of the child
> By whose descent among us
> The worlds are reconciled.

Stafford is content with natural imagery—the leap of fish between sky and water, the arcs of realization. Wilbur is too, but here he uncovers the strong foundation of the new approach. His poetry in theme and technique more and more rests upon truth as this hypostasis "Where word with world is one / And nothing dies" ("Games Two"), rather than concept or judgment or proposition.

As Eliot says in the preface to his translation of Saint John Perse, "there is a logic of the imagination as well as a logic of concepts"; it is the logic of the imagination that Heidegger and contemporary poets find true. Heidegger would recognize poetic perceptions of his own insight in Wilbur's work. "Attention Makes Infinity" is an obvious example but there are many others, such as "Love Calls Us to the Things of This World," or here, "A Problem from Milton":

> Poor Adam, deviled by your energy,
> What power egged you on to feed your brains?
> Envy the gorgeous gallops of the sea,
> Whose horses never know their lunar reins.

or "La Rose des Vents":

> Forsake those roses
> Of the mind

> And tend the true,
> The mortal flower.

and certainly "Epistemology":

> We milk the cow of the world, and as we do
> We whisper in her ear, "You are not true."

Someone remarked of Wordsworth that he combines John Locke and St. Francis. Whether we can substitute Martin Heidegger for Locke in an estimation of Wilbur, or not, still what is true in Wordsworth is true in Wilbur: "We see into the life of things."

DONALD L. HILL

From "Studies and Aversions"

. . . I turn to Wilbur's prose writings on two poets of the last century in whose views he has shown a special interest. . . .

The first of the prose pieces is an essay on Poe, published in 1959 as an introduction to the complete poems of Poe in the Dell Laurel Poetry Series, of which Wilbur has been general editor for several years. He begins by conceding that Poe's poems after his twenty-first year "ceased to be efforts at full statement; they became in effect addenda to the prose pieces, embroideries, cryptic distillations" (7). For this reason one must go to the prose for an adequate understanding of the poems, and Wilbur does so in his essay. First, he points out that Poe drastically limited by his theories the scope and nature of poetry. Believing that "the scientific spirit and the universal prosaism which accompanies it have inherited the earth," Poe held that the poet's "sole present recourse is to repudiate all human and mundane subject-matter, all 'dull realities,' and to pursue visions of those realms in which beauty was or is inviolate: the remote Earthly past, in which Naiad and Hamadryad went unchallenged, and the distant 'happier star' to which they now have flown" (9). The poet's object is "to get away from Earth and men" rather than to use in his poems a maximum of worldly experience. Wilbur remarks that in this respect Poe's ideas run counter to the aims of most poets today.

This is true, and ultimately Wilbur stands with most modern poets against Poe; but it is also true that Wilbur shares with Poe not only a mistrust of "the scientific spirit and the universal prosaism which accompanies it" but also that vivid sense of

---

Chapter 5 of *Richard Wilbur* (New York: Twayne, 1967), pp. 163–69. Page numbers in parentheses are from the Introduction to *Poe: Complete Poems,* edited by Richard Wilbur (New York: Dell, 1959).

other realms for which Poe was ready to abandon the Earth. In "All These Birds," Wilbur gives some illustrations of the way in which, in the eye of creeping science, "the monsters of the sky / Dwindle to habit, habitat, and song." His dismay is, I should think, very much in the spirit of Poe (as in that of most other poets from Blake to the present moment). But the counter-measures Wilbur proposes are entirely different. Instead of surrendering the Earth in despair to science and prose, he stakes everything on the power of the imagination to recover what has been lost; he urges that, even while we grant the validity of science within its province, we

> . . . tell the imagination it is wrong
> Till, let it be undone,
>> it spin a lie
> So fresh, so pure, so rare
> As to possess the air.

Instead of seeking out ancient or unearthly or supernatural realms, the imagination, as "a natural thing" itself, should establish itself on earth and become a refuge for all natural things:

> Oh, let it climb wherever it can cling
> Like some great trumpet-vine, a natural thing
> To which all birds that fly
> > come natural.

The motive of the imagination as it does so will be very different from Poe's aversion to the natural world and different also from the disinterested curiosity of science that diminishes its objects as it studies them. The poem concludes

> Come, stranger, sister, dove:
> Put on the reins of love.

"The reins of love" do not constrain or diminish; they dignify and magnify objects through the power of the myth-making imagination. The poem is one of a number of Wilbur's poems that exalt the imagination over mere fact, but I think its thematic kinship with "Cigales," "In a Bird Sanctuary," "Objects," "Poplar, Sycamore," "'A World Without Objects . . . ,'" "Merlin Enthralled," and "Love Calls Us to the Things of This World" is especially clear.

Poe and Wilbur both take for granted the conception of two worlds, one here and now, the other elsewhere and timeless. Poe regards this world as diseased and damned; Wilbur might share this view without ceasing to accept the world as the human estate and to strive for closer bonds with it. Poe never doubts the value of striving to enter the other world; Wilbur remembers that we can enter it only by—in some sense—dying. Poe's dream voyages are all "escapes from corrupt mundane consciousness into visionary wholeness and freedom" (23); more skeptical, Wilbur is aware of the danger of false dreams that may weaken our hold on life. "Poe," says Wilbur, "offered always the same account of the poetic process. Straining after a supernal beauty which might restore the unity of the diffused universe— and of his own shattered soul—the poet begins with earthly things (Rowena, Mary Chaworth, the City, the Sea), subverts their identities, and accomplishes their imaginative destruction. The supposition is that melodious and rhythmic destruction of the earthly must be heavenly" (19). Wilbur begins and ends by cleaving to the things of this world. But, as I have often insisted, the spiritual state reflected in his poems is not so simple as that. A good many of Wilbur's poems bear the marks, often "lightly hid," of a profound effort to resist the charm of some such ghostly siren as Poe's contempt for the world. He concludes his account of Poe's poetic purposes with a dictum that exactly reflects the ambivalence revealed in his own poems: "There has never been a grander conception of poetry, nor a more impoverished one" (39).

A reader who is familiar with Wilbur's poetry might reasonably gather from a lecture he gave at Amherst College, October 23, 1959,[1] that he owes a more grateful debt to Emily Dickinson than to Poe. From her, perhaps, he learned something of the active role of consciousness in coloring, shaping, or apprehending whatever we are conscious *of*. Emily Dickinson, says Wilbur, discovered personally in writing her psychological poems "that the aspect of the world is in no way constant, that the power of external things depends on our state of mind, that the soul selects its own society and may, if granted strength to do so, select a superior order and scope of consciousness which will render it finally invulnerable" (36). To act by these insights is not to destroy the world, like Poe, but through a discipline to make it serve our purposes. Wilbur's statement reminds us of the recurrent insistence in his poems on the power of mind or imagination to construct and to give value to reality.

Most of the lecture consists of an account of Emily Dickinson's "sumptuous destitution," the tactics she adopted in adjusting to her "sense of privation." In her outer and in her inner life "she came to keep the world's images, even the images of things passionately desired, at the remove which renunciation makes; and her poetry at its most mature continually proclaims that to lose or forego what we desire is somehow to gain" (39). Wilbur cites her poem "Undue Significance" as one with the moral: "Once an object has been magnified by desire, it cannot be wholly possessed by appetite." The moral recalls Wilbur's "A Voice from under the Table," "Ballade for the Duke of Orléans," and a number of other poems. In "Success is counted sweetest," he says, it seems likely that Emily Dickinson "is arguing the *superiority* of defeat to victory, of frustration to satisfaction, and of anguished comprehension to mere possession . . . that food, or victory, or any other good thing is best comprehended by the eye of desire from the vantage of privation" (40–41).

How can desire define things? Wilbur asks the question and draws from Traherne a distinction between "the way of appetite and the way of desire. . . . The creature of appetite . . . pursues satisfaction, and strives to possess the object in itself; it cannot imagine the vaster economy of desire, in which the pain of abstinence is justified by moments of infinite joy, and the object is spiritually possessed, not merely for itself, but more truly as an index of the All. . . . Emily Dickinson elected the economy of desire, and called her privation good, rendering it positive by renunciation. And so she came to live in a huge world of delectable distances. . . . 'Heaven,' she said, 'is what I cannot reach'" (41–43). Poe abandoned the world as diseased and damned; but Emily Dickinson, equally desperate, we imagine, but not so drastic, looked past or through it as less than sufficient. Wilbur quotes a sentence from her correspondence: "Enough is of so vast a sweetness, I suppose it never occurs, only pathetic counterfeits"; and he comments that "The writer of that sentence could not invest her longings in any finite object" (43).

I do not mean to suggest that there is any very close correspondence between Wilbur's views and moods and those he attributes to Emily Dickinson. It is only that this lecture, like many of his poems, shows an unusually sympathetic understanding of the relationship between the thirst for perfection and a sense of the insufficiency of this world. It might be said that Wilbur characteristically strives in his own poems to record a moment of joy in which "the object is spiritually possessed, not merely for itself, but more truly as an index of the All." On the other hand, Wilbur is always on guard against an undervaluation of the finite object. This struggle between an inclination to unworldliness, moral and metaphysical, and a determination to give the world its due is, as I have argued earlier, perhaps the chief motive of his poems. Now and then, as in "'A World Without Objects . . . ,'" "Love Calls Us to the Things of This World," and "A Christmas Hymn" in honor of "the child / By whose descent among us / The worlds are reconciled," he seems to have hinted at or adopted a Christian solution. But he is much more interested in the tension or paradox of the two worlds than in solutions, and he remains wary of ready-made patterns of thought and language. He begins his lecture on Emily Dickinson by saying that what he found most remarkable in her is that she would not let her inherited Calvinist vocabulary "write her poems for her." Instead, she forced it to "subserve her own sense of things" (35).

In Emily Dickinson, if not in Poe, the yearning for another mode of existence was matched and counterbalanced at times by an equally strong capacity for taking pleasure in the world around her; hence the humor, the happiness, and the vivid natural detail of many of her poems. The same balance is kept by Dante, by Milton, by Wordsworth, Keats, Hopkins, Yeats—all otherworldly poets who (as Wilbur says of his old people in "Next Door") "will not cheat the world of their regard, / Even as they let it go." Yeats struggled all his life with the problem posed by the rival claims of the ideal and the actual. When in Yeats' poem "Vacillation" the religious Soul advises, "Seek out reality, leave things that seem," the secular Heart replies: "What, be a singer born and lack a theme?" Rejecting Von Hügel's view that the way of the artist and the way of the Christian are the same, Yeats chooses this world, saying "Homer is my example and his unchristened heart." This passage from "Vacillation" might be paraphrased to echo Wilbur: "Art calls us to the things of this world." It is true that Yeats in other moods can represent himself as turning away from this world with relief, as he does in "Sailing to Byzantium"; but Wilbur, though haunted by his own vision of "the dreamt land / Toward which all hungers leap, all pleasures pass," responds again and again to the injunction expressed in the happy slogan, "Love calls us to the things of this world."

The abstract pattern of this oscillation is that of the familiar doctrine of liberal Christianity in which the love of God implies a love of his creations and vice versa. In this view of things "The worlds are reconciled," and due honor can be done to both. But poets are not philosophers, even though they may, like Wilbur, have philosophical interests; in any case, even to mention the doctrine suggests the difficulty of holding it today as an article of faith. It will be better to keep our terms secular and to say only that, unlike many of his thoughtful contemporaries, Wilbur has managed to entertain his visions of perfection without paying the price of alienation from the "damned universe."

Wilbur's studies of Poe and Dickinson thus show something of his interest in keeping the two worlds of the ideal and the actual in balance, without withdrawal and without despair. They also illustrate his capacity for drawing sympathetically on the world of the past without getting out of touch with that of the present. The general aim and spirit of his study of earlier poets is well expressed in "Looking into History," where he promises himself that he will, if he can,

> . . . by some fervent fraud
> Father the waiting past,
>
> Resembling at the last
> The self-established tree

That draws all waters toward
Its live formality.

The poet's "live formality" is not an isolated growth but the product of his active search for spiritual ancestors. Like Proteus, "by some fervent fraud," he takes the shape of his chosen dead and helps them to find their voices again. He does not relinquish his own individuality, which guides his choice of shapes and stands "self-established" in the end, but instead enriches it by entering at will into the minds and feelings of others. In the final image the poet-Proteus becomes a tree, and the voices become the nourishing waters of the tradition. The image of the tree is as important a clue to Wilbur's conception of the poet as is the image of Proteus. While every tree is an individual, it is not free to become anything it pleases; it is limited by its kind and by the soil and climate in which it finds itself. Unlike a tree, a poet can do something to choose his soil and climate (becoming in this sense "self-established") by seeking out the life-giving waters that flow from the past into the present. Wilbur is not afraid of academicism, of a poetry of echoes and allusions. Instead he conceives of the poet as one whose "live formality" depends on establishing, through the necessary effort of study, a significant relationship with older poets and with other great spirits of the past.

NOTE

1. In *Emily Dickinson: Three Views* (Amherst: Amherst College Press, 1960). Page citations following are from this text. Wilbur's paper, "Sumptuous Destitution," was later reprinted in *Responses—Prose Pieces: 1953–1976* (New York: Harcourt Brace Jovanovich, 1976), pp. 3–15. —ED.

CHARLES F. DUFFY

"Intricate Neural Grace"
The Esthetic of Richard Wilbur

Readers have been often struck by the large number of Richard Wilbur's poems on the arts, especially painting and sculpture. These poems in turn form part of an even larger group on literature and the imagination. Since Wilbur is often at his best in the visual art poems and since they provide us with a manageable group, I propose to map Wilbur's esthetic by exploring these poems where, as with Keats' "Ode on a Grecian Urn," contemplation of the art object engenders speculation on art itself and its relationship to life.

It is by no accident, I think, that the eleven or so poems of Wilbur's on the visual arts are mostly from his early work when his esthetic was naturally shaping itself. "The Giaour and the Pacha," "Objects," "A Dutch Courtyard," "My Father Paints the Summer," "The Waters," and "L'Etoile" are from Wilbur's first book, *The Beautiful Changes* (1947); "Museum Piece," "Giacometti," and "Ceremony" are from *Ceremony* (1950); "A Baroque Wall-Fountain in the Villa Sciarra" is from *Things of This World* (1956); and "A Hole in the Floor," which is only indirectly on painting, from *Advice to a Prophet* (1961). We notice then six from the first volume, three from the second, only one from the third, and just barely one from the fourth. *Walking to Sleep* (1969), his most recent volume, has none, unless we include "A Miltonic Sonnet for Mr. Johnson" which is only indirectly on the Peter Hurd portrait of Lyndon Johnson. As Wilbur moved from the beautiful changes which art effects out to the things of this world in the later poems, he left behind his poems

Concerning Poetry 4 (Spring 1971):41–50.

on works of art. But their significance for his later work should not be overlooked.

Even in the very early poems, though, Wilbur is concerned with the things of the world, and so he treats of the superb seventeenth century Dutch painter of objects, Pieter de Hooch, in two poems, "Objects" and "A Dutch Courtyard." After a somewhat mannered and overly allusive opening, the poet stands us squarely in front of de Hooch's *A Dutch Courtyard* (officially referred to as *Courtyard with Two Officers and a Woman Drinking*) in the Mellon Collection at the National Gallery in Washington:

> Guard and gild what's common, and forget
> Uses and prices and names; have objects speak.
>
> There's classic and there's quaint,
> And then there is that devout intransitive eye
> Of Pieter de Hooch: see feinting from his plot of paint
> The trench of light on boards, the much-mended dry
>
> Courtyard wall of brick,
> And sun submerged in beer, and streaming in glasses,
> The weave of a sleeve, the careful and undulant tile.[1]

The eye of the painter and poet is devout because it guards the things of this world as sacred objects which cannot be bought or used. And the eye is also "intransitive" (a superb word) because the poet commands us to stop naming the objects and instead "have objects speak." We must forget the "I" and realize the object itself as de Hooch did. The poet's own recreation of the painting carefully selects salient and yet varied details so that we hardly need to see the painting itself to visualize the poem, and thus gives us a testament in a different medium of the quality he praises in the painter's eye.

Wilbur has obeyed his own command to "Guard and gild what's common" and goes on:

> A quick
> Change of the eye and all this passes

Into a day, into magic.
For is there any end to true textures, to true
Integuments; do they never desist from tacit, tragic
Fading away? Oh maculate, cracked, askew,

Gay-pocked and potsherd world
I voyage, where in every tangible tree
I see afloat among the leaves, all calm and curled,
The Cheshire smile which sets me fearfully free.

Precisely because the painting is "feinting" (deceiving us by illusion) with a possible pun on "fainting" (archaic for fading), the poet is compelled to voyage back out to the world of real objects. But he sees it anew now because de Hooch has taught him to observe the textures of the world. This very process is "magic," and yet "day" also, that is, both real and yet imagined.

The poem immediately following, "A Dutch Courtyard," is a look at the same painting differently. A more whimsical poem, it contrasts the ideal observer who engages in the "blameless fun" of simply enjoying the painting, and those who, like the capitalist art collector Andrew Mellon, can't abide by the "strict / propriety" of life and art.

In despair,

Consumed with greedy ire,
Old Andrew Mellon glowered at this Dutch
Courtyard, until it bothered him so much
He bought the thing entire.

Unlike the blameless observer, Mellon commits three of the deadly sins by failing to observe the instructions of "Objects." I say "sins" quite seriously because it is Mellon's attitude toward the painting (and the world by extension) which desecrates the object to the status of a "thing." He neither realizes the object nor employs his imagination. He buys.

So far, then, we can clearly posit acceptance of the world of objects as a *sine qua non* for Wilbur. But "Objects" ends with a strange shift of focus:

> in every tangible tree
> I see afloat among the leaves, all calm and curled,
> The Cheshire smile which sets me fearfully free.

These lines are a real teaser on Wilbur's part: looking at the trees above the courtyard in the actual painting I swear I now see, like Alice, the Cheshire cat leering at me after reading Wilbur's description. The relationship between the painting and viewer is now complicated by the poet, just as the trees in his own real world are now complicated by the painting. We agree with Stephen Stephanchev to "the possibility that the celebration of the things of this world is, in reality, a celebration of the individual imagination, the power of the mind that creates the world."[2]

As a result, dreams of the ideal or eternal occupy a place in Wilbur's esthetic, although he is usually against them as in the superb "A Problem from Milton" and "Beasts." But he lays his strictures on the idealist only when the dream is destructive. If the dream is ennobling or at least a momentary refuge from the hideousness of triviality, then it is allowed a place as in "L'Etoile (Degas, 1876)."

> A rushing music, seizing on her dance,
> Now lifts it from her, blind into the light;
> And blind the dancer, tiptoe on the boards
> Reaches a moment toward her dance's flight.
>
> Even as she aspires in loudening shine
> The music pales and sweetens, sinks away;
> And past her arabesque in shadow show
> The fixt feet of the maître de ballet.
>
> So she will turn and walk through metal halls
> To where some ancient woman will unmesh
> Her small strict shape, and yawns will turn her face
> Into a little wilderness of flesh.
>
> (208)

Ordinarily this aspiring of the human to a state almost superterrestrial is scorned by Wilbur. But here the terrestrial is adamantine in the "fixt feet of the maître de ballet," metallic, and utterly dull. It is, in fact, a hell where things of the world, even the human face, become "a little wilderness of flesh" (a chilling echo of "in flesh their wilderness" in "On the Eyes of an S. S. Officer," p. 183) when the moment of creative energy and shaping dream is over and ennui regains its hold on us.

In "My Father Paints the Summer" Wilbur enlarges this vision of art as a valid land of dreams by entering a new note: the necessity of love. The poem, which immediately follows the de Hooch poems, opens with random glimpses of bored tourists shut in a hotel by a rainy day, and then shifts to the poet's father:

> But up in his room by artificial light
> My father paints the summer, and his brush
> Tricks into sight
> The prosperous sleep, the girdling stir and clear steep hush
> Of a summer never seen,
> A granted green. . . .
>
> Caught summer is always an imagined time.
> Time gave it, yes, but time out of any mind.
> There must be prime
> In the heart to beget that season, to reach past rain and find
> Riding the palest days
> Its perfect blaze.
>
> (198)

The "perfect blaze" must be held as an ideal, almost a mystical one, to make sense of the "palest days" which only spell ennui. An "imagined time" is outside the things of this world, for it springs from the "prime / In the heart." This highly esthetic (in the late nineteenth-century sense) note is important in Wilbur's vision, but unlike the cold or decadent esthete, Wilbur's art must spring from love of the world as he puts it in "Love Calls Us to the Things of This World." Nature is not abandoned, but gilded in the best sense of that word. The vision is neither correctly "classic" nor sentimentally "quaint," but devout and impersonal as we saw in "Objects."

If he admires the possible dream, Wilbur also knows of nightmare and writes revealingly in Kunitz's *Twentieth Century Authors* (First Supplement) that he started writing poetry in earnest when on the battlefields of Europe. He adds: "One does not use poetry for its major purposes, as a means of organizing oneself and the world, until one's world somehow gets out of hand. A general cataclysm is not required; the disorder must be personal and may be wholly so, but poetry, to be vital, does seem to need a periodic acquaintance with the threat of Chaos." This statement may explain Wilbur's strange fascination for Poe whom we would ordinarily think of as several removes from Wilbur. It also explains the dedication of "A Hole in the Floor" to the French Surrealist painter René Magritte. Looking through a carpenter's hole in the parlor, the room of conscious social life, he sees in the second half of his poem:

> The radiator-pipe
> Rises in middle distance
> Like a shuttered kiosk, standing
> Where the only news is night.
> Here it's not painted green,
> As it is in the visible world.
>
> For God's sake, what am I after?
> Some treasure, or tiny garden?
> Or that untrodden place,
> The house's very soul,
> Where time has stored our footbeats
> And the long skein of our voices?
>
> Not these, but the buried strangeness
> Which nourishes the known:
> That spring from which the floor-lamp
> Drinks now a wilder bloom,
> Inflaming the damask love-seat
> And the whole dangerous room

(15, 16)

Like Magritte's surrealist paintings, the objects of dreams are vividly real, but in isolation from their conscious use or configuration, and a return to the conscious world makes him aware of its roots in the subconscious. But the objects of the dream are clearly seen: "A pure street, faintly littered / With bits and strokes of light." Rather than merging into each other, they retain their utter separateness and are thus controlled to some extent in the manner of nonsense verse according to Elizabeth Sewell.

Acceptance of the world, the validity of imaginative recreation, the value of love, the glimpse into the underside of consciousness—all these are important areas in Wilbur's esthetic. But perhaps his major concern is the need for order and control and so the semi-Impressionist Bazille interests him in "Ceremony."

> A striped blouse in a clearing by Bazille
> Is, you may say, a patroness of boughs
> Too queenly kind toward nature to be kin.
> But ceremony never did conceal,
> Save to the silly eye, which all allows,
> How much we are the woods we wander in. . . .

> I am for wit and wakefulness,
> And love this feigning lady by Bazille.
> What's lightly hid is deepest understood,
> And when with social smile and formal dress
> She teaches leaves to curtsey and quadrille,
> I think there are most tigers in the wood.

(167)

Recently Wilbur has said on Boston's WGBH-FM (March 21, 1970) that he had no particular Bazille work in mind, but in fact the poem bears a striking resemblance to Bazille's *Family Reunion* in which a group sits for its portrait in a clearing in the woods. A girl wearing a striped blouse looks intently, impersonally, and almost fiercely at the painter. In her ceremonial, almost stiff, pose and with her most unnatural stripes she yet paradoxically joins nature by her very separateness, as the striped tiger is avoided by other animals. The indiscriminate eye is silly because it fails to see differences and cannot particularize each object in its own uniqueness. But the person of wit and wakefulness, like this alert, highly conscious girl, by her resistance reveals herself.

Definition by resistance and struggle is the theme also of "The Giaour and the Pacha (Eugène Delacroix, 1856)." After describing the painting (by taking some liberty, I think), Wilbur has the conquering giaour say to himself as he debates whether to shoot his enemy:

> Is this my anger, and is this the end
> Of gaudy sword and jeweled harness, joy
> In strength and heat and swiftness, that I must
> Now bend, and with a slaughtering shot destroy
>
> The counterpoise of all my force and pride?
> These falling hills and piteous mists; O sky,
> Come loose the light of fury on this height,
> That I may end the chase, and ask not why.

To kill would be the easy way, and also the nonrational way: "and ask not why." The giaour realizes that his humanity, joy, and pride has been most engaged in the hunt, and that if he kills he must paradoxically bend and destroy his "counter-poise." There is thus a moral note entered here about the necessity of striving toward perfection, of willing it. Keeping his enemy alive for another hunt and battle is to realize the necessity of the world as our moral arena.

I would like to end with a more detailed commentary on "Giacometti" (162), one of Wilbur's most ambitious and brilliant poems, because it pulls together many of the themes we have been tracing, and develops a vision of history as well. The poem opens with an admiring account of how the traditional stone sculptor (I think he has Michelangelo in mind) would work in stone precisely because it resists us. Man's magnificent pride would battle the stone down to his own image and form. But what of today?

> So we can baffle rock, and in our will
> Can clothe and keep it. But if our will, though locked

In stone it clutches, change,
Then we are much worse mocked
Than cliffs can do: then we ourselves are strange
To what we were, which lowers on us still.

Man in stone, man working on stone, he goes on, was religious,
philosophical, and heroic. But witness our condition now:

look where Giacometti in a room
Dim as a cave of the sea, has built the man
We are, and made him walk:
Towering like a thin
Coral, out of a reef of plaster chalk,
This is the single form we can assume.

We are this man unspeakably alone
Yet stripped of the singular utterly, shaved and scraped
Of all but being there,
Whose fulness is escaped
Like a burst balloon's: no nakedness so bare
As flesh gone in inquiring of the bone.

He is pruned of every gesture, saving only
The habit of coming and going. Every pace
Shuffles a million feet.
The faces in this face
Are all forgotten faces of the street
Gathered to one anonymous and lonely.

No prince and no Leviathan, he is made
Of infinite farewells. Oh never more
Diminished, nonetheless
Embodied here, we are
This starless walker, one who cannot guess
His will, his keel his nose's bony blade.

And volumes hover round like future shades
This least of man, in whom we join and take
A pilgrim's step behind,

And in whose guise we make
Our grim departures now, walking to find
What railleries of rock, what palisades?

Wilbur as art interpreter is at his descriptive and insightful best here in this elegiac masterpiece. But notice how many of our themes are here. He laments modern man's condition as interpreted by Giacometti by first of all saying that modern man is ironically not a part of this world: "no nakedness so bare / As flesh gone in inquiring of the bone," and "pruned of every gesture," these skeletal structures are "shaved and scraped / Of all but being there." Secondly, Giacometti's man is a "starless walker," that is, without a dream, and by implication without direction: "one who cannot guess / His will, his keel his nose's bony blade." He follows his nose, not his imagination; his skeleton, and not his will. It is the will which Wilbur posits at the bottom of it all—the will to combat intransigent matter, to differentiate, to love and accept the self and the world. To be overwhelmed by the world of matter is to await our fate at the "railleries of rock."

We have hardly done justice to this rich, complex, and astonishingly hieroglyphic poem. But "Giacometti" demonstrates clearly the value Wilbur places on form and control in poetry as the signets of man's achievement. He affirms in both idea and execution his belief in art as above all conscious form. (It would be instructive to read all his poems which stress the need for *balance,* physical, moral, and artistic.)

I think we can now draw some further tentative conclusions about Wilbur's esthetic by surveying his favorite artists. One thing common to the painters de Hooch, Delacroix, Bazille, Degas, and Magritte is the clear representationalism of their styles. They are all, even the romantic Delacroix, basically careful observers of what the eye sees; even Magritte's surrealist paintings place absolutely clear objects next to each other. Wilbur thus avoids abstract art, but also murky painting such as Turner's. Secondly, the human figure occupies a central figure position in all the painters (with the possible exception of Magritte on occasion). It is perhaps not irrelevant that Wilbur's father was basically a portrait painter. The people are caught in moments of dramatic decision as in Delacroix, or exquisite poise as in Bazille and Degas, or a moment of innocent pleasure as in de Hooch. In all, however, man is not degraded or distorted but caught in moments of delight or heroism. Only in Giacometti's art do we find man "diminished" because that is the state of modern man; but the heroic ideal of Michelangelo in "the image of man" is upheld at the beginning of the poem as an ironic reminder of our possible greatness. Thus, Wilbur's esthetic by inference is a balanced, humanist representationalism which is neither photographic realism (not even de Hooch's is—remember the "magic" of it) nor man-obliterating abstractionism. As Robert Horan puts it, Wilbur's subjects and allusions are "clear and personal uses of a sense of history and event."[3] Wilbur has stated his admiration of Eliot, but has spared us in his own recreation of history and art the need of extensive footnotes. He demands a sensitive, educated reader, but believes far more than Eliot himself in the autotelic principle in the poem as he recreates, interprets, and reveals the work of art and something about himself.

NOTES

1. *The Poems of Richard Wilbur* (New York: Harcourt, Brace and World, 1963), p. 95. Subsequent references are in parentheses.

2. *American Poetry Since 1945* (New York: Harper and Row, 1965), p. 99.

3. *Contemporary Poet as Artist and Critic,* ed. Anthony Ostroff (Boston: Little, Brown, 1964), p. 10.

JOHN P. FARRELL

The Beautiful Changes in
Richard Wilbur's Poetry

The time is past when Richard Wilbur could be dismissed as a
poet who writes "prayers on pinheads."[1] But we still hear of his
"ignoring of the dark," and, in general, it may be said that he is
not yet quite taken seriously even by readers who admire his
work. The feeling has been that, in the long run, Wilbur's poetry, for all its qualities, doesn't matter, or doesn't matter in a
large way. It has not that range and power that makes some
poetry, as Eliot would say, part of the consciousness of one's
age. The doubts about Wilbur (whose craftsmanship has been
universally commended) have always centered on the depth of
his vision and, most particularly, on his apparent insensitivity to
the issues of our time.[2] The truth is, however, that while Wilbur
is not a poet for the dark nights of the soul, neither is he a poet
for the soul's Sunday afternoons. If he seems to have made peace
with the modern world, he has not bargained blindly: he knows
with astonishing lucidity both the terms of his compact and its
attendant perils.[3]

Wilbur has recently said that a good part of his work could
"be understood as a public quarrel with the aesthetics of Edgar
Allan Poe."[4] He has conducted this quarrel, quite explicitly, in
two brilliant essays, and his comments throw a good deal of
light on the themes of his poetry. He says, for example, that for
Poe "the poet is not concerned with the imaginative shaping of
human life on the existing earth; his sole present recourse is to
repudiate all human and mundane subject-matter, all 'dull realities,' and to pursue visions of those realms in which beauty was
or is inviolate."[5] It is to this quest for visionary knowledge that

Contemporary Literature 12 (Winter 1971):74–84.

Wilbur objects. His own poetry accepts the things of this world; it does not honor their imperfections, as the poetry of a jejune optimist might; rather, it celebrates the ineffaceable beauty which subsists in an imperfect universe, a beauty which is both created by imperfection and in adamant conflict with it.[6] The relation Wilbur sees between beauty and imperfection is suggested by the title of his first volume, *The Beautiful Changes*. In the poem which gave the volume its title, he says: "The beautiful changes as a forest is changed / By a chameleon's turning his skin to it. . . ."[7] The import of these lines Wilbur has explored in numerous poems; he has made the chameleon everywhere visible.

What mattered to Poe about change was that it indicated a fallen world, from which escape was the only recourse. Wilbur points to the result of this thinking in Poe's aesthetic philosophy:

> Poe distinguishes in his criticism three divisions of mind—Intellect, Taste, and the Moral Sense—and bars the first and last from the poetic act on the ground that poetry has nothing to do with Truth or Duty. If the poet's object is to get away from Earth and men, he is plainly bound to disregard the Moral Sense, which is involved with the conduct and passions of men; and he must also degrade the Intellect (which defers to fact and "dull realities"), restricting its function to rationalization.[8]

Wilbur does not suppose, as Poe does, that the intellect and the moral sense are inimical to the apprehension of beauty. Quite the contrary. In Wilbur's poetry beauty is realized only upon the exercise of man's intellectual and moral faculties. This condition has much to do with Wilbur's style and tone. The poems have, characteristically, a moral design, and this design is, if anything, emphasized rather than merely insinuated. Similarly, the poems are deliberate meditations. They rely heavily on argument and debate and they use much intellectual irony, paradox, and ambiguity. These techniques are not employed in slavish imitation of what was, in Wilbur's formative years, a fashion in poetry. They reflect, rather, the value he places on the life of the mind.

In general, Wilbur's poems envision two kinds of change, disintegrative and metamorphic. Wilbur suggests that a genuine reverence for life can be attained if one has the capacity to see beyond disintegrative change, into the metamorphic and regenerative life of the universe. Metamorphic change is not without its own tragic consequences, but the tragedy is always redeemed by the fulness of being which metamorphosis effects. Insight into this redemptive process is possible only when both the intellect and the moral sense are intact. Wilbur's poetry is therefore much concerned with a certain quality of vision, a certain way of seeing into things. The presence of this vision is registered by perception of what he calls the beautiful changes. (Both syntactical senses of the phrase are important.) Here, once again, his poetry contrasts with Poe's. Wilbur has commented on Poe's capitulation to the "hypnogogic state":

> The hypnogogic state, about which there is strangely little said in the literature of psychology, is a condition of semi-consciousness in which *the closed eye beholds a continuous procession of vivid and constantly changing forms.* These forms sometimes have color, and are often abstract in character. Poe regarded the hypnogogic state as the visionary condition *par excellence,* and he considered its rapidly shifting abstract images to be—as he put it—"glimpses of the spirit's outer world" (my italics).[9]

Altogether the opposite condition obtains in Wilbur's poetry. His poems present to the *open eye* a procession of constantly changing forms. These are never abstract, for they are the things of this world. And they are, or at least can be if the eye is educated, beautiful in their actuality.

Wilbur deals with the problem of change in a variety of contexts, but there is one context which, in the light of his alleged aloofness from the realities of the modern world, is particularly worth our attention. Since the nineteenth century, the most dramatic perceptions of the world's mutability have been linked to what we have come to call the historical consciousness. Although once a source of benign optimism, the historical consciousness has more and more been an agent of despair. Stephen

Dedalus cursed history as a nightmare from which he was trying to awake, and the remark has become a contemporary slogan. The issue was summed up by Philip Rahv when he said that "modern life is above all an historical life producing changes with vertiginous speed, changes difficult to understand and even more difficult to control. And to some people it appears as though the past, all of it together with its gods and sacred books, were being ground to pieces in the powerhouse of change, senselessly used up as so much raw material in the fabrication of an unthinkable future."[10] Wilbur's treatment of historical change is in every way remarkable. Sensitive as he is to the nature of change in general, he is able to write about historical change with far more penetration than the host of critics who demand from the modern poet endless tokens of torment.

"Speech for the Repeal of the McCarran Act" gives a clear view of the difference between disintegration and metamorphosis as modes of change, and it serves as a convenient introduction to Wilbur's poems on history. The theme is set in the first stanza:

> As Wulfstan said on another occasion,
> The strong net bellies in the wind and the spider rides it out;
> But history, that sure blunderer,
> Ruins the unkempt web, however silver.

(100)

History as "blunderer" turns out to have a special meaning, and Wilbur alerts us to it by first saying what he does not mean:

> I am not speaking of rose windows
> Shattered by bomb-shock; the leads tousselled; the glass-
>   grains broadcast;
> If the rose be living at all
> A gay gravel shall be pollen of churches.

Here is metamorphosis the way Wilbur sees it. If the value is true, it will survive in other forms and the process of its survival is beautiful. History is a blunderer when "oathbreach, faith-breach, lovebreach / Bring the invaders into the estuaries." In other words, history becomes a wanton agent of disorder only when men's moral sense has broken down: "I speak / Of the spirit's weaving the neural / Web, the self-true mind, the trusty reflex."

The theme is amplified in Wilbur's "Advice to a Prophet": the prophet will come, no doubt, "mad-eyed from stating the obvious," but he is asked not to recite "the long numbers that rocket the mind" nor to "talk of the death of the race." These horrors are so unreal that we, being "unable to fear what is too strange," will ignore him. Therefore, the prophet is advised to "speak of the world's own change." By this Wilbur means that the prophet ought to instruct men in terms of those disintegrative processes which they have observed in Nature and which are fearfully familiar:

> Though we cannot conceive
> Of an undreamt thing, we know to our cost
> How the dreamt cloud crumbles, the vines are blackened
>> by frost,
> How the view alters.

(6)

Men will be able to see their destruction in Nature's destruction because they have always used Nature as a mirror of experience:

> Ask us, prophet, how we shall call
> Our natures forth when that live tongue is all
> Dispelled, that glass obscured or broken
>
> In which we have said the rose of our love and the clean
> Horse of our courage, in which beheld
> The singing locust of the soul unshelled
> And all we mean or wish to mean.

The image of the locust's metamorphosis is crucial. Though we have known to our cost how the cloud crumbles and the vine blackens, we have also known change as metamorphosis. The prophet will do his work best if he forces us to imagine a world that is not only the victim of disintegration, but which is also incapable of metamorphic revival. As Wilbur says at the end of the poem, there shall no longer be "lofty or long standing / When the bronze annals of the oak-tree close."

The closing of the oak-tree's annals brings history to a halt, but there is, of course, no solace in the act, since metamorphosis is brought to a halt as well. This is precisely the predicament which is visited upon those who succumb to the seductions of the hypnogogic state. "Merlin Enthralled" confesses to the hypnogogic state's temptations, but not without defining the punishment which submission always exacts. Wilbur connects Merlin's surrender to Vivien with the collapse of Arthur's kingdom, suggesting that Merlin's will was weakened by the imminence of general disaster. A sense of history's lugubrious operations is conveyed in the picture of the Round Table's last survivors. The knights, obviously sensing imminent catastrophe, set out under Gawain to find Merlin. He is, in their minds, the only one who might be able to return to them the enchantment they knew in the past. But Merlin, bewitched by Vivien, is beyond helping himself, much less his friends:

> And Merlin slept, who had imagined her
> Of water-sounds and the deep unsoundable swell. . . .

> Slowly the shapes of searching men and horses
> Escaped him as he dreamt on that high bed:
> History died; he gathered in its forces;
> The mists of time condensed in the still head. . . .

(77)

With Merlin's retreat from history into dream, the world loses its natural magic. The enervation this brings is reflected in the poem's closing lines, which portray the knights fading away into mere fabulous characters: "Their mail grew quainter as they clopped along. / The sky became a still and woven blue."

Merlin's attempt to unify time is heroic, but to do so by destroying history is, at best, a pyrrhic victory. Transcendence of time's disintegrative processes is, nevertheless, possible. This is what "Looking into History" affirms. If Wilbur writes prayers on pinheads, "Looking into History" approximates an oratorio.

The poem has three major motifs: it stresses the idea of optics, as the title suggests; it stresses the idea of posing and assuming postures; and it uses tree images extensively. These motifs are made to serve Wilbur's basic interest, which is to show that although history is far more than a catalogue of events embedded in an inert past, although it has, indeed, enormous vitality in the human consciousness, men are not destined to perform a role which history has cast for them. Instead, Wilbur suggests, man asserts his dominion over history by a miraculous capacity to discover his human identity in all the bewildering modes of existence that history can prepare for him. The poem, then, rests on a paradox: the upheavals, changes, and entanglements of history confront men with a wilderness which threatens to smother the personal will, but in doing so they elicit from man's creative imagination the very powers which allow him to order his world and sharpen his sense of his human identity.

The poem begins with a contemplation of the past as inert fact: the speaker is looking at one of Mathew Brady's Civil War photographs. Everything about the photograph confirms the static quality of the past. The five soldiers "stand in a land subdued beyond belief." They are captured in "their amber atmosphere" and "show but the postures men affected then." They are the remnants of "a finished year." The speaker is at a loss to see his "spellbound fathers in these men" and pictures himself as "orphaned Hamlet."

History as rendered by the photograph presents no threat, but neither does it afford an orphan any sense of his identity. The speaker must seek further. Noticing a file of trees in the background of the photograph, he awakens to what lies beyond the range of Brady's camera. Looking into history in this way gives him a connection with the past that the photograph is incapable of producing:

> The long-abated breeze

> Flares in those boughs I know, and hauls the sound
> Of guns and a great forest in distress.
> Fathers, I know my cause, and we are bound
> Beyond that hill to fight at Wilderness.

(84)

Besides being the scene of a Civil War battle, Wilderness is a perfect metaphor for the unstructured world of changes, both disintegrative and metamorphic, through which all must find their way.

The purpose of the second movement of the poem is to explore the implications of looking into history with full consciousness of history as a force rather than as a series of facts. The movement is inaugurated by a dramatic development of the "Wilderness" metaphor and the tree imagery of the first stanzas:

> But trick your eyes with Birnam Wood, or think
> How fire-cast shadows of the bankside trees
> Rode on the back of Simois to sink
> In the wide waters.

These references to historical events as seen by great imaginative writers immediately alert us to the extraordinary significance of the historical process. The allusions redefine the meaning of "Wilderness" and recall that Homer and Shakespeare found it appropriate to understand man's inner life within the context of climactic historical events. With this reminder, we are led to the poem's central reflection:

> Reflect how history's

> Changes are like the sea's, which mauls and mulls
> Its salvage of the world in shifty waves,
> Shrouding in evergreen the oldest hulls
> And yielding views of its confounded graves

> To the new moon, the sun, or any eye
> That in its shallow shoreward version sees
> The pebbles charging with a deathless cry
> And carageen memorials of trees.

As opposed to "Mathew Brady's eye," which could only record an inert past, the eye of Homer or Shakespeare or any man with insight can see the great shaping forces of history. These forces are destructive in the changes they produce, but, to the acute eye, history's changes finally issue in an affirmation of life. The "carageen memorials of trees," while they constitute, as Keats might say, only a shadow of the magnitude that was, are still inherently more appropriate as historical records than the photographic memorabilia of the first stanza. They achieve this distinction by virtue of the metamorphic process which they reflect. History's changes are like the sea's, and the sea's changes are ones in which new forms of life are evolved out of old forms. Liberation from history comprehended as a blind concatenation of events depends on the ability to see these "carageen memorials."

Wilbur, however, is aware of the elusiveness of this kind of perception. The poem clearly suggests that what our eye beholds in the sea's "shallow shoreward version" must not blind us to the tumult that goes on in the great deeps. Similarly, the "carageen memorials" are themselves a very fragile form of life, and the "charging pebbles," as we are surely meant to remember, sounded grating to Matthew Arnold.

Tenuous though it is, the perception is possible, and the poem, in its third section, undertakes to show how it is possible. This last section can, in fact, be read as an elaboration on what Wilbur means by that moral fiber which in "Speech for the Repeal of the McCarran Act" he offers as the only sure defense against the flux of time. One makes this defense by refusing to become imprisoned in the self, by opening oneself to all the forms of life that are external, and by drawing from those forms an increased measure of one's human identity. In short, perception of the world's beautiful changes becomes possible if we do not deny to our own being the instinct for metamorphosis.

Having established in the poem's second section an analogy between history's changes and the sea's, Wilbur begins the final section with an address to Proteus, the presiding deity of his verse:

> Now, old man of the sea,
> I start to understand:
> The will will find no stillness
> Back in a stilled land.

The play on "still" recalls Brady's photograph. History as the photograph conveys it is rejected, for the will insists on using the past as a living force in shaping its own identity. "The dead give no command . . . / Till they be mustered by / Some present fatal choice." But the will, in exposing itself to history as a living force, does not invite its own annihilation, not, that is, if one can "rejoice / In all impostures, take / The shape of lion or leopard, / Boar, or watery snake. . . ." This protean disposition makes accessible the sources of renewed vitality which, as the poem implies, are immanent in history's changes. Thus do we "by some fervent fraud / Father the waiting past. . . ." If the "spellbound fathers" of Brady's photograph showed "but the postures men affected then," we are not, on that account, condemned to be orphans in the universe. We have within us the potential to establish our kinship with the past by undergoing transformation ourselves. Though this may seem a fraud, an affectation of postures, the ultimate effect is, paradoxically, a fuller comprehension of our identity. To contain oneself within the limits of the self-regarding life is a greater fraud, a greater affectation. It is in the "Wilderness" that we find our cause. And so the poem comes to its conclusion with an image that precisely expresses the paradox it has developed. Under the aegis of Proteus, we discover ourselves

> Resembling at the last
> The self-established tree
> That draws all waters toward
> Its live formality.

The protean disposition, nurturing itself on all the forces of vitality around it, becomes, in the end, firm and stable. From our perception of the "memorials of trees," we build the tree itself, and from our ability to undergo metamorphosis, we impose coherence on history's "shifty waves."

It is useful to place "Looking into History" alongside "The Aspen and the Stream," a poem that takes the form of a dialogue between a tree and the stream which it borders. The aspen expresses dramatically the idea which the self-established tree of "Looking into History" represents symbolically. Beholding the stream, on whose surface all creation is reflected, the aspen aspires to what it believes is the stream's "deep surrendered mind," and says: "Teach me, like you, to drink creation whole /

And, casting out my self, become a soul" (p. 32). But the stream, it turns out, takes no pleasure in its capacity for assimilating the life of things external to it:

> I seek an empty mind.
> Reflection is my curse.
> Oh, never have I been blind
> To the damned universe. . . .

The stream is another version of Merlin and of Poe's protagonists; it is weary of the world. But the point I wish to make in comparing the two poems is evident in the last stanza, in which the aspen concludes the poignant dialogue:

> Out of your sullen flux I shall distil
> A gayer spirit and a clambering will,
> And reach toward all about me, and ensnare
> With roots the earth, with branches all the air—
> Even if that blind groping but achieves
> A darker head, a few more aspen-leaves.

One needs no further gloss on the meaning of the last image in "Looking into History." The aspen's beautiful changes are accomplished by its openness to the sullen flux. And if the process entails exposure to tragic experience (the "darker head"), once again it is fulness of being, not annihilation, that results.

The bearing of "The Aspen and the Stream" on "Looking into History" illustrates the point that Wilbur's poems on history are actually part of a wider preoccupation with change itself. And both of these poems, as well as "Advice to a Prophet," illustrate Wilbur's tendency to comprehend change by means of the heuristic power he finds in Nature. His exploration of change, in the context of natural forms, is effectively conducted in "Driftwood." The poem contrasts disintegration and metamorphosis as processes that are equally real. And it advises us that our capacity to perceive the difference between these alternatives depends on our willingness to reject the overweening self and to embrace the universe.

The poem attempts to reconstruct the lineage of some miscellaneous driftwood:

> In greenwoods once these relics must have known
> A rapt, gradual growing,
> That are cast here like slag of the old
> Engine of grief. . . .

(153)

The speaker has here been struck by the mortal—and natural—process of erosion. But as he muses with regret on the changes suffered by these relics, an entirely different view of the changes begins to form itself. He sees that in their pristine condition the driftwood could merely have "affirmed in annual increase / Their close selves, knowing / Their own nature only. . . ." The rapt, gradual growing, it now appears, has the falsity of Poe's hypnogogic state. It was better, the poem indicates, that "their solitude was taken" and that they were "milled into / Oar and plank. . . ." Though metamorphosis into ships exposed them to a hostile world in which they "smashed or sank," still, they did not disintegrate. Instead, release from their self-regarding lives made available to them a revelation of their essential identity which they could never have won in the greenwoods:

> Then on the great generality of waters
> Floated their singleness,
> And in all that deep subsumption they were
> Never dissolved. . . .

Thus, far from reducing them to slag, the changes imposed on these relics have wrought in them a hallowed purity and beauty:

> Curious crowns and scepters they look to me
> Here on the gold sand,
> Warped, wry, but having the beauty of
> Excellence earned.

That the excellence is at once aesthetic and moral and that these qualities are inseparable, as Keats affirmed and Poe denied, is the point on which the poem concludes. Though the pieces of drift-wood "have ridden to homeless wreck" and have been "long revolved / In the lathe of all the seas," still they "have saved in spite of it all their dense / Ingenerate grain."

Another subject about which Wilbur has written with profound skill is children, whom he neither patronizes nor romanticizes. Children experience change in quite radical ways, and Wilbur understands how the imaginative life of children reflects their delight in change on the one hand, and their sense of its painful mysteries on the other. Children in Wilbur's poems, however, are never victimized by this conflict. They are paragons of the open self, the self that is amenable to transformation. As a result, their lives are a pattern of the way in which the conflict between beauty and tragedy in change can be reconciled through an instinctive capacity for metamorphosis.

In "Statues" Wilbur discovers an almost ritualistic significance in the well-known children's game. The children refuse to be caught in the sculptured *rigor mortis* that characterizes both the adults who observe them and the scientifically designed playground that has been constructed for them.

> in a planned
> And planted grove they fling from the swinger's hand
> Across the giddy grass and then hold still
>
> In gargoyle attitudes,—as if
> All definition were outrageous. Then
> They melt in giggles and begin again.
>
> (83)

The earth itself is dazzled by their performance and the "planted grove" is released from its bondage to the Park Department's empty vision. Rediscovering their immemorial capacity for beautiful changes, the maples "with a stiff / Compliance" begin to "entertain the air" and lose the "look of trees / In rushed and cloudy metamorphoses. . . ." As the children and trees dance to their splendidly "fickle" rhythm, something is touched and aroused in the bric-a-brac adults who watch them:

> The soldier breaks his iron pace;
> Linked lovers pause to gaze; and every rôle
> Relents,—until the feet begin to stroll
> Or stride again.

Their withdrawal before metamorphosis, their instinctive retreat back into their familiar attitudes, are gestures which pay
ironic homage to the children's superior wisdom. It is left to
"one aging bum," himself a victim of a contrary debility, "adamantine shapelessness," to grasp something of the children's real
significance as he "stares at the image of his kingdom come."
    In "Boy at the Window" a child is in terrible anguish as he
looks out from the sanctuary of his home at a snowman whom
he knows is about to be assaulted by "a night of gnashings and
enormous moan." What he sees in the snowman is, of course, a
reflection of his own situation as a human being. Wilbur univer-
salizes their common tragedy:

> His tearful sight can hardly reach to where
> The pale-faced figure with bitumen eyes
> Returns him such a god-forsaken stare
> As outcast Adam gave to paradise.

(99)

The meaning of being cast out of paradise is that one inherits a
world whose imperfections are inevitable and omnipresent. The
boy's feeling of security in his warm home is an innocent illusion, and the illusion is partly exposed by the snowman's "having no wish to go inside and die." The fundamental nature of
this illusion does not, however, become clear until the snowman
responds with sadness to the boy's love and is

> moved to see the youngster cry.
> Though frozen water is his element,
> He melts enough to drop from one soft eye
> A trickle of the purest rain, a tear. . . .

The snowman begins to dissolve as he begins to love. This
condition, rather than the bitter night, reflects the true nature of

the world. The boy at the window, who is "surrounded by / Such warmth, such light, such love, and so much fear," has not yet realized that these qualities, which have shielded him from the world's brutality, are but imperfect gifts. Unutterable love will be for him, as it has always been, the cause of crushing pain. He is even now being introduced to this pain: "Seeing the snowman standing all alone / In dusk and cold is more than he can bear."

Nevertheless, if the snowman's act of love reveals the real nature of the boy's illusions, it also illuminates both for him and for the reader how the willingness to bestow love, in spite of the pain, is redemptive. The snowman in dissolving does not, after all, die. He is metamorphosed into "the purest rain." His love exacts an enormous cost, but the effect on him is, finally, beautiful, both in itself and because it rescues him from the "night of gnashings and enormous moan."

Kenneth Burke has claimed that "a rationale of history is the first step whereby the dispossessed repossess the world."[11] It may be said that Wilbur makes this claim with reference to change in general. The rationale which informs his effort to repossess the world, the rationale of the beautiful changes, has obvious limitations. It assumes, for example, a world that is imperfect, not a world that is meaningless. But Wilbur makes the possibility of repossessing an imperfect world decidedly real and palpable, and that is the achievement of his poetry.

NOTES

1. Excerpts from the poetry of Richard Wilbur are from *The Poems of Richard Wilbur* (New York: Harcourt Brace, 1963). Page references are to this edition.

2. This view of Wilbur is reflected in such a standard work as M. L. Rosenthal, *The Modern Poets: A Critical Introduction* (New York: Oxford University Press, 1960), pp. 253–55.

3. Wilbur himself has indirectly replied to his critics by saying that no poet should "adjust his concerns to what others consider the great thought-currents of the times: the *Zeitgeist*, after all, is only a spook invented by the critics." "Round About a Poem of Housman's," in

Don Cameron Allen, ed., *The Moment of Poetry* (Baltimore: Johns Hopkins University Press, 1962), p. 97.

4. "On My Own Work," *Shenandoah* 17 (1956):66.

5. Introduction to *Poe* (New York: Dell, 1959):9.

6. On this aspect of Wilbur's poetry, see A. K. Weatherhead's fine essay, "Richard Wilbur: Poetry of Things," *ELH* 35 (1968):606–17.

7. *Poems,* p. 226. Sister M. Bernetta Quinn quotes "The Beautiful Changes" in her study of *The Metamorphic Tradition in Modern Poetry* (New Brunswick, N.J.: Rutgers University Press, 1955), pp. 7–8. She does not, however, deal with Wilbur in the book, though I suspect she would have if Wilbur's key work, *Things of This World* (1956), had been available to her.

8. Introduction to *Poe,* p. 10.

9. "The House of Poe," Library of Congress Anniversary Lecture, May 4, 1959, reprinted in Eric W. Carlson, *The Recognition of Edgar Allan Poe* (Ann Arbor: University of Michigan Press, 1966), p. 265.

10. Philip Rahv, *The Myth and the Powerhouse* (New York: Farrar, Straus and Giroux, 1965), pp. 13–14.

11. *Attitudes Toward History* (Los Altos, Calif.: Hermes, 1959), p. 315.

JOSEPH BRODSKY

On Richard Wilbur

I doubt that I will succeed in adding anything to what has already been said about Richard Wilbur's works by American critics. Moreover, my conclusions are obviously inadequate, because they are based only on his two early books of poems (one of which—*Things of This World*—incidentally, won a Pulitzer Prize) and a few poems which I managed to find in anthologies which reached me.

Therefore, the things which I can discuss are rather the impressions of a reader than the opinions of a specialist, the only difference from an ordinary reader perhaps being that I am a Russian reader, and also the translator of several of the poems. The latter circumstance probably gave me the opportunity to look into the poems I did read more deeply than the average reader.

It all began with reading, I no longer remember where, one short poem by Wilbur which I would like to quote here. It is only eight lines long, so it does not take much space. If one equates the "I" of the poem with its author (which I suggest doing), despite the fact that the grass is speaking, we will find the poet's stylistic and sensual credo.

> Anonymous as cherubs
> Over the crib of God,
> White seeds are floating
> Out of my burst pod.
> What power had I
> Before I learned to yield?
> Shatter me, great wind:
> I shall possess the field.

Translated by Carl R. Proffer, *The American Poetry Review* 2 (January–February 1972):52.

The quality which attracted my attention to Wilbur is his dramatism, camouflaged by excellence of form. I am more or less aware that Wilbur's technical skill has been the subject of critical comment—both positive and negative. Some people marvel at it, others suppose it is clichéd. But one should not be too haughty even about clichés—let us recall how significant a role the cliché plays in our daily lives. The meaning which we put into the cliché endows it with life, the right to existence. Therefore, every time we run into a cliché (or what seems to us a cliché) while analyzing any work, it is more useful not to shake our heads, but to determine to what degree it is functional.

In my opinion a regular meter and exact rhymes shaping an uncomfortable thought are far more functional than any form of free verse. Because in the former case the reader gets a sense of chaos being organized, while in the latter a sense of dependence on and being determined by chaos. From what one could call a moral point of view, the former is more important than the latter. Even in the event that it is not organization, but nothing more than a form of resistance to chaos. For in the physical world only resistance is possible.

I make these objections not at all because the opinions of the second group of critics strike me as unrealistic, but because it is far more interesting to deal with criticism than praise. Although, as I see it, the two approaches to Wilbur's work are equally unrewarding. His is a pure, sometimes sardonic voice which speaks as a rule in a regular meter about the drama of human existence, and this narration, conducted according to the rather harsh laws of his *Ars poetica,* acquires an independent value and is transformed into one of those extremely vital "things of the given world."

Into a thing, moreover, which possesses a rather attractive form. But one might note that for Wilbur attractiveness and beauty are never goals in themselves. Even when he describes a thing which is obviously beautiful, as for example in "A Baroque Wall-Fountain in the Villa Sciarra," where halfway through the poem the author's eye, observing the stepped fall of the water, is transformed into an idea which makes a stepped ascent to:

That land of tolerable flowers, that state

> As near and far as grass
> Where eyes become the sunlight, and the hand
>   Is worthy of water, the dreamt land
> Toward which all hungers leap, all pleasures pass.

Maybe this is not a new device under God's sun, but at least it is proof again that for this author beauty is not the ultimate aim of his feelings and thoughts, that it is just a means or opportunity to journey into higher spheres. At very best it is a secondary result of such a journey.

The formal perfection of Wilbur's poems is nothing more than a mask—one of those masks that was used in the Greek theater, the only difference being that there the mask expressed character, while here it conceals it, or rather, underlines it because of the difference between the external features and what is being said. Frost's quiet didacticism and rural irony were the same kind of mask. Constantin Cavafy's excursions into antiquity were the same kind of mask.

For it is impossible to speak of life in an open text. In Wilbur the idea is far away from the perfection of the text. It is at approximately as great a distance as that which separates our life from the ideal. The modern art of the mask is the art of creating a scale against which things can be measured.

Perhaps none of this is right, and perhaps Mr. Wilbur himself would be offended to read this. But these are the same feelings and same ideas which spun through my head when I was reading and translating his poetry in Russia. Or rather, this is all only one idea—the idea that the laws of art, including the laws of an *Ars poetica,* when they are observed, render a greater gain in quality than any breaking of these laws in the name of intellectual freedom or the name of freedom of self-expression. And what kind of freedom can we speak of once we have experienced fear?

To Wilbur's laurels as Molière's translator (though generally poets do not like to be talked about as translators, "post-horses of civilization" as Pushkin called them), I would like to add one for his translations of several poems by Anna Akhmatova, in my opinion the greatest Russian poetess of the twentieth century. These translations, published in Olga Carlisle's quite wretched book *Poets on Street Corners,* were a genuine surprise, all the more surprising since the translator does not know Russian.

From my point of view, in the twentieth century America has been very lucky with poetry—more than any other country in the world, including Russia. Therefore, there is nothing surprising about the existence of a poet such as Richard Wilbur, but it is always pleasant to convince oneself of his existence.

RAYMOND OLIVER

Verse Translation and
Richard Wilbur

I

To read poetry, as everyone knows, is to read it in the original
language. This is obvious because any good poem fully exploits
the sounds, rhythms, meanings, and nuances of the particular
language in which it is written; and all languages are different,
even the most closely related. To say that Baudelaire's poems
exist in English or German would be like claiming that steak is
steak, though it may at times consist of pork or salmon. In
poetry, as in food, flavor and texture are of the essence.

   Then what do we mean by translating poetry? I am not referring to the logical or psychological processes involved, though
these things certainly need clarification; I am interested in eval-
uating translations and in asking how they relate to their originals, particularly regarding fidelity. These are not modest questions and I have no final answers. But they must be asked from
time to time because for those who value poetry, the art of
translation is vitally important. It has been practiced by a vast
number of poets, including the greatest, and at no time more
than the present; some of the best poems in our language are
translations of one kind or another. And according to Paul Valéry, the most illustrious but not the only spokesman for this
view, any thoughtful act of writing is essentially an act of translation. In the introduction to his verse translation of Virgil's
Bucolics, Valéry comments: *"To write anything whatsoever,* as
soon as the act of writing demands reflection and is not the

The Southern Review 11 (April 1975):318–30.

mechanical, uninterrupted transcription of completely spontaneous inner speech, is an effort of translation exactly comparable to that which effects the transmutation of a text from one language into another."

That is, translation is the generic term and poetry the special case, not vice versa. This makes a great deal of sense if we think about the continuum that goes from literal to free translation to paraphrase, adaptation, and the like, to variations on a theme or the borrowing of plots and commonplaces, and finally ends at "original" writing, which means the translation of our experience into whatever style we've learned. Even the most spontaneous style is learned, probably at second or tenth remove from someone like Walt Whitman, but learned nonetheless, and adapted—in other words, translated. It is no accident that *translation* and *tradition* are etymologically so close—the one having to do with carrying over, the other with giving over. Every poet, from a Wyatt to a Whitman, has to learn some tradition in order to write, just as we have to learn English before we can speak it. And writing or speaking we are translators, transmutors, bearers of tradition.

These remarks are themselves commonplace, but at the present in this country traditional lore of all kinds is not competing very well with the cult of spontaneity, so I hope I will be pardoned for belaboring what used to be the obvious and for enlisting champions on my side. Valéry has, in fact, put forth another argument for the primacy of translation, this one even more eulogistic than the first:

This former Inspector of Finances . . . turned Carmelite [Father Cyprian, translator of St. John of the Cross] was accomplished in the fine art of writing verse in the pure state. I say *writing verse in the pure state,* and by that I mean that in the work I am discussing, his share is limited to fashioning the form. All the rest—ideas, images, and choice of terms—belongs to St. John of the Cross . . . . he makes a kind of masterpiece by producing poems whose substance is not his own and each word of which is prescribed by a given text. I can hardly refrain from claiming that the merit of so successfully completing such a task is greater (as it is rarer) than that of an author entirely free to choose his means. [From Jackson Mathews' essay, "Third Thoughts on Translating Poetry."]

I do not know to what extent Valéry is here trying to *épater les poètes*—he is certainly taking a swipe at all manner of Romantics—but the argument has, if we make one concession, a hard kernel of logic. The concession is that the translator should be as faithful as possible to the original. Once we grant this it becomes immediately clear that a translator of this sort, as Valéry says, is working with the essence, the differentia of poetry; his medium is pure style, which is the choice of appropriate words and rhythms as distinguished from depth and sharpness of insight, reasoning power, and so forth. He is the ultimate practitioner of *poésie pure*. But at this point my argument seems in danger of becoming parochial. Why should a translator accept the doctrine of *poésie pure?* Do I expect everyone to write like Valéry? (I don't.) Haven't we heard a lot recently about "imitations" and "free adaptations"? Traditional virtues are indeed on the defensive; the problem is to define and justify fidelity.

It may be less difficult to justify than to define. In the first place, I have no objection to those who practice the looser forms of translation, as long as they make no exclusive claims for their approach. Poets have a right to be inspired by anything, including someone else's poem. But the exponents of free translation have gone too far. Robert Lowell, who has brilliantly translated Hugo and Baudelaire, among others, into strict metrical verse (unexpectedly, as will appear), has given us his translator's credo in the introduction to *Imitations:* "Strict metrical translators still exist. They seem to live in a pure world untouched by modern poetry. . . . A better strategy would seem to be the now fashionable translations into free or irregular verse. Yet this method commonly turns out a sprawl of language, neither faithful nor distinguished. . . ." Lowell does not resolve his dilemma, he merely adds, "I believe that poetic translation—I would call it imitation—must be expert and inspired. . . ." Yet surely the resolution is in plain sight: metrical verse should be translated metrically, free verse freely. To proclaim that even strict metrical poems should be translated into free verse is to say that the form of a poem, its rhythmic, patterned shape, is merely external, like ribbons and wrapping paper. This puts Lowell into less fashionable company than he might wish, that of the pedants, who disregard form in their search for messages. And if irregular translations of strictly metrical poems are all right (Lowell's very pallid version of Villon's "Dictes moy ou," for example), then why not translate, say, Allen Ginsberg into the strictest French classical Alexandrines? Questions of possible improvement aside, the degree of change would be equally dramatic.

Galway Kinnell, commenting on his translations of Villon, whose poems make superb use of rhyme and meter, argues even more extremely than Lowell:

> I decided against using rhyme and meter. . . . What is more expressive of a poet than his images? Yet in rhyming translations we can't even be sure the images are the poet's. . . . And I wonder, do rhyme and meter mean for us what they meant for Villon? It may be that in our day these formal devices have become a dead hand, which it is just as well not to lay on any poetry.

Formal devices are certainly dead for the poet who does not understand their nature and use. Like Lowell, Kinnell appeals to an implicit faith in historical determinism, according to which we are all provincials, powerless to reject the reigning values of the moment and incapable of seeking forms and values in the past. Thus, the opinion that imagery is essential to poetry, and meter adventitious, happens to be current doctrine and is probably true for the poetry of Ezra Pound; but it is not true for Ben Jonson, and I do not see that Jonson's poems are therefore inferior to Pound's. This insistence on the contemporary leads logically to solipsism, seen at its most pathetic and suicidal in the case of Sylvia Plath, who lived these ideas to the end (see Joyce Carol Oates's valuable study, "The Death Throes of Romanticism," *Southern Review,* Summer 1973): each individual, like each period, asserts his own private values, which need have no bearing on anyone else's and hence are indisputable. Persuasion becomes a matter of force and uncritical acceptance (fashion), because there are no common grounds for rational argument. The theories of people like Kinnell and Lowell—not always their practice—deny the possibility of faithful translations and criticism, depriving us of all but the most limited, self-centered relations with other cultures and the past.

II

This is one reason why it is good to make translations as faithful as possible, in meter, imagery, thought, overall structure, and whatever else the original may contain. We need to get out of ourselves, to practice the clear, sensitive objectivity required to understand the words of other people on their own terms. And this is why the translations of Richard Wilbur are so important. Though I have not read all the candidates for this distinction, I suspect that Wilbur is the best verse translator of our time, in the full sense I have been describing above; his best work is extremely faithful and it is fine poetry in its own right, achieving a kind of absolute in that it probably cannot be surpassed. I would like to discuss and evaluate some of Wilbur's translations in order to illustrate his faithful approach to this craft and discover, in some degree, how a master goes about his work.

As I have said, it is easier to justify fidelity than define it. In a sense all translations are perfectly unfaithful because every word in the original is changed. There are maxims about how poetry is what gets lost in translation, Italian puns linking *traduttore* (translator) to *traditore* (traitor), and a parable by Borges in which someone finally achieves the perfect translation by rendering *Don Quixote* verbatim into the original Spanish. But I think a working ideal of fidelity is possible since it must exist somewhere between the two extremes of word-for-word literalness and absolute freedom, and these are easy to identify. The truly faithful verse translation is neither arbitrarily "free" and therefore untrue to the original, nor ruthlessly "literal," therefore not worth reading (or writing) for its own sake. The goal of accurate verse translation is the equivalence of stylistic effect; one translates form, not language. And what that equivalent will be, specifically, depends on the poem in question; translation is a matter of bargaining, of gains and losses, of sacrificing and compensating.

Wilbur is especially adroit at striking these subtle bargains and he also is good at the first task of any translator—choosing a poem that is both excellent and translatable. I think the choicest fruits of his talent are five sonnets, four from modern Spanish and one from French: "The Horses" and "Death, from a Distance" by Jorge Guillén, "Everness" and "Ewigkeit" by Jorge Luís Borges, and Valéry's "Helen." Also excellent but perhaps below the first rank are three ballades by Villon ("Ballade of the Ladies of Time Past," "Ballade of Forgiveness," and "Ballade in Old French"), Andrei Voznesensky's "Foggy Street," and "The Pelican," from Philippe de Thaun's *Bestiaire*. And several are more clearly below the first rank but still very good: "The Avowal" and "The Gifts" (Villiers de l'Isle Adam), "Invitation to the Voyage" (Baudelaire), "Compass" (Borges), "To N.V. Rikov-Gukovski" and "Lot's Wife" (Anna Akhmatova), "Antiworlds" (Voznesensky), and "Heureux, Qui, Comme Ulysse" (Du Bellay). There may be others as good as these eighteen poems and I neither can nor wish to rank them any more precisely; but I am sure that these, at least, are worth careful study as accurate translations and as good poems. Wilbur's translations of Molière are widely regarded as masterpieces of their kind and I agree with this judgment, but they are in a different category from the short poems, and I will discuss them separately.

To read a verse translation requires at best three distinct readings: one of the translation, one of the original, and a comparison of the two. I will try to combine these procedures in a discussion of "Helen" by Paul Valéry and Richard Wilbur:

> It is I, O Azure, come from the caves below
> To hear the waves clamber the loudening shores,
> And see those barks again in the dawn's glow
> 4 Borne out of darkness, swept by golden oars.
>
> My solitary hands call back the lords
> Whose salty beards beguiled my finger-tips;
> I wept. They sang the prowess of their swords
> 8 And what great bays fled sternward of their ships.
>
> I hear the martial trumpets and the deep-
> Sea conches cry a cadence to the sweeps;
> The oarsmen's chantey holds the storm in sway;

12   And high on the hero prows the Gods I see,
      Their antique smiles insulted by the spray,
      Reaching their carved, indulgent arms to me.

I think this is a fine poem, quite apart from its high value as a translation. I can find no flaws—not even the two extra syllables in the first line, coming before the iambic norm has been firmly established. To eliminate *the* would make "hear the waves" echo "come from caves" in a sing-song rather than suggestive manner, and it would destroy the truly suggestive echo in "clámbĕr thĕ lóud—," which juxtaposes the forward and upward movement of the waves with the similar movement of Helen ascending from the "grottes de la mort." And there is more internal rhyming, so appropriate in a poem about memories and resonant trumpet-calls: barks/darkness, dawn's/Borne, solitary/salty, Sea/sweeps, high/smiles. Yet this is a translation; most of the superb local effects have their French equivalents and sometimes even improve the original. In lines 9 and 10, for instance, Wilbur enriches "les conques profondes et les clairons / Militaires" with a wordplay that makes ingenious use of the line break: the sound of the conches is deep and they are from the deep sea, though not from the depths that Helen has come to know. Wilbur also understands Wallace Stevens' dictum that "French and English constitute a single language," but he understands equally well that English is derived from Anglo-Saxon. Thus while "chantey" in line 11—he might have spelled it "shanty"—clearly reflects "Le chant," the really strong pun in that line could have no parallel in French: the chantey holds the storm in its power, its sway, but *swey* is also an Anglo-Saxon word meaning "harmony," "melody." This is a finer verbal stroke than Valéry's straightforward "Le chant . . . enchaîne le tumulte," in spite of the play on chant/-chaîne. Elsewhere Wilbur and Valéry make equally good use of the Latin substratum partly shared by French and English; in line 13, "insulte(d)" has the same primary meaning in both languages, as well as the root meaning of "leap at," which is what the spray is doing to the smile of the Gods.

In addition to finding parallels for the sonorous internal rhymes of the French, and equalling or surpassing the French wordplays (not all—"high" in line 12 is not as rich as "exaltés"),

Wilbur has added some resonance from his own literary tradition. The Yeatsian "what great bays" of line 8 carries an echo of the grand manner, well suited to this poem about a heroic literary past.

Wilbur then has created a poem of very fine texture and balance in which the union of sound and sense appears inevitable; and yet this poem was begotten on a French original and preserves most of that original through (1) verbatim, (2) equivalent-substitute, and (3) implicit translations (by implicit I mean, for instance, that the "triomphes" of line 7 imply or can imply "the prowess of their swords," and the "degrés" in line 2 imply or at least suggest "clamber"). The English also renders the measured, dignified tone of the original and its rhythm of syntax, meter, and thought. I submit that this is a very high level of accomplishment, worthy of emulation.

Robert Lowell has tried something else in his own translation of "Hélène"; it is, as he would say, an "imitation." I quote the first stanza, followed by the original French:

> I am the blue! I come from the lower world
> to hear the serene erosion of the surf;
> once more I see the galleys bleed with dawn,
> and shark with muffled rowlocks into Troy.
>
> Azur! c'est moi . . . Je viens des grottes de la mort
> Entendre l'onde se rompre aux degrés sonores,
> Et je revois les galères dans les aurores
> Ressusciter de l'ombre au fil des rames d'or.

The third line contains a striking image, though it is very different from the French, and "the serene erosion of the surf" is also vivid, with its oxymoronic sense of destruction reinforced by the soothing repetition of *s* and *r* sounds; but this phrase is at best remotely implicit in the French. None of the details in the fourth line has anything to do with the original wording and in this case I find the change quite arbitrary. But the first sentence, "I am the blue," seems a simple mistranslation with no hint of a raison d'être. Why such a shrill outcry and what could it mean? Helen is not the sea or the sky; and the rest of Lowell's version does not explain in what sense she is "the blue." My point is not that Robert Lowell is a bad poet and translator—he has done much better elsewhere—but that he has succeeded, according to his own lights, and that this success is inferior. He has written an "imitation" by using Valéry's poem as a springboard for his own verbal gymnastics. The result is a seriously flawed poem with good but not redeeming features, and a translation that betrays its original again and again. And while he has skillfully written all but one line in iambic pentameter, Lowell has done away with the patterned end-rhymes that one associates with sonnets. Richard Wilbur has preserved the rhymes, handled the meter even more skillfully, *and* translated far more accurately—in every sense—than Lowell. Wilbur had the good judgment and humility to grant that Valéry's poem deserved faithful translation; Lowell took more of a risk and trusted in his own talent. It may be that "imitations" should be made only of poems that could stand improvement, or perhaps they should just be made more carefully; in any case, I think that on grounds of sheer economy Wilbur's approach is better. Why aim merely for a good poem related vaguely to a foreign original, if you can try for a good poem that also reveals the foreign one?

III

I have also checked the rest of Wilbur's translations carefully against the originals; his degree of accuracy is almost always very high and his technical skill as a poet is just about equal to that of the people he translates. When his performance is relatively weak it is usually the result of picking a weak original. For instance, Francis Jammes's "A Prayer to Go to Paradise with the Donkeys," based on the charming conceit stated in the title, is an easygoing poem full of tender humility, but it is also full of undistinguished phrasing in both English and French. The looseness of Wilbur's iambic pentameter fits the looseness of the phrasing but has no other justification I can discern. He probably chose this poem because he liked the theme and tone (cf. his own "A Baroque Wall-Fountain in the Villa Sciarra" and "Praise in Summer," among others). The same thematic interest would account for his translation of La Fontaine's "Ode to Pleasure," which is as agreeable as the Jammes and smoother—Wilbur conveys its leisurely periodic movement—but also very soft. His single ventures into Italian and Anglo-Saxon also seem ordinary. "The Agrigentum Road" by Salvatore Quasimodo is a fairly literal version of an unrhymed poem; some of the imagery is sharp, some of it sentimental, and the rhythms are roughly iambic, measured off with no clear rationale in lines of irregular length. As to the Anglo-Saxon, Wilbur rightly omitted from his collected poems the passage translated from lines 210–24 of *Beowulf,* but it shows something of his interest in the roots of English, an interest that appears elsewhere in his writings. Oddly though, he fails to exploit a few figures of the sort that he often puts into his own poems; thus "wudu bundenne" becomes merely "hardy vessel."

Otherwise, Wilbur's translations range from reasonably good to superlative. He does very well with Latin, the other language he has quarried only once, in his "Eight Riddles from Symphosius." This minor poet of the fourth century A.D. is very ingenious, but Wilbur equals him in this and surpasses him in at least one department of verbal dexterity: he introduces an *a-a-a* rhyme scheme where Symphosius has no rhyme at all. Far from being a mistake through excess of technical zeal, this is a fine example of translating literary *form;* whereas the epigram in classical Latin does not rhyme, it does in the English tradition, to reinforce the sense of inevitability and the final point. Wilbur has translated epigram into epigram. The only poor line of the group is the first one in the eighth riddle: "To me, and through me [a chain], Fortune is unkind" for "Nexa ligor ferro, multos habitura ligatos"; the English is too generalized, too obviously in need of a rhyme, and pretty remote from the Latin. Another illustrates the translator's device of rearranging syntax or lines, as well as Wilbur's normal accuracy:

> Mordeo mordentes, ultro non mordeo quemquam;
> Sed sunt mordentem multi mordere parati;
> Nemo timet morsum, dentes quia non habeo ullos.

> I bite, when bitten [an onion]; but because I lack
> For teeth, no biter scruples to attack,
> And many bite me to be bitten back.

The third line of the Latin is redistributed between the first and second lines of the English; the second line ends up third; and the second half of line 1 is omitted (at a slight loss), but it is largely implicit in the translation. These riddles are merely exercises in cleverness, but they are well done, in English as in Latin.

The four sonnets from the Spanish of Guillén and Borges are, I believe, approximately as good as the Valéry, and at least three of them are on broader, deeper themes than "Helen." The horses in Guillén's poem of that name are "heavily natural," which adds a sense of physical weight to the Spanish "tristamente naturales"; and Wilbur's final line, an understated gesture, seems more powerful to me than Guillén's laconic statement: "Ahí están: ya sobrehumanos"; "Serene now, superhuman, they crop their field." In general Wilbur's syntax is more hypertactic than the Spanish, but with no weakening of effect.

Among the Russian translations, Voznesensky's "Foggy Street" is probably the best. But like the two others from Voznesensky ("Antiworlds" and "Dead Still"), it is rather different in style from the original. The Russian is concise and elliptical, lacking in connectives; this is partly a function of the Russian language, but it also results from Voznesensky's choice. Wilbur's translations supply the connectives, complete the sentences, and add a good many comments and descriptive details. The effect is much more articulate than Voznesensky, more social, conversational, and finally more literary than the abrupt manner of the Russian. In translating Anna Akhmatova, Wilbur has stayed closer to the original, possibly because Akhmatova's style is more congenial to him. He makes brilliant compensations, as usual: "Chornoi smerti mel'kalo krylo" (the wing of black death flashed) becomes "Death's wing has swept the sky of color," in which death is not black but is causally linked, by a strong metaphor, to the colorless sky. There are more readings I would dispute in the Russian translations than elsewhere, but they are still more accurate than free.

In spite of his often marvelous work, sometimes tours de force, with these five languages—Spanish, Italian, Latin, Anglo-Saxon, and Russian—Wilbur remains principally a translator of French. He ranges through all periods, beginning with the twelfth-century writer of bestiary lore, Philippe de Thaun, whose droll (to us) didacticism Wilbur transcribes very precisely in "The Pelican" ("PELLICANUS is the word / For a certain breed of bird / Who truly is a crane"). His versions of Villon's ballades, especially "Ballade of the Ladies of Time Past" ("Dictes moy ou"), are perhaps more dramatic than the French and less melodious, but certainly skillful. The English for "Dictes moy ou, n'en quel pays," incidentally, displays what I would call *analysis,* another very useful trick from the translator's repertory: "O tell me where, in lands or seas." The general term *pays* (country) is resolved into its parts; the reverse procedure, synthesis, is of course equally useful.

There are also several poems (or prose-poems) each, by Villiers de l'Isle Adam, Baudelaire, René Char, and Francis Ponge; but Wilbur makes no attempt to give us the gist of anyone's whole *oeuvre.* He is explicitly concerned with single poems. In "On My Own Work" (1965), he wrote "The unit of my poetry, as I experience it, is not the *Collected Poems* which I may some day publish; nor is it the individual volume, or the sequence or group within the volume; it is the single poem." This is also the proper attitude for translators concerned with excellence and fidelity, since an attempt to translate the complete works of any poet is bound to produce a great deal of mediocre writing. Even so, Wilbur's *Tartuffe* and *The Misanthrope,* because they are sizable pieces of work and superbly translated, do, I think, give us a good idea of Molière at his best.

Virtually everything I have said about the short poems also applies to these plays, but there are a few comments to add. Wilbur himself has supplied most of them in his introduction to *The Misanthrope* (1955):

To duplicate this parody-tragic effect in English [of "Cornelian *tirade*"] it was clearly necessary to keep the play in verse, where it would be possible to control the tone more sharply, and to recall our own tragic tradition. There were other reasons, too, for approximating Molière's form. The constant of rhythm and rhyme was needed, in the translation as in the original, for bridging great gaps between high comedy and farce, lofty diction and ordinary talk, deep character and shallow. Again, while prose might preserve the thematic structure of the play, other "musical" elements would be lost, in particular the frequently intricate arrangements of balancing half-lines, couplets, quatrains, and sestets.

He goes on to explain that two of the most striking features of Molière's dialogue, its redundancy and logic, can be rendered much better in verse than prose. I would agree that all of these are important stylistic goals, and add that in my opinion Wilbur has achieved them. His general point is that strict metrical verse allows more subtle, rapid, and intense variations of tone and meaning, since the norm is so precisely defined—like a violin string rather than a clothesline. This is true, but easier to observe in a short, dense poem like "Helen" than in the Molière plays, which are very closely written compared to prose, but loose compared to the best short poems. I'm sure this is the only reason why either Molière or Wilbur could keep it up at such a high level for hundreds of pages. The relatively prosaic norm of the verse gives them some room for maneuvering.

Still, there are plenty of high points. The section from act 1, scene 4 of *Tartuffe,* which Wilbur chose to include in his *Poems,* is a small masterpiece of narrative, characterization, and controlled irony. In *The Misanthrope,* when Alceste tells Philinte he ought to hang himself for being a hypocrite, Philinte responds:

> Je ne vois pas, pour moi, que le cas soit pendable,
> Et je vous supplierai d'avoir pour agréable
> Que je me fasse un peu grâce sur votre arrêt.
> Et ne me pende pas pour cela, s'il vous plaît.

> It hardly seems a hanging matter to me;
> I hope that you will take it graciously
> If I extend myself a slight reprieve,
> And live a little longer, by your leave.

Wilbur has made some of the usual adjustments, but the precise, formal irony seems as good in English as in French; as elsewhere, it would be hard to say which was the original and which the translation. Again, Dorine is perversely and sarcastically telling Mariane she must marry Tartuffe:

MARIANE:	Not Tartuffe! You know I think him . . .
DORINE:	Tartuffe's your cup of tea, and you shall drink him.
MARIANE:	I've always told you everything, and re-lied . . .
DORINE:	No. You deserve to be tartuffified.

Here Wilbur both translates exactly and improves on Molière, who has Dorine say, less outrageously: "Tartuffe est votre homme et vous en tâterez." (By "improve" I mean that the translator sees the stylistic purpose of the original and does a better job of accomplishing it.) Wilbur's rhyming is consistently brilliant; he keeps the paraphrasable content of Molière to a remarkable degree; he preserves the meter and closed couplets of the originals; he is sometimes more colloquial, succinct, and vivid than Molière, sometimes less—on balance, I suppose the French and English are about equal as verse.

What Richard Wilbur does not manage to do in his intelligent, live translations is what Robert Lowell would expect him to do: "Strict metrical translators . . . . are taxidermists, not poets, and their poems are likely to be stuffed birds." Wilbur does not create stuffed birds. In one and the same act of translation he shows himself a perceptive critic by picking a good text and deciding which parts of it must be kept and which can be sacrificed; an accurate philologist by grasping the sense of the original; and a good poet by writing a good poem. These skills are worth cultivating, especially in our time; and I can think of no better encouragement and model than Richard Wilbur.

CHARLES R. WOODARD

Richard Wilbur's Critical Condition

Critical commentaries on Wilbur's poetry have come to seem
rather highly stylized and predictable, like bullfighting. First
there is the ritual praise of his technical virtuosity (music, diction, imagery, metrics), to show that the critic is not devoid of
the appreciation of beauty, followed quickly by the disclaimers
which establish his awareness of its irrelevance to contemporary
life. Objections to Wilbur's poetry, to phrase them in the sim-
plest terms, take the following forms: (1) He thinks too much.
(2) He does not suffer enough.

Strictly speaking, it is not Wilbur's thought so much as his
imagination that is derogated. Clearly we cannot condemn him
for his epistemological interests if we are to permit them to
Wallace Stevens. It is Wilbur's use of the things of this world, his
chosen poetic province, which gets him into trouble; he is not
tough enough with them, not sufficiently insistent upon their
thinginess, but persists in allowing them to pass through his
mind, where his recalcitrant imagination may act upon them.
Back of such criticism there hover the dicta and practice of
William Carlos Williams, whose followers put their faith in an
objective "rendering" of reality or experience as little tampered
with by mind as possible. The chief emphasis is on outwitting
the mind's insidious attempts to impose its own patterns on
reality or to substitute them *for* reality—an end accomplished by
limiting its reported activities to acts of perception or "prereflec-
tive cognition." It is as if the poet were arrested in his linguistic
development on the verge of the invention of language, striving
for an arrangement of shells on the shore from which we as
readers are to deduce an idea, rather as Deism could deduce

Contemporary Poetry: A Journal of Criticism 2 (Autumn 1977):16–24.

God's existence from an inspection of the natural world. Perhaps it is not quite so primitive as this; a better comparison would be the still-life tableau of such objects as apples, pears, and freshly killed hare, except that the seemingly arbitrary grouping must "mean" something, without saying it. With a red wheelbarrow, glazed with rain, and white chickens, Williams takes us back to an approximation of pictographic writing. Thus the snares and delusions of discursive thought and emotive language are avoided, but only until we read an analysis of such symbols by one of Williams' exegetes. The reader is permitted to use his mind, we are tempted to say, but not the poet, except in the most rigorous "demonstrative" sense. It was Williams' insistence that there be no new wine in old bottles, and thus Wilbur is condemned for using older forms and conventions. Paradoxically, it is acceptable for Williams' imitators to put their wine in his old bottles, but Wilbur may not put his in Eliot's and certainly not in those of Pope and Donne. If wit and cleverness were not generally outside the laws governing the works of the Williams school, one of its members might write a satire on Wilbur, similar to that written by Dryden on Shadwell—no doubt it would be entitled "MacDonne."

The second complaint, which appears to have its origin in the vogue for "confessional" poetry, may at times be viewed as a result of the first; if Wilbur did not take refuge so habitually in his own mind, he would see the world for the pit of horror that everyone else knows it to be. Lowell and his followers, with their categories of "cooked" and "raw" poetry, take it as a priori that the good poet will suffer and, further, that good poetry consists precisely in the reporting of this suffering. Emotional Jacksonians, the critics who take this position, want no one whistling within hearing of their misery. They appear to view poetry as having some therapeutic function, but if poets are their physicians how can it profit them to be prescribed continuing doses of their own sickness? The answer must be that misery continues to love company; they want the assurance that the poet is not sunny or happy—that he is, in fact, exactly like themselves. They want it reaffirmed that man is beastly, the "human condition" hopeless. Thus assured, they may turn out the light and fall into dreamless sleep. In such a critical environment, Wilbur is a kind of Mauberley, born out of his due time in "a half-savage country, out of date"—a country with a taste, where a taste can be discerned, for meat not merely rare but raw.

The effect of such criticism is to confine poetry to immediate sensation and emotion. We appear to have reared a race of critics who go about with their tongues probing their aching teeth, hungering to see lepers, monstrosities, freaks, wounds, blood, madness. We require to be told that we are mad, or have at least the rich potential for going mad. We still, in some strange perversion of Victorianism, require our poets to be sages, but sages of a very rare and specialized breed, sages of suffering. Their hands display their stigmata, their wrists their slashes. The lurid path cut through our skies by the Welsh comet Dylan Thomas, Eliot's resigned nerveless suffering, Auden's frequent reminders of "the suffering to which we are fairly accustomed," Yeats even, with his cyclic cataclysms, our own grim expectations of life in the twentieth century, the dreadful tragedies of our younger poets—all these have led us to believe that the poet's role requires that he put the stamp of sincerity upon his work by stepping in front of an automobile or leaping off a bridge.

We seem, in fact, to have arrived, in recent years, at a kind of unwritten contract with our poets. Were it formalized, it might read more or less as follows: "You may be a poet, and we will reward you with grants and fellowships and readings if you are fashionable, and publish your doings in the papers, like those of football players and television performers, but never forget that it is your suffering for which you are being paid. We will begin to take most interest in your work precisely when it shows clearest symptoms of your breaking down. We want to know of every visit to a sanitarium, every cut, cuddled, and sucked thumb, your bouts with alcohol and depression, your flirtations with suicide. And then to prove your seriousness, you must write a final poem, in the form of a leap from a bridge or a pulled trigger. Then we will believe. Then we will establish a cult and proclaim you unreservedly a poet."

Confessional poetry may be quite as much a result of this attitude as its cause. The wounds! we cry, all the wounds, licked by so many bloody tongues. Knowledge is sorrow, but must art be pain? Must we now have suffering only, without catharsis?

Unused to hearing confessionals, knowing only our own local pain, we are overwhelmed. This is what life is, we say, like the blind man laying hold of some part of the elephant. Granted that life is grim, that this may be, as Elizabeth Bishop said, "our worst century yet," must our poetry continue compulsively to rehearse this one obsessive fact? The mind's indwelling powers are capable of more; the vulture reminds the alert of Noah; another world opens through a hole in the floor. Even a man on the way to a madhouse may smile at a girl in the street.

Arnold criticized the Romantics for not knowing enough; another generation of critics condemns Wilbur for not suffering enough. He comes and sets up shop before us, dazzling us with displays of virtuosity such as to make him seem a creature from another world—or from another age, at the very least. His technical skill is immense. His poems stand apart from him in the independent world of art; both he and they are like cats, licking their fur in total self-sufficiency, self-possession. It is almost as if he were too blessed with talent. We may be tempted to see him as a kind of happy fool, a "natural," into whose pockets apples fall as he dawdles cheerfully across the verdancy of an outmoded romantic landscape. "How graceful," we say, "but does he go through life without pain?" His poetry is a reminder that the tragic vision which we prize so highly in our poets need not rule out the "wit and wakefulness," the free play of the mind delighting in itself, which Wilbur proclaims as his own. "It's pretty," say Kipling's Philistines doubtfully, "but is it art?" "It's art," we say of Wilbur's poetry, shaking our heads with equal doubt, "but is it life? Does he not suffer?" He does not say, overtly, and thus we conclude that he *has* nothing to say. We might pay him the compliment, however, of thinking that he is perhaps not trying to say so much as to make, and with materials subtler than oyster-shells. The play of his mind, as shimmering and translucent as the spray of his fountains, may be a delight to the reader; if it is an equal delight to Wilbur, so much the better. It was once considered a virtue to suffer in silence; if Wilbur suffers, it is thus he does. Socialized suffering can only be ruinous; shared property dwindles; shared pain multiplies until every emotional reservoir is overflowing. The giver retains a full store, no matter how fully he burdens his recipients. It would be tragic indeed if we forced Wilbur, as the price of our adulation, to take to drink and end a suicide in some peaceful New England summer, and thus to become overnight another of our cult-heroes.

In lamenting man's tragic circumstance, however, and supposing that Wilbur is unaware of it, we do him a very real injustice. Apart from man's mortality, with its attendant suffering, there is perhaps no more tragic situation in his life than the discrepancy between the world he perceives and the world which he knows intellectually to exist. A study of Wilbur's poetry—we may confine ourselves to the collection *The Poems of Richard Wilbur* (New York: Harcourt, Brace & World, 1963)—shows how often the things of this world which he celebrates are shadowed by an awareness of this discrepancy. His little poem "Epistemology" states a theme implicit in much of his writing:

I

Kick at the rock, Sam Johnson, break your bones:
But cloudy, cloudy is the stuff of stones.

II

We milk the cow of the world, and as we do
We whisper in her ear, "You are not true."

This is not merely the cow of Berkeley's idealism but the cow of current science, without milking machines. Nothing can bridge the gap between appearance and the reality which we know to exist but cannot perceive. Wilbur for his poetry chooses the cow he can see and milk rather than some molecular cow which cloudily fails to abide our question. Nevertheless, he is far removed in his epistemology from Williams and his followers. Though he knows, as the title of one of his poems tells us, that "a world without objects is a sensible emptiness," his poetry is ironically informed with the further knowledge that a red wheelbarrow possesses no quality of redness and that the chickens in a barnyard are cloudy stuff indeed, as is his cow. His poetry itself, the milk from that cow, must thus partake of the general untruth of those things whose fragile beauty it celebrates; and that fragility is more moving than the traditional theme of mutability. The Williams school accepts without question the world as our senses give it to us, while rejecting the validity of any Wordsworthian recollection in tranquillity. It is as if Margaret Fuller had said, "I accept the universe, but I will not allow my mind to contaminate it." Wilbur permits the entry of mind into the reality-equation, and not without logic. If the world which the Williams school uses as the materials of poetry is "unreal," as scientifically viewed, then it is difficult to see that the senses are more reliable than the intellect for poetry or more valid than the imagination. How can the mind contaminate in any significant way a world which the mind knows already not to exist except as invisible particles awhirl in infinite immensities of space? Poets, after all, are not philosophers or scientists; their observations are neither methodologically nor logically immaculate. If on the other hand the world is "unreal" in philosophic terms, with no existence outside mind, then intellection is not only the order of the day—it *is* the day, and the night.

We may, if we please, insist upon the validity of sensations and the "reality" of sensible objects; but such an assumption, in the context of modern scientific knowledge, is in itself a denial of the validity of the mind's operations; and thus we are returned to a primitive state of existence—a precortical state, we are tempted to say—scratching or painting our visual perceptions on the wall of the cave. Such a state is not Wilbur's. In a world eternally in motion, where nothing is stable, where even atomic particles are beset with an uncertainty principle, the play of the individual mind, itself reducible to the activity of chemically generated electrical impulses, may be as good a model of reality as we have. If it imposes its own patterns on the outer world, perhaps that is not a calamitous event after all, since those patterns are a part of that world. Beneath the sensible surface of Wilbur's world another threatens, like the crack in Auden's teacup, to open into unspeakable voids—"the buried strangeness / Which nourishes the known" ("A Hole in the Floor"). His is a landscape of ephemera, of "opulent bric-a-brac," mined country, touched with a fatal "seeming" of the Edenic pear in "June Light," which constantly erodes the "truth and new delight" of the visible world. Each poem is a temporary victory over our knowledge of the nature of things; in each, like his juggler, he "has won for once over the world's weight," even as his prophet is being rehearsed to preach the "worldless rose" of an atomized earth ("Advice to a Prophet"). In this connection, Wilbur's tendency to concentrate on things rather than on dramatic situations (people) is perhaps not without its own sinister implications, as much a commentary by omission as Housman's excluding the fully adult and the aged from *A Shropshire Lad.*

Wilbur's concern is not mutability alone (although this too is a central theme) but the precariousness of a physical world which is known to be different from what our physical senses tell us it is, as we know that sand may be a component of glass, without being able to see it ("Junk"). A tension is set up between eye and mind. Wilbur must praise appearance even as he is being hoodwinked by it, because a molecular world is not a workable stuff for poetry, though it is always there, an undeniable adjunct to the assertions made by the poetry. His is not the too-solid flesh of Hamlet; things of summer growth "raise / Plainly their seeming into seamless air" ("June Light"); the erratic flight of birds suggests a world "dreamt" by "cross purposes" ("An Event"), and misty weather brings a fear of the loss of the physical world ("A Chronic Condition").

If Wilbur is to be criticized for being "too happy," for employing his mind too much, it might be well for those who do so to consider the poised fragility of his world as set against the "bloody loam," apparently eternal, which is the basis of Williams'. Both Williams and the confessional school appear to accept the sensible world at face value; in his later work Williams' world is poised between the mythic primal slime on the one hand and the momentary display of spirit on the other. The uneasy ground of Wilbur's poetry is the irreconcilable oppositions of appearance and knowledge. It is not immediately apparent that Williams' world is more "real," and thus more unhappy, than Wilbur's, or that it deals more rigorously with its facts and artifacts, since it does not show any inclination to question the evidence of the senses as the basis of its epistemology.

Between the two poles of sensation and knowledge, Wilbur's mind functions as mediator. Its graceful error may "correct the cave" of reality ("Mind"); it milks the cow of the world which it knows to be untrue. The perceived world, with its fine gauzy shimmer of fountains and its colored juggling balls, is equally a world of the fine shimmer and juggling of mind. His poetry constitutes a realm of its own, with its own truth, constantly reiterating that the mind's reflections are hardly less substantial or valid than the objects of its perceptions. If a critic, standing at the edge of one of Wilbur's displays, cries, "Unreal!" Wilbur need only allow a wider spin of the lariat to rope him into the scene whose existence he is denying. After all, Wilbur has denied it from the beginning.

CHARLES R. WOODARD

"Happiest Intellection"
The Mind of Richard Wilbur

Richard Wilbur's poem "Mind," in *The Poems of Richard Wilbur* (New York: Harcourt Brace, 1963), which compares the mind to a bat in a cave, "Contriving by a kind of senseless wit / Not to conclude against a wall of stone," ends with an examination of his trope:

> And has this simile a like perfection?
> The mind is like a bat. Precisely. Save
> That in the very happiest intellection
> A graceful error may correct the cave.

It would appear, then, that the figure is "precisely" *im*perfect, since the mind enjoys an advantage not possessed by the bat, confined within its unyielding boundaries. Indeed, it is not immediately apparent what the mind's cave is, if it is subject to correction by error, however graceful. When asked about this difficulty on one occasion after a public reading, Wilbur, somewhat in the manner of Browning, professed not to know what he meant. The answer is in keeping with the generally playful nature of Wilbur's mind—playful in the best sense, sometimes very seriously so—and it is with a full appreciation of that mind and of Wilbur's reiterated concern with questions of cognition that we need to approach the poem's conclusion.

Wilbur's universe is one in which the real and the apparent exist in a highly tentative relationship. His little poem "Epistemology" makes reference to Samuel Johnson's kicking of a stone to refute Berkeley and concludes, "But cloudy, cloudy is

Notes on Modern American Literature 2 (Winter 1977): item 7.

the stuff of stones." The second part of the poem reads, "We milk the cow of the world, and as we do / We whisper in her ear, 'You are not true.'" "Cloudiness" is a word Wilbur uses with some frequency, to denote both the opacity of matter, so far as the senses are concerned, and its shifting, colorless insubstantiality as the mind knows it. The latter quality is generally not so much the result of philosophic idealism as of atomic theory. In a poem called "The Eye," in his new volume *The Mind-Reader* (New York: Harcourt Brace Jovanovich, 1976), his eye, looking through binoculars, is "Giddy with godhead or with nonexistence." The eye, in fact, may be no more than "folly's loophole," whether scientifically assisted or not. The world appearance, in the light of scientific knowledge, is not only misleading but infinitely fragile, threatening at any moment to break up into meaningless abstractions of mathematics and physics, as when he writes in "The Fourth of July," (in *The Mind-Reader*),

> The sun is not a concept but a star. . . .
> Though, as for that, what grand arcanum saves
> Appearances, what word
> Holds all from foundering in points and waves?

It is this distrust of "appearances," overlying the shifting chaos of the twentieth-century scientific world-picture, which leads him to speak of the mind's "graceful error." The cave is knowledge itself, including scientific knowledge, but Wilbur is aware how much that cave is subject to alteration by the mind which creates it. The great discoveries which bring about such alterations are frequently accidental, intuitive, "graceful errors" which controvert received opinion but result finally in a cave enlarged or "corrected." Today's unthinkable is tomorrow's theory and next year's law, as Wilbur seems to be suggesting in "April 5, 1974," in the new volume, when, remarking on the changing appearance wrought by rising mist ("cloudiness") over a thawing landscape, he asks, "Was matter getting out of hand / And making free with natural law?"

Matter, for all its sensuous appeal, is perilous stuff for Wilbur, far too subject to the mind's revisionism to be fully trusted or taken always with full seriousness; and thus, in "The Fourth of July," though he pays tribute to Copernicus, "Not hesitant to risk / His dream-stuff in the fitting-room of fact," he earlier says, "Praise to all fire-fledged knowledge of the kind / That, stooped beneath a hospitable roof, / Brings only hunch and gaiety for proof." The world exists for each of us, finally, as a cave fashioned by our own flittering bat Mind; in "The Mind-Reader" Wilbur speaks of the pain of being "pent / In the dream-cache or stony oubliette / Of someone's head" where "Nothing can be forgotten." The interdependency of matter and mind, the former a series of ever-shifting schemata as conceived by the latter through the surges and recessions of intellectual history, makes Wilbur, for all his warmth and appeal, a more skeptical poet than is generally recognized. In the privacy of our mental caves, there is no point in taking with absolute seriousness either mind or the matter subject to its changes. In one of his most impressive poems, "A Hole in the Floor" (in *Poems*), he playfully uncovers part of a lost city between the floor joists, complete with street and kiosk, then realizes that he has done so in search of "the buried strangeness / Which nourishes the known" and renders "dangerous" our comfortable daily environment. Faced with such danger, Wilbur falls back upon a kind of Cartesian certainty. Things do not exist for his mind to make poetry of them, as some critics have charged; rather his mind exists to make poetry, as gracefully as possible, of things whose existence is subject to no final certainty in the "dream-cache" of the most enlightened head. Apparently, however, there may be also a kind of tribal cave of experience where Wilbur's heuristic bats come to perform before us, with juggling "wit and wakefulness" and "hunch and gaiety," not merely to correct but also to color and brighten.

HOWARD NEMEROV

From "What Was Modern Poetry?"

In my first lecture, I spent almost all the time on what I called imagism—not the movement called Des Imagistes, but, much more broadly, the many and recurrent movements in modernist poetry that had in common a wish to exalt the senses, especially the sense of sight at the expense of the mind. Indeed, these movements, like some movements in philosophy (and not in the branch of aesthetics alone), found themselves impelled, by the necessities of rhetoric if by nothing more serious, to a contempt for mind, and since this contempt for mind in general had to include of necessity the mind that was being contemptuous, not to mention the mind that was writing the poems that exalted the senses at the mind's expense, some contradiction was always involved, though it was not always acknowledged. For to proclaim, as the first Imagists did, that one must do away with "Cosmic Poetry" is to proclaim that one must do away with metaphysics, which is, however, a metaphysical decision; and as Owen Barfield says, "It is a failing common to a good many contemporary metaphysical theories that they can be applied to all things except themselves but that, when so applied, they extinguish themselves" (*Poetic Diction* [New York: McGraw-Hill, 1964], p. 16).

Having tried to illustrate by certain poems of William Carlos Williams what theoretical considerations, what problems, and what solutions belonged to this movement of the mind, I wish now to ask why. Why should it have happened to so many talented men and women, in poetry, in the novel, not to mention in painting, to put such an exclusive emphasis upon sensing,

Figures of Thought—Speculations on the Meaning of Poetry and Other Essays (Boston: David R. Godine, 1978), pp. 149–98. Excerpts: pp. 166–70, 174–5, 188–92.

so exclusive that it led them in many instances to a contemptuous or fierce rejection of mind and thinking and explicitly stated meaning? One would have thought there could never have been a poet or novelist or painter so foolish as to be *against* accuracy of perception, accuracy of notation, or *against* the sympathetic concentration upon nature which alone could enable such accuracy—but why was it, why is it, this stress on seeing, almost always as if of necessity accompanied by an assault on the still and mental parts?

I remind you of some of the forms this twinned attitude took during the early part of the period, where the stress is upon immediacy of experience either in neglect of reason or more often in denial or contradiction of reason. Eliot, who gave us the "objective correlative," also praised Donne because his thought was as immediate to him as the odor of a rose. Hopkins, whose visionary contemplation of divinity both in and behind nature proceeded by an "instress" in the self that corresponded with an "inscape" in the object, made an appealing slogan for his procedures: What you look hard at seems to look hard at you. D. H. Lawrence interested himself fiercely in a relation to the universe that should proceed directly to and from the genitals and the solar plexus, omitting as entirely as might be the brain he thought responsible for the world's damage; he wanted, poetically and piously, to see process instead of result—"the perfect rose is only a running flame," he said—and cursed the mind with all his mind. Even Proust in his great work yields an example of this strange contradiction: a man patiently and laboriously researching the past in minutest detail, and constructing by the habit of the hardest daily work a book whose two main principles are that voluntary memory is futile and that habit prevents us from seeing truly. Many more instances, among the great and the not-so-great, will occur to you. But I must now try to say why it was so.

My answer is a hypothesis, and it can take form both simple and complex. Most simply: history was—and still is—becoming elusive as well as ever more uncomfortable. Poets and novelists are people whose vocation it is to see and say as much as possible the whole of things rather than their division into categories; they are sensitive to a wholeness they believe to be really there and really prepotent over appearances even if it can be grasped only by synoptic and symbolic vision attending to minute particulars.

When one tries to specify a little more this elusiveness of history, the same hypothesis takes a more complicated, more problematic, maybe even a more dubious form. This form has to do with the amazing growth of the scientific way of viewing the world, and with the corresponding growth of the technological way of changing the world that went along with it. Most plainly, the poets have never been happy under the reign of Newtonian mechanics and Kantian criticism. Their distrust of, their protests against, the consequences entailed upon life and thought by this physics and this philosophy form a major strand in the movement known as Romanticism, which indeed may not be over yet. For it was the effect of Newton to remove mind from the cosmos except as a passive recording instrument, and the effect of the dominance of Kant's philosophy to remove from remaining mind any access whatever to ultimate reality. Whereas poetic thought can proceed beyond the minimal affirmation of parlor verse only upon the supposition that the world is equally and simultaneously perceivable as real and as transpicuous, or sacramental, and that no percept is ever divorced entirely from concept. Poetic thought is indeed in this respect primitive, though its primitivism may take highly sophisticated forms; and it is beautifully described by Claude Lévi-Strauss in talking about savage thought, "definable," he says, "both by a consuming symbolic ambition such as humanity has never again seen rivalled, and by scrupulous attention directed entirely toward the concrete, and finally by the implicit conviction that these two attitudes are one." A page earlier, indeed, he makes the parallel in a piquant and illuminating way: "Whether one deplores or rejoices in the fact, there are still zones in which savage thought, like savage species, is relatively protected. This is the case of art, to which our civilization accords the status of a national park, with all the advantages and inconveniences attending so artificial a formula" (*The Savage Mind* [Chicago: University of Chicago Press, 1967], pp. 220, 219).

I am neither historian nor philosopher, and this is not the

occasion for a philosophical discourse or one on the history of mind. One proposition that follows from my hypothesis is that imagism in its varieties arose as one response of the imagination to a development that saw mind—often by the hardest thought—progressively being read out of the universe along with gods, devils, spirits, the spirit, and so much else. As I tried to show in the first lecture, imagism seems to me a crippled and crippling response, though it has its rare triumphs; what it amounts to is abandoning what has been lost and making costume jewelry of the little that remains; and its ultimate effect is in a sense on the side of technology, as poetry becomes simply one more specialization. A linguistic philosopher said to me, in the course not of trying to convert me but of showing that I was in fact already one of the happy flock, "You could still write your poetry, so long as you were quite clear it was . . . poetry." Where he paused I silently supplied the word "only," and I don't think I was in error to do so.

What I hope to do in this chapter is to discuss examples of other kinds of poetic response to the question of history. For reasons of time, though, as well as for the prevention of tedium, I am not going to bother with the biggest examples, which have in common not only their size and other things formidable about them but also the fact that they are extremely well-known to all who do not read them; I mean the *Cantos, Paterson, The Dynasts, Finnegans Wake, The Anathemata,* . . . even *The Waste Land,* whose compactness allows it to be read even though it is in other respects comparable to the works I have named, is not to my purpose, for it has been too much discussed. Instead, I shall use smaller and more compassable examples, short poems that appear to me to grow from within, by the reader's meditation upon them, rather than by accretions and additions from without.

Before presenting my examples, however, I should say a word or so about science, for it is very likely that some of you will accuse me of being against it. And so far as a somewhat called *science* can be isolated for inspection—and that is fairly far—I should feel sorry, as well as look silly, to be thought against something so massively and so brilliantly present and part of reality; anyhow, it would be unbecoming for anyone to stand in an air-conditioned room and say mean things about science through a microphone.

But owing to that sense of wholeness I spoke of earlier, the poets whose poems I have chosen to bring evidence for my hypothesis do not separate out, at least in their poems, a somewhat called science to be for or against. They seem to me to be looking at, and trying to phrase in the lightning instant of their figured speech, as much as possible of what happened in the world since, say, the Renaissance. What they see is terrible, and what they say ranges from the neutrally diagnostic to prophetic sorrow and prophetic rage, but it is not, I think, against science, if only for the reason that in poetic thought science cannot stand alone but must be taken along with many other forces and their results. There may be much gold, the poets seem to say, though even of that we are sometimes doubtful; but you will be plain foolish if you pretend that the gold is not guarded by a dragon, or if you pretend that the gold is real and the dragon is not. *Satis quod sufficit. . . .*

It is a striking thing about many of the intellectual heroes of the present age, that those of them that lived long were able to experience two quite different worlds; their childhood and youth were passed in the old world, their productive maturity and age in the new. In some instances, too, the new they experienced was the new they had in part themselves created. I think here especially of Einstein and Freud, but would also bring into this category the literary and artistic folk whose works are both diagnostic and prophetic of what I shall call The Great Change.

I hope to stress this point without overstressing it. No doubt history was present to the man of 1890 as to the man of 1920; or maybe not quite so present, not quite so immediate, not quite so overwhelming. And the world has always been a sufficiently terrible place for most of the people in it. Yet there did come The Great Change, and there is ample evidence of its having been experienced as such by the writers and artists that lived through it. The War of 1914–1918 in part *was* this great change, and in part was but the astounding revelation of its more continuous and subtle workings over a long time. History swallows so much so easily, that it may take a considerable effort of the mind for us to place ourselves in a situation so unprecedented as then confronted the most civilized intelligences of Europe. It seemed to Freud to reveal that "the state has forbidden to the individual the practice of wrong-doing, not because it desired to abolish it, but because it desires to monopolize it, like salt and tobacco" ("Thoughts for the Times on War and Death," 1915). And to Valéry, beginning an essay in 1919, the lesson was as clear as it was somber: "We know now, we other civilizations, that we too are mortal." The recent histories by Barbara Tuchman are most helpful on this theme, *The Guns of August* showing how utterly surprising and unforeseen were the events let loose upon 1914, even among those most responsible for the decisions immediately leading to them, *The Proud Tower* recording with picturesque charm and in much detail some of the ways in which Before was decisively different from After. In fiction, it is perhaps Ford Madox Ford's great tetralogy *No More Parades* that more than any other work will give us a sense of this incredible discontinuity in experience, and not more by the events it records than by the stylistic substitutions and dissolutions of the successive volumes. . . .

Richard Wilbur has a beautiful poem called "Merlin Enthralled," in which he views what I am calling The Great Change by means of legend. Again, the poem is too long to quote entire, and I must summarize with the help of phrases here and there. The story tells how, when Merlin was seduced and locked away by Niniane, something went out of the enterprise of the round table, and out of the world, too. Arthur and Gawen go out riding, aimlessly riding, the poem says:

> Merlin, Merlin, their hearts cried, where are you hiding?
> In all the world was no unnatural sound.
>
> Mystery watched them riding glade by glade;
> They saw it darkle from under leafy brows;
> But leaves were all its voice, and squirrels made
> An alien fracas in the ancient boughs.
>
> Once by a lake-edge something made them stop.
> Yet what they found was the thumping of a frog,

> Bugs skating on the shut water-top,
> Some hairlike algae bleaching on a log.

There follows a middle section dealing with Merlin's sleep and his forgetfulness of Arthur and the Court:

> Slowly the shapes of searching men and horses
> Escaped him as he dreamt on that high bed:
> History died. . . .

And as he ceased from dreaming into deeper and simple sleep, we are to understand, a certain great reality departed from the world because he no longer had the world in mind. The poem ends with Arthur's being made aware that this is so, though not of why it is so:

> Fate would be fated; dreams desire to sleep.
> This the forsaken will not understand.
> Arthur upon the road began to weep
> And said to Gawen *Remember when this hand*
>
> *Once haled a sword from stone; now no less strong*
> *It cannot dream of such a thing to do.*
> Their mail grew quainter as they clopped along.
> The sky became a still and woven blue.
>
> In Things of This World (New York:
Harcourt, Brace & Company, 1956)

It is hard for me to discuss this poem with you, though I shall have to try. Apart from the tact, skill, and modest assurance with which it is written—all qualities very easily and often disparaged these days in favor of various unbuttoned alternatives—it makes a strong and personal appeal to me. I think I experience this appeal whenever—and it isn't so often—a modern poet returns to legendary figures and themes not for decoration but in order that we shall see deeply into their present truth. When this happens, when, as here, the poet has heard the very footsteps of Astraea leaving the earth, I feel that literary criticism is scarcely to the point, and I answer with love and sorrow to his thought, as well as with that impersonal gladness, that elation, that comes when beautiful and accurate saying seems to overcome the sorrow of what is said. I do not believe it is the lecturer's office to persuade his hearers of the beauty of something he thinks beautiful; it gets him into all sorts of ridiculous postures; but I couldn't resist saying that much.

How is this poem about what I am calling The Great Change? It is timeless and mythological rather than historical. Perhaps, for me, that is one of its many excellences, that by its legendary setting it tells me that The Great Change is not historical only, but primarily metaphysical and psychological; something we have a certain experience of under today's historical conditions, and yesterday's, but also something we should have experienced, though in other terms perhaps, whenever and wherever we lived; a change that can become historical, in fact, only because it is first the experience of every individual at all times.

Merlin is a remote and deep and powerful figure. As far as I know no one, not Malory certainly and not even T. H. White, has truly told the story as Merlin saw it, though maybe before making so round a statement I should go back and read again Tennyson's attempt, and Robinson's. He is a magician, whose magic is for the most part not identifiably of any practical use to people; his capture by Niniane, or Nimue, or Vivien, is also a most mysterious business, for it suggests his magic is mediate, it brings to the earth powers derived elsewhere and subordinated to someone else. In Wilbur's poem the magic that Merlin did is seen to be imagination, relating to will, to dream, to spirit, with their incredible power of overcoming the visible and natural world as it were by poetizing it full of spirits. When Merlin fades from the world, the supernatural entities fade also, leaving bewilderment behind. For these supernatural entities may be easily enough derided and mocked into nonexistence by the skeptical under their traditional names, such names as Jehovah, Lucifer, Michael, Ahriman, and so on; but at some peril to all of us, for if those names are fictitious names, and they are, they nevertheless name perfectly real forces able to produce perfectly real and spectacular results in what we call the real world. The names presently given to such beings—mind, spirit, will, soul, imagination, intellectual light—are also under the attack of a skeptical reasoning power minded to daylight alone and entire; and like the giant forms of mythology and legend these too are being driven out of poetry—for most poets shamefacedly acquiesce in the skepticism around them, careless or unaware that they are acquiescing in the destruction of their art and their vocation together. But here, says Gerard Manley Hopkins, "the faithful waver, the faithless fable and miss." And Shakespeare in a wonderful passage shows us again that this question is not a question simply for our own day alone, but for always:

> They say miracles are past; and we have our
> philosophical persons, to make modern and
> familiar, things supernatural and causeless.
> Hence it is that we make trifles of terrors,
> ensconcing ourselves into seeming knowledge,
> when we should submit ourselves to an unknown fear.
>
> Lafeu, *All's Well,* act 2 scene 3, *ll.* 1–6

Erich Heller (*The Disinherited Mind* [New York: Meridian Books, 1959], p. 205), applying that passage to the writings of Franz Kafka, adds that "our age has witnessed the abdication of the philosophical persons." I think I see what he means. But it just doesn't seem to be so, though it ought to be. Devils and angels together, goblins and nymphs alike, appear to be progressively forbidden the poets just as they have progressively been exiled from the world, in the interest, it is supposed, of evidence, reason, clear thinking, common sense; but I rather doubt the poets are in a better position for that; and the last state of them is like enough to be worse than the first. For poetry was once the place where these entities did their proper work, where the exact degree of their fictitiousness could be measured against the exact degree of their quite real powers, and both could be experienced ideally, not fatally in the world of action. As Rudolf Steiner said so shrewdly, Think these thoughts without believing them. Which is like what Keats said about the poetical character taking no harm from either the dark or the bright side of things—because, he said, they both end in speculation. In that sense, poetry would be the good place for experiencing mankind's brightest and his darkest mythological fantasies—poetry, and not the newspapers, the Congress, and so on. As Blake said in the Preface to *Jerusalem,* "We who live on earth can do nothing of ourselves, everything is done by spirits" . . . and just as we are about to say brightly, Aw, come off it, Willy, there ain't no spirits, he adds: "No less than digestion or sleep."

The great difficulty or impossibility—the hazard, as Heller calls it—for modern poetry has been in attaining to a view of the universe which shall be equally and simultaneously real and transpicuous, physical and mental, and to do this—here is the tightrope part of the act—without on the one hand becoming a religion fully outfitted with priesthood and theology (or criticism), and without, on the other hand, pretending that science either doesn't exist or doesn't matter. I do not think, myself, that our resolutions of this difficulty have been triumphant ones; indeed, it is perhaps a built-in feature of "the modern" in poetry to couple ever more extravagant and hysterical claims to save the world with the actual products—those little poems, remember?—that appear as ever more marginal and incapable of saving even themselves.

So perhaps what I am responding so deeply to in Wilbur's poem about Merlin is his steadfast and poignant acknowledgment of what magic, and what poetry, are about. It is part of the pathos, maybe, that this acknowledgment can be made precisely and only because magic, and poetry, have gone out of the world; just as Freud said that certain thoughts can be admitted to consciousness only under pain of being denied. It is not that Arthur is older, his hand less strong to hale a sword from stone; but now "it cannot *dream* of such a thing to do." And those quiet concluding lines:

> Their mail grew quainter as they clopped along.
> The sky became a still and woven blue.

I like to think, though I've never asked the poet about it, that their decisive effect on me is produced by a particular association; that is, to those movies we used to see in childhood, where the camera at the beginning shows us the naive and storybook illustration, whence gradually emerge the real persons, who however at the end are absorbed back into such an illustration, becoming, ever so quietly and finally, storybook persons again. Arthur and Gawen have become obsolete to life, their mail grew quainter as they clopped along—"clopped" especially makes them out a bit toylike and diminutive—but they also, with an effect at once sorrowful and consoling—as the grownups used to say to us, whispering and holding hands, "Don't worry, dear, it's only a movie"—they also merge seamlessly into the ground, the work of art, the story.

EJNER J. JENSEN

Encounters with Experience
The Poems of Richard Wilbur

Our strengths betray us. Nowhere in modern poetry is that axiom demonstrated more convincingly than in the case of Richard Wilbur. Elegance, sophistication, wit, learning, technical skill of a high order—these are the qualities that define the poet's current reputation. But the very phrases that sum up Wilbur's achievement have become for his detractors the measure of his limitations. Thus Randall Jarrell, in *Poetry and the Age*, wrote that Wilbur's poems "not only make you use, but make you eager to use, words like *attractive* and *appealing* and *engaging*." Wilbur in this view is the perfect gentleman-poet:

> the reader notices that the poet never gets so lost either in his subjects or in his emotions that he forgets to mix in the usual judicious proportions of all these things: his manners and manner never fail.

Jarrell's remarks, which begin as criticism, end in a sneering class denunciation. The careful poet becomes a well-tutored, genteel scholar; but in courses that matter—in philosophy (hard thought) and poetry (tough feelings)—he will probably never earn more than a *B*+.

Jarrell's evaluation, set down over two decades ago, reflects a widely shared view. Most of the commentators on Wilbur's poetry judge him to be a master craftsman, but less than a complete artist—a brilliant manipulator of language and rhythm, but a poet somehow not in touch with life. Herbert Leibowitz, in a review of *The Mind-Reader*, parrots the standard evaluation: the

New England Review 2 (Summer 1980):594–613.

poet "rhymes adroitly, fashions polished epigrams, commands a suave syntax, and he entertains with an edifying wit. De Tocqueville would have judged him more an aristocratic writer than a democratic one, for Wilbur strives to please more than to astonish, to charm taste rather than to stir passion." Nor is this a judgment of the critics alone. In teaching Wilbur to undergraduates, I have found that they come by their own means to similar negative judgments of his work. The sophisticated among them analyze his technical skills; the less gifted praise the way his poems "flow." But they are united in the view that he is too "artistic" and that his poems fail to provide a direct experience of life. Even when his subject is the things of this world, argues Theodore Holmes, Wilbur assumes an

> attitude that can only be satisfactory for the privileged and unthinking. . . . It is the purview of things seen from the Parnassian heights of wealth, privilege, ease, refinement, and education, looking down on the permanent sufferings of mankind without being part of them.

The charge that an artist is remote from life is serious enough in any age. In this generation, which seems particularly obsessed with a sense of darkness in all things, the demand for contact between art and life easily becomes a demand for the irrational and the violent in art. Critics searching for manifestations of our darker impulses find horrors in Shakespeare's Athenian forest and signs of profoundest evil in the woods of Robert Frost. When they turn to contemporary poets they find life in abundance—but it is life seen as a source of anguish, a battleground of elemental forces, a compound of blood and sex and dung. Judged in this context Wilbur seems elegant, stylish, aloof: the artist's style is mistaken for his vision.

Wilbur is, in fact, aware of the darker elements of human experience, and he is in every way a more complete and a more significant poet than his detractors suggest. At the heart of his achievement is a willingness to face the full implications of our humanness, to confront not merely that paradoxical creature, man, but to encounter as well those structures—both physical and intellectual—that man has created for himself. Again and again, this requires that the poet respond to contradictions of the most disturbing sort. At the one extreme he discovers an immense, nearly heart-rending potential for beauty and love; at the other, mindless violence and inexplicable evil. In facing this paradox Wilbur explores its tensions and ambiguities with the careful attention only a poet can summon to such a task. If the result of such exploration seems controlled and poetically sure, that is, after all, what we have a right to expect from our artists. Wilbur's poems create beautiful shapes for the experiences they record; but often the very beauty of the designs may conceal from us the struggle and anguish of the experiences themselves.

I want to begin by discussing some poems from *Walking to Sleep* (1969), poems whose quietness and apparent simplicity make them seem removed from the strains and conflicts of life. A recurrent theme of these poems declares itself in Wilbur's elegy for Dudley Fitts, where he remarks the light on a vase of flowers and moves from that impression to imagine how we humans might look "perceived / From a black ship." The answering vision is typical of Wilbur in its depth of implication:

> A small knot of island folk,
> The Light-Dwellers, pouring
>
> A life to the dark sea—
> All that we do
> Is touched with ocean, yet we remain
> On the shore of what we know.

These lines are the most poignant and concentrated expression of the poem's central design, a contrast of light and shadow. The loss of "an exceptional man" and the incompleteness of his labors now give place in our awareness to a simple human action:

> It is the straight back
> Of a good woman
> Which now we notice.

In setting the table for her guests, she seems to call forth the sun, which illuminates "a chair, a vase of flowers / Which had stood

till then in shadow." But this light, "the light of which /
Achilles spoke," is less than real; it is instead a teasing, evanescent reminder of "The splendor of mere being." Like the shadows in Plato's cave, it exists at some remove from the life it
represents. This contrast of light and shadow returns again at the
poem's close when the speaker imagines himself "waiting / For
the deft, lucid answer" that the dead poet might impart. He
hears nothing; but

> At the sound of that voice's deep
> Specific silence,
> The sun winks and fails in the window.

This is the gentlest of elegies, and when Wilbur closes the
final stanza with a benediction ("Light perpetual keep him.") he
takes us to a point where no more can be said. But the questions
remain, anguished yearnings of "island folk," puny creatures
whose chief awareness is of the ocean around us and whose most
awesome mystery is the sacrifice of life to that dark sea. "For
Dudley" seems a perfectly appropriate memorial for the scholar
and poet it honors. It is elegant and correct, with something of
the precision of the man "whose coats hang in black procession." But the poem expresses pain as well—the pain of awareness, of a mind charged with grief yet unable to release its burden. Decorum is observed, but at a cost; and the cost is dearer to
one who sees and feels the desperation of man's inadequacy.
Wilbur finds no easy release through anger or rant. He achieves a
benediction even as he acknowledges that "we remain / On the
shore of what we know."

The movement of "For Dudley," which progresses from
quiet observation through a tortuous intellectual anguish, ending finally in a sort of religious calm, appears again in "On the
Marginal Way." Here, though, the contrasts are steeper. The
observer's imagination, ranging over a beach scene, transforms
it now into a scene reported by George Borrow—"a hundred
women basking in the raw"—now into "a Géricault of blood
and rape," and again into "a heap" of "poor slaty flesh," remnants of "a death. . . / Like that of Auschwitz' final kill." These
successive visions, products of "the time's fright within me,"

drive the speaker to "take cover in the facts" of geology and recall how by the processes of nature "these forms were made." For a moment, the facts give protection as the "strange rock" that gave rise to the poem's earlier visions of horror becomes "bright boulders"

> That now recline and burn
> Comely as Eve and Adam, near a sea
> Transfigured by the sun's return.

But the tension between such opposed visions is made explicit once again in stanza ten:

> Though, high above the shore
> On someone's porch, spread wings of newsprint flap
> The tidings of some dirty war,
> It is a perfect day: the waters clap
> Their hands and kindle, and the gull in flight
> Loses himself at moments, white in white.

The grotesque newspaper bird presents a striking contrast to the Yeatsian images of the last three lines, where nature itself seems to "clap its hands and sing. . . / For every tatter in its mortal dress."

Again, Wilbur closes this poem on a religious note, a sort of benediction. But the joy that "for a moment floods into the mind" promises no security. It is but a last fluctuation in a poem that is never still, that reflects the capacity of man to see fully both the magnificence and the horror of the world around him. The excursion into geology provides an escape from the modern world, which "distracts / Least fancies into violence." It also provides the poet with the opportunity to convey the power and the mystery of a force that "Hove ages up." But this too is only an interval, and the speaker must return to a world of paradoxes and anomalies, a world that hosts "dirty wars" and sponsors the magnificence of the gull in his perfect radiance. Intellect and illusion may permit some temporary refuge, but "the time's fright" stands ready to seize the mind and senses and to focus them on a world of horrors.

"In the Field," a poem whose surface reflects both learning and an apparently easy elegance, moves again through a process of struggle. The major opposition of night and day—"Wading as through . . . cloudy dregs" over against "beheld in gold"—is reflected in other oppositions that shape the poem—imagination-reason, doubt-faith, fear-assurance. "Last night" the poem's speaker was a caricature of the critics' Wilbur—knowledge-able and allusive, delighting in his ability to summon the relevant myths (Andromeda, Arion) and thus confirm his understanding of "the grand, kept appointments of the air." The assurance this learning provides is, however, short-lived. Abruptly, the poem tells us that "none of that was true"; and we are jarred from our assurance into a vision of total chaos, "As if a form of type should fall / And dash itself like hail." The startling rush of this figure gives point to its implication. The source of communication, the very material for creating printed words, is irrationally scattered; and what seemed capable of aiding in our perception of order becomes frustratingly the symbol of a disjointed universe.

One's response is not to accept such a vision of disorder but to enlist reason as a means of reining in the imagination, and thus "We . . . trued / Our talk awhile to words of the real sky." The verb recalls the final line of "O," where particular objects ("hawk or hickory") are called to the speaker's aid ("to true my run") when abstractions will not suffice. But the struggle of imagination and reason is not so easily resolved. Imagination can still catch "The feel of what we said," touch upon "The school-book thoughts we thought," and produce a Yeatsian nightmare of "All worlds dashed out without a trace, / The very light unmade."

"Today, in the same field, / The sun takes all," and the "scan of space / Blown black and hollow" gives way to "the heal-all's minor blue / In chasms of the grass." So far the oppositions seem obvious. Night fears give place to the easy certitudes of day. Nature, in the light of perfect sunshine, surrounds us with richness and seems a source of physical as well as spiritual elevation:

> we, beheld in gold,
> See nothing starry but these galaxies

Of flowers, dense and manifold,
Which lift about our knees—

Day and night, fear and faith, are locked in a perpetual alterna-
tion. While "We could no doubt mistake / These flowers for
some answer," they are clearly not *the* answer; and to accept
them as such would be a willful delusion. Nevertheless, such a
response may be the closest approach to certainty available to us;
and it stems from "the heart's wish for life, which" . . .

Beats on from sphere to sphere
And pounds beyond the sun,
Where nothing less peremptory can go,
And is ourselves, and is the one
Unbounded thing we know.

What the poem asserts, finally, is the heroism of being
human, the heroism of facing up to the inadequacy of the answers we can discover with all our powers of thought and imagination. Like the "starless walker" of Giacometti whom Wilbur
sees as the paradigmatic figure of modern man, the heroic self
moves without limits into a future of uncertain knowing. Only a
careless reading of "In the Field" could see it as a poem of easy
contrasts. The night scene is immensely varied as it moves from
a rehearsal of myths to a reading of the universe as mere chance,
catches hold of the certitude booklearning provides, and ends
with a vision of total chaos created by the imagination working
on observable neutral facts. The day too, though it is conven-
tionally sunny and reassuring, provides only the appearance of
an answer. There is no primitive fright here, no shouts of out-
rage from a poet confused and terrified by nature's immensity
and its too-apparent contradictions. What Wilbur shows us is
the struggle of man who knows too much, whose learning and
wit conspire to multiply both nature's horrors and its wonders.
If the perfect meter of "without a trace / The very light unmade" seems too ordered and precise for the apocalyptic vision
the words convey, the sound of "dashed out without a trace"
surely suggests the intrusion of violence and disorder kept from
the full exercise of their power only through a great effort of

intellect and will. Similarly, the skillful management of the quatrains and the range of allusion in the total poem do not minimize this struggle; they give it additional point. The minor things are under control. Beyond us, and testing us always, is a world that baffles our perceptions: "we remain / On the shore of what we know."

The title poem of *Walking to Sleep* urges a voluntary descent into the world of the unknown: "Step off assuredly into the blank of your mind. / Something will come to you." As a prescription for insomnia, however, the cure offered by the poem is more dangerous than the complaint. Innocuous at first, the mind's landscape holds potential for grotesque collocations. One who gives himself over to such a vision must be circumspect and selective, but easy choices or too great care may produce unintended effects. One's desire for a sanitized and precise domesticity may produce instead, from the comfortable "Potempkin barns / With their . . . / . . . sweet breath of silage . . . / The trotting cat whose head is but a skull." A narrowed, attentive consciousness may bring one to a point where, all unexpectedly, he is "crossing / An unseen gorge upon a rotten trestle."

With its emphasis on the imagination, its abrupt transitions in space and tone, and its surreal juxtapositions of imagery, "Walking to Sleep" is in part a poem about the writing of poetry and not merely a jumble of dream images. As such, it speaks finally of poems as gifts. It celebrates the joyous release one may feel "In the strong dream by which you have been chosen"; and it closes with a vision of that perfect moment of achievement, when

> if you are in luck, you may be granted
> As, inland, one can sometimes smell the sea,
> A moment's perfect carelessness, in which
> To stumble a few steps and sink to sleep
> In the same clearing where, in the old story,
> A holy man discovered Vishnu sleeping,
> Wrapped in his maya, dreaming by a pool
> On whose calm face all images whatever
> Lay clear, unfathomed, taken as they came.

Other, less restful visions appear as well, not merely "The trotting cat," but "the known stranger," curious hoists which allow one the choice of emerging in pyramids or mining camps, all sorts of grotesque and threatening confrontations to which one may be delivered by "the claws of nightmare." Although the walk to poetry may lead through unimaginable grandeur, though it may reward one with the "jetsam beauty" of the stars, it may also involve less pleasurable confrontations:

> When, as you may, you find yourself approaching
> A crossroads and its laden gallows tree,
> Do not with hooded eyes allow the shadow
> Of a man moored in air to bruise your forehead,
> But lift your gaze and stare your brother down,
> Though the swart crows have pecked his sockets hollow.

So much happens in these lines that only the context of the dream explains their multiple significance. The walker is both the Christian pilgrim-knight ("long errantry") and the dragon, both the serpent who destroys man and the beneficiary of Christ's sacrifice ("Stare your brother down"). The poem's intensity gathers here with all the power of nightmare, and the release that follows seems therefore both more welcome and less reassuring. One must walk to sleep as one walks into life. An infinite range of possibilities awaits, but they may be illusive or treacherous. The easiest answers—perfect landscapes, domestic content—offer no promise of sustenance; indeed, they are the very homes of dread. No final choice seems possible; the walker is doomed "to pursue an ever-dimming course / Of pure transition." This vision of man's existence and of his quest for sleep and poetry—rest and creation—must enlarge our sense of Wilbur's capacity as a poet. The familiar qualities are here—the elegance, the range of allusion, the precision. But these qualities only serve to emphasize the poem's immense power, which comes from its daring to confront all that man may be without ever suggesting the easy answer of reconciliation. Our literature is filled with attempts to respond to the paradox of man. Shakespeare in his most distrustful period has Isabella rail at the spectacle of a creature who "Plays such fantastic tricks before high heaven / As makes the angels weep," and he allows Iago to diagnose the nature of this profound division in man: "If the balance of our lives had not one scale of reason to poise another of sensuality, the blood and baseness of our natures would conduct us to the most prepost'rous conclusions." In most of Western literature, rational man is viewed approvingly and his triumphs celebrated. More recently, particularly in poets who reject modern society, the higher value attaches to instinctual man, to man in nature. In a way, each of these answers is false; certainly they are both too easy. The more daring vision is the one that maintains the paradox and confronts it with full awareness of its extremes.

But many of Wilbur's critics cannot respond to the complexity of his vision. In their reservations about him there is something peculiarly American, something which distrusts intellectual control and prefers instead the simple and direct sensory apprehension of experience. In its crudest form this attitude appears in Reed Whittemore's wish to "find . . . a great big personal Wilburian burp or yawp," though it may also find expression in Peter Viereck's elegant complaint that "Wilbur lacks a saving vulgarity." It is this belief in the unmediated response that maintains the reputation of Walt Whitman as the quintessentially American poet. A second example, however, is more to the point in this discussion. When Robert Frost seemed in danger—not so many years ago—of sinking from critical favor under the weight of excessive and sometimes unthinking popular acclaim, Randall Jarrell and Lionell Trilling rescued him by proclaiming that the New England poet had, in fact, a profound sense of evil. Frost, claimed Trilling, was a "terrifying poet"; and Jarrell argued that Frost's poetry was at its best "grotesquely and . . . mercilessly disenchanting." To support this view, Jarrell offered in evidence such poems as "The Witch of Coos," "Home Burial," "Design," and others which "begin with a flat and terrible reproduction of the evil in the world and end by saying: 'It's so, and there's nothing you can do about it; and if there were, would *you* ever do it?'"

Now, whatever may be said of these poems, I trust that few attentive readers will wish to call them subtle. The sense of evil that they illustrate is in many instances no more profound than the response which labels as "tragic" such random and senseless events as accidental drownings and airplane crashes. But the evil in Frost's poems does communicate horror and an immediate, chilling recognition of the brute facts of blood, pain, and violent (even grotesque) endings. In responding to this way of presenting evil, Jarrell claimed for Frost a new status as a poet of the widest vision. He might also have claimed for him, although he did not, a new status as an American seer. For there is a strain in American thought and feeling that makes us want to identify our experiences as unique. If America began as an Eden, then the intrusions of society upon that Eden are unexampled in their destructiveness. This is the way Frost sees evil. He recoils from its power and seems baffled by its randomness; and his response is immediate, and instinctive, and definably American.

It is no part of my task here to denigrate the achievement of Frost, but I do want to suggest that there is a bias in our country that may lead us to favor the sort of response that his poems record as over against the sort of response one finds in the poems of Wilbur. Michael Novak has analyzed the manifestation of that bias in another context, but his remarks may be helpful here. In *The Experience of Nothingness,* Novak argues that although "the experience of nothingness swept through the educated class of Europe" for seventy years beginning in 1870, it was not a major topic in American philosophy. Here, the idea of nothingness collided with our guiding myths and was incomprehensible in a nation whose beliefs were grounded in "progress, pragmatism, and fulfillment." Frost's response to evil is like the typical American response to the problem of nothingness: he records, in wonderment, the effects of the state; and he marvels at the horror and the devastation of it all. Wilbur's response is more self-aware and analytical: in Novak's terms, European. The result is a poetry that comes from awareness; evil may be terrifying, but to such a consciousness it can never be merely anomalous. Wilbur's sense of evil in some of the poems that precede *Walking to Sleep* manifests itself in part in the extraordinary emphasis on movement in his poems. Stasis of any sort seems a condition out of nature: the rule of life is movement dictated by the tension of opposites. Often this tension—between two states of being, between the known world and a world of mystery, between security and risk—is imaged in the figure of a walker. An early use of the figure appears in "Water Walker." The poem's title refers to the caddis fly, a creature whose life cycle and peculiar role in nature enables or condemns him to "breathe / Air and know water." Beyond that primary identification, the poem treats "Paulsaul the Jew born in Tarshish" and the speaker himself, who is torn between the appeals of domesticity and the familiar and, on the other hand, the recognition that accepting such appeals could mean that "I might never come forth any more." A poem about identity, "Water Walker"may seem vitiated by its excessive self-awareness; but this would only be true if the poem remained focused on the speaker, and such self-reflexiveness is a danger it quite neatly avoids. The penultimate stanza concludes with a question: "what stays?" The bridging line to the final stanza (itself a "water walker" like the other bridge lines, poised between two stanzas and partaking of both) opens to the answer:

> Lives that the caddis fly lays
>
> Twixt air and water, must lie
> Long under water—how Saul
> Cursed once the market babblers,
> Righteous could watch them die!
> Who learns
> How hid the trick is of justice, cannot go home, nor can leave,
> But the dilemma, cherished, tyrannical,
> While he despairs and burns
>
> Da capo da capo returns.

The poem presents no terrible vision of evil; it describes, without shrillness, the desperate complexity of being fully human. Retreat from that complexity to some larval state—"Dreaming the stream-bottom tides, / Writhing at times to respire"—is unthinkable. Man's fate is defined by the paradoxical, nearly oxymoronic dilemma of his existence, a dilemma at once "cherished" and "tyrannical."

Other figures walk through the poems of *The Beautiful Changes*. In "Mined Country,"

the boys come swinging slow over the grass
(Like playing pendulum) their silver plates,
Stepping with care and listening
Hard for hid metal's cry.

Prostitutes "stroll and loll / Amid the glares and glass" in "Place Pigalle," while in the Cambridge of "Violet and Jasper," "the heirs of purity pick by / Pecked by petite damnations." The speaker's imperative in "Up, Jack!" is shadowed by his own awareness that "those who walk away are dying men"; and women too are walking toward death like the dancer in "L'Etoile (Degas, 1876)":

So she will turn and walk through metal halls
To where some ancient woman will unmesh
Her small strict shape, and yawns will turn her face
Into a little wilderness of flesh.

What one sees in these poems are the first anticipations of the powerful imagery that closes "Giacometti" and of the hypnotic and terrible movement that pulses through "Walking to Sleep." The settings are constructed to suggest disequilibrium and confusion, worlds of uncertainty and types of hell. The lesson of "Mined Country" is that "the whole world's wild"; and "Place Pigalle" juxtaposes in the most grotesque fashion the modern and classical, a juxtaposition marked by outrageous puns: "electric graces," and "Ionized innocence." The scene of "Violet and Jasper" opens upon a Miltonic infernal landscape, "the burning marle of Cambridge."

The Beautiful Changes is not, of course, a book given over to images of death and confusion. It is a young man's book: it has its share of merely witty poems—"Walgh Vogel," "Potato"— and of others that seem undecided about their own significance. The book has its romantic elements as well, and these are wonderfully crystallized in its title poem. But the theme of "The Beautiful Changes," its emphasis on heightened perception brought about by a sort of emotional transfer, affords in the context of other poems a no less wonderful but altogether more sinister interpretation. In these poems one's chief awareness is of certain mysteries that lie just beyond our usual perception—a sense of an evil that may be unnameable but is nevertheless real. One sees this in the dissolution that awaits Degas' dancer and in the inescapable movement of "Water Walker." In "Sunlight Is Imagination" the mysteries that the speaker's hand can touch are "each / Of a special shadow." To confront "The various world" successfully one must know that "All creatures are, and are undone"—that the response to such awareness must be acceptance, even an heroic acceptance of the paradox of death in life:

> Then lose them, lose
> With love each one,
> And choose
> To welcome love in the lively wasting sun.

This too is a cherished and tyrannical dilemma, that we must delight in evanescent things even as we recognize their transience. The world of flux and our longing for patterns are forever in contest, and Wilbur reveals that struggle most poignantly in "Caserta Garden." The enclosed garden is immutable, a place where one might "hear the fountain falling in the shade / Tell changelesss time upon the garden pool" and where purity of design might give one "faith that the unjustest thing / Had geometric grace past what one sees." Beyond the stone boundaries of this place of rest, the rule is change and disorder and, finally, paradox:

> The garden of the world, which no one sees,
> Never had walls, is fugitive with lives;
> Its shapes escape our simpler symmetries;
> There is no resting where it rots and thrives.

The poems in *Ceremony* restate the major themes of *The Beautiful Changes,* but they do so with a specific emphasis. While the earlier poems illustrate aspects of the struggle between order and flux, these poems describe the various sorts of ceremonies—of art, of civility, of legerdemain—used to conceal change and disorder. Such ceremonies not only fail in their purpose, they often serve only to emphasize the very factors they are designed to limit or control. Thus in Bazille's painting—the subject of the poem "Ceremony"—the "feigning lady" may teach the "leaves to curtsey and quadrille," but her presence and organizing force merely lead the speaker to "think there are most tigers in the wood." "The Terrace" celebrates the elegance of a world which all other human activity seems designed to serve, but darkness brings an awareness of hostile forces—"real mountains / Hulking in proper might," and "the black wind's / Regardless cleave." The magic of the "Juggler" is such that

> For him we batter our hands
> Who has won for once over the world's weight,

but reality nevertheless asserts itself: "the broom stands / In the dust again," and "the plate / Lies flat on the table top."

The other side of Wilbur's presentation of this theme appears in such poems as "Still, Citizen Sparrow" and "'A World Without Objects Is a Sensible Emptiness.'" In the latter, the ceremony of art becomes efficacious only when it grounds its observations in reality: "auras, lustres / And all shinings need to be shaped and borne." In the former poem, the meek, protesting "Citizen Sparrow" rejects the "rotten office" of the vulture. Yet such labor, like the "wheezy gnaw" of Noah's saw and "the slam of his hammer all the day," though unceremonious and vulgar, is yet necessary. There is a sort of heroism in one who

> could bear
> To see the towns like coral under the keel,
> And the fields so dismal deep.

Without the mediation of ceremony, he faced reality. The result for us is both a triumph and a tragic understanding: "he rode that tide / To Ararat; all men are Noah's sons." We share in God's promise, but we also share with the sons of the ark-builder the cruel knowledge of our father's weaknesses.

If the world of Bazille's elegant art intensifies our sense of the world's evil and the immediate vision of reality in "Still, Citizen Sparrow" asserts the need for direct encounter with evil, then

"Giacometti" shows the modern artist fashioning in heroic honesty not a means of coping with life but the very figure of man himself in the act of contending with a universe that remains ever in flux. The poem begins with a witty inversion of Michelangelo's theory of sculpture. Here, instead of releasing the form concealed within the rock, those who work in stone

> down to the image of man
> Batter and shape the rock's
> Fierce composure, closing its veins within
> That outside man, itself its captive cage.

Wilbur then moves from this opening to address the issue of the poem. Sculptures in stone, all those majestic figures that

> Look heavenward, lean to a thought, or stride
> Toward some concluded war,

misrepresent our condition altogether, for

> we on every side,
> Random as shells the sea drops down ashore,
> Are walking, walking, many and alone.

Such disproportion demands an answer, and it is provided "in a room / Dim as the cave of the sea" where Giacometti "has built the man / We are, and made him walk." The art of Giacometti is no elegant concealment. It is an art that confronts reality, facing both its known evil and its terrible uncertainties. In this figure, "stripped of the singular utterly, shaved and scraped / Of all but being there," Giacometti has given us—in our isolation and our sameness—the very image of our selves:

> Oh never more
> Diminished, nonetheless
> Embodied here, we are
> This starless walker, one who cannot guess
> His will, his keel his nose's bony blade.

And volumes hover round like future shades
This least of man, in whom we join and take
A pilgrim's step behind,
And in whose guise we make
Our grim departures now, walking to find
What railleries of rock, what palisades?

Rarely has an artist in one medium drawn from a master working in another with so little sacrifice of power and truth. Verdi's levying on Shakespeare might be a comparable instance. Such re-creation is on one level an act of criticism; but on another level, as in "Giacometti," it is an intensification of our experience of the original joined to the experience of the new form. That new form, in the case of Wilbur's poem, uses Giacometti's familiar walking figures to confront us with our tragic and problematic condition. Wilbur's artistry in "Giacometti" is accessible to nearly any diligent student of the poem. What is more difficult of notice is the tragic awareness, an awareness nearly Shakespearean in its depth of implication, of man's isolation and his awful understanding of how little the traditional forms can help. All the heroic past—those massive figures of stone, the grand celebratory figures, testimonials to triumph—all of it is gone. No ceremony now can disguise our separation from the past and from its characteristic assurance: "we are / This starless walker."

Things of This World (1956) and *Advice to a Prophet* (1961) contain a slighter proportion of poems that engage the basic issues of man's tragic situation than do the other books I have discussed here. But in the strongest poems from these two volumes one sees again the complexity of Wilbur's view of man. In the first of these books, Wilbur demonstrates a wonderful skill in poetic closure. Certain of the poems—especially "Piazza di Spagna, Early Morning," "The Beacon," "Mind," and "A Plain Song for Comadre"—end with a memorable and resonant justness. The most haunting conclusion, however, comprises the last four lines of "Marginalia." Here Wilbur defines the condition of man—his need to struggle and to know set over against his impotence and the prevailing forces of history and nature:

> those are our own voices whose remote
> Consummate chorus rides on the whirlpool's rim,
> Past which we flog our sails, toward which we drift,
> Plying our trades, in hopes of a good drowning.

This is the vision of "For Dudley" and "Giacometti"; it is Wilbur's version of tragedy. To deny its power or to assert that such a poem lacks a significant connection with life is to reject poetry itself as a means of feeling knowledge. The second stanza of "Marginalia" describes the shared intuitions that help us to know "Our riches are centrifugal":

> Descending into sleep (as when the night-lift
> Falls past a brilliant floor), we glimpse a sublime
> Décor and hear, perhaps, a complete music,
> But this evades us, as in the night meadows
> The crickets' million roundsong dies away
> From all advances, rising in every distance.

This is Prufrock's "music from a farther room" brought to a higher power and given tragic relevance as it applies to a shared condition of mankind.

It would be impossible to treat the elements of Wilbur's poetry under discussion here without reference to "Beasts," a poem that contrasts the paradoxical harmonies of nature—

> the lyric water,
>
> In which the spotless feet
> Of deer make dulcet splashes, and to which
> The ripped mouse, safe in the owl's talon, cries
> Concordance

—to the discord of "The werewolf's painful change" and the amusical isolation of "suitors of excellence." "Beasts" focuses at last upon tragic aloneness and man's inability to locate any source of assurance; its overall design is controlled by a movement from "lyric water," to "the degradation / Of the heavy streams," to "the dark / Unbridled waters." The poem's progress, in other words, is from concord, to decay, to a state of chaos. Once again, the question of a governing order is introduced, and once again man is seen to be a "starless walker" who remains "On the shore of what we know." The difference here is in the quality of horror that emerges at the close. All the labor of the "suitors of excellence," their construing "the painful / Beauty of heaven, the lucid moon / And the risen hunter," seems only to underscore and make more painful the discrepancy between the luminous order of the heavenly bodies and the reality of earthly life. They make

> such dreams for men
> As told will break their hearts as always, bringing
> Monsters into the city, crows on the public statues,
> Navies fed to the fish in the dark
> Unbridled waters.

In *Advice to a Prophet* Wilbur brings together thirty-one poems, seven of them translations or stage-pieces. This is not a strong collection with respect to the themes considered here, and it is arguable that it contains fewer first-rate poems than any of the other books Wilbur has published. Yet even here one finds poems that touch life directly, that confront a reader with some striking insight into experience. In the short poem "Stop," the revelation is conveyed through the most ordinary experience, the halting of a train as it pulls into a station; yet the quality of seeing that it communicates is altogether astounding. On the station platform are "Three chipped-at blocks of ice / Sprawled on a baggage-truck." The ice lies "glintless"; but the truck— "painted blue / On side, wheels, and tongue"—gives off potent meanings:

> A purple, glowering blue
> Like the phosphorus of Lethe
> Or Queen Persephone's gaze
> In the numb fields of the dark.

Wilbur builds this compelling image out of a commonplace event, contriving to add to the poem's force a reader's own memory of similar occasions when the random detritus of our urban landscape came to us as a vision of hell.

Other poems in this volume are less dramatic in their images and concerns, though some, like "In the Smoking-Car," "Someone Talking to Himself," and perhaps "Fall in Corrales" deal in a thoughtful way with too-familiar horrors of life—with weakness, shame, and the fear of change. Only in "The Undead" does Wilbur offer a telling and reverberant statement of the theme of isolation. "The Undead" are vampires; but they also suggest those whose impulses are wholly self-directed. Even their frenzies are "negative," and they are "Secret, unfriendly, pale, possessed / Of the one wish, the thirst for mere survival." Judging them over against a thrush "Who has sung his few summers truly," or considering their worth as we think of "an old scholar resting his eyes at last," they seem things of little value. And yet, in the poem's conclusion, we are asked to pity them:

> Think how sad it must be
> To thirst always for a scorned elixir,
> The salt quotidian blood
>
> Which, if mistrusted, has no savor;
> To prey on life forever and not possess it,
> As rock-hollows, tide after tide,
> Glassily strand the sea.

Here again, as in "Marginalia," life remains in motion and elusive, beyond our capture; like "the crickets' million round-song," it "dies away / From our advances."

The Mind-Reader, Wilbur's latest collection, contains something like a representative sampling of the poet's interests and skills: comic poems, translations, poems of natural description, reminiscence. Both the title poem—a subtle, continuously rewarding dramatic monologue—and "In Limbo," which recapitulates themes and imagery from earlier poems (especially "Walking to Sleep") provide additional support for my view of Wilbur. But the case I wish to make is by now, I trust, sufficiently clear; and perhaps I can point the issue by turning finally to "The Writer." This poem is a kind of narrative which has two major divisions. The first of these involves the poet, who hears from outside his daughter's closed door the sounds of her writing. He listens, interprets both the clatter and the silence of her typewriter, and reports the episode in a self-consciously elaborate figure which concludes, "I wish her a lucky passage." The second section involves a remembered episode in which a "dazed starling / . . . was trapped in that very room." Girl and bird then become the two terms of a comparison. The speaker recalls how a sash was lifted and how "we" (he and the daughter, perhaps the entire family) retreated to watch "through the crack of the door" the bird's struggle to escape.

> We watched the sleek, wild, dark
>
> And iridescent creature
> Batter against the brilliance, drop like a glove
> To the hard floor, or the desk-top,
>
> And wait then, humped and bloody,
> For the wits to try it again; and how our spirits
> Rose when, suddenly sure,
>
> It lifted off from a chair-back,
> Beating a smooth course for the right window
> And clearing the sill of the world.
>
> It is always a matter, my darling,
> Of life or death, as I had forgotten. I wish
> What I wished you before, but harder.

Here Wilbur comes as close as he ever does to involving himself in the human struggle at the center of a poem. That he remains in some measure outside of it suggests to me not aloofness but rather, in this intensely personal poem, his commitment to a certain understanding of the function of poetry and the role of the poet. His sympathy for his daughter is like the care of Prospero for Miranda. He knows, finally, that her experience of life must be hers alone and that he can protect her from nothing.

He comes to the awareness that we cannot share either our wisdom or our disenchantment: "Tis new to thee."

In arguing for a view of Wilbur that stresses the depth and seriousness of his concern with basic issues, I find "The Writer" a most helpful and persuasive poem. Each of us, finally, is alone. Old certainties prove ineffectual or disappear altogether; the quest for something we can affirm and cling to and be sustained by—something that we might call life—is beset by difficulties and shrouded in confusion. In such a world it would seem a shameless vanity for the poet to act out our needs or our desires. He cannot alter our condition nor mitigate our aloneness. What he shares, he must share as a poet; and he does this by helping us to see ourselves as we go on our curious, undirected pilgrimage, "walking to find / What railleries of rock, what palisades?"

BRUCE MICHELSON

Wilbur's Words

While we acknowledge his erudition and urbanity, we regretfully liken his mildness to the amiable normality of the bourgeois citizen. Emergencies are absent in his poems; he is unseduced by the romantic equation of knowledge and power; he seldom rails at the world. Suspicious of grandiose gestures, of parading the ego, he mediates experience through reason.[1]

He is a bell too conscious of its clapper, clapper-happy. Pert but proper, always safe rather than sorry, his poetry is completely without risks, a prize pupil's performance. His ideas are always cut exactly to the size of his poems; he is never puzzled. And the ideas are all sentiments, aware of their potential high-minded emotional value and determined to snuggle into it.[2]

Richard Wilbur is still talked about with this kind of condescension; he gets such treatment more commonly than any other major poet alive. One grows used to hearing of Wilbur as the "mannered" poet, the "amiable," "clever," "elegant" poet, the "bourgeois citizen" verse-maker, the "safe" artist. People condescend to Wilbur because they misunderstand his taste for rich and echoing language, for that word-play which everyone notices in his poetry and many readers suspect. It is not hard to misread or misvalue Wilbur. It is easy to take his word-play for ornament, for poetic bric-a-brac dressing up an imperfect sensibility, a comfortable optimism, a childish showing-off. It is easy to confuse his puns and spreads of meaning with the famil-

The Massachusetts Review 23 (Spring 1982):97–111.

iar game of undermining the validity of language. We are well stocked, after all, with poems which "prove" that poems can really say nothing, and poets who indulge in what Roland Barthes calls the *jouissance* of ambiguity which tells us again and again what a hopeless thing language actually is.

I intend to show here however, that Wilbur's poetry is neither charming ornament, nor gimmick, nor fashionable confusion. I believe that Wilbur's use of language—especially his famous word-play—has everything to do with his most urgent reasons for being an artist, that it is as daring an experiment in poetry as we have seen in the past three decades. Wilbur's language is not some handsome machine for carrying messages or dressing up safe little observations. It is an attempt to use words as magical, incantatory, creative forces. His famous word-play is in fact the very essence of his imaginative transcendence of the world, as well as his reconciliation *with* the world. If we cannot understand this, the paramount seriousness of Wilbur's word-play, we cannot appreciate what Wilbur is doing.

To see what Wilbur's word-play is meant to be, we must first understand Wilbur's idea of how the imagination makes sense of the world. As some readers have noted,[3] Wilbur's conception is that the mind reaches cosmic awareness only by an imaginative and intellectual tightrope act. His recurring theme is that our best hope for understanding where in the world we are lies in balancing the dreaming with the waking consciousness, in reconciling dim, momentary intimations of something beyond us with full awareness of the now. Wilbur is sometimes sniffed at as "optimistic," which seems to me another condescending, misleading label. Borrowing an apt phrase from Loren Eiseley, we would do better to call him a "midnight optimist"; for amid the constant shape-shifting of nature, Wilbur, much like Eiseley, finds cause for a guarded, cautious hope. For Wilbur, those moments, when imaginative engagement with the world flashes out at us like a discovery *in* the world, give cause for keeping one's faith alive. Wilbur accepts man as a creature who *may* have a place in other realities—but only by understanding who and where he is now—as a creature of flesh and spirit—can one hope to comprehend anything more of one's place in the universe.

Consequently Wilbur is a nature poet, a superb nature poet,

writing about a nature which constantly changes and recreates itself, awakening that wonder in which one seems to transcend, for a moment at least, separation from the general scheme of things. This much every close reader of Wilbur's poetry will grant; and I hold that Wilbur's use of language has everything to do with this intention. His words are meant to be regenerative forces, catching not just diversity, but the unity beyond diversity. A few years ago, when Wilbur spoke of his conception of language in a short essay called "Poetry and the Landscape," he wrote of language as "recreating the creation, giving each creature a relation to himself," and bringing the speaker "a kind of symbolic control over what lay around him."[4] Just as the balanced imagination can see in nature both time and timelessness, the individual word can conjure up the same kind of encounter. The right ambiguous word at the right time provides not proliferation of meaning, but *reconvergence* of meaning, all possibilities drawing towards one.

Like most of the major verse since World War II, Wilbur's verse is the performance of a self-consciously fictive imagination—but it is also an act of hopeful conjuring, done with a wish that the order created in the poem might somehow become an order perceived. Wilbur's word-play, therefore, expresses his conception of our ontological condition, his role as a careful, insightful nature poet, and his idea of the re-creative power of language itself. I cannot think of three more serious reasons for a poet to play with words. A look at five poems, spanning the thirty years of Wilbur's career, will indicate how this is so; and they will show that Wilbur's language, far from being a vehicle for themes, changes like nature itself from poem to poem and even from moment to moment *in* the poem, enacting again and again the miracle of transcendence. Further, Wilbur's use of language has undergone a subtle evolution, and lately a radical change, as the poet continues to mature and expand.

"The Regatta" (1947) is a young man's poem—Wilbur was in his mid-twenties when he wrote it—which no one has said much about, perhaps because at first look it may seem too young, too word-dizzy, to be taken seriously. It is a good poem to begin with, however, for although it might seem over-rich, Wilbur's word-play already shows itself not to be preciousness, mechanism, or showing-off. It is not hard to see that "The Regatta" is about hope amid hopelessness, evasive intuitions, and the stubborn duality of human consciousness and the persistent knack of that consciousness for dreaming arrangements beyond the chaotic surface of things. We get all this in a short poem about an elderly couple watching a boat race. It is the multiple meanings of Wilbur's key words, and the fact that all these meanings achieve a common resonance, which make the poem succeed, and which make a punning, puzzling description of the regatta both handsome and right. Here is "The Regatta" in full:

A rowdy wind pushed out the sky,
Now swoops the lake and booms in sails;
Sunlight can plummet, when it fails,
Brighten on boats which pitch and fly.

Out on the dock-end, Mrs. Vane,
Seated with friends, lifts lenses to
Delighted eyes, and sweeps the view
Of "galleons" on the "raging main."

A heeling boat invades the glass
To turn a buoy; figures duck
The crossing sail—"There's Midge and Buck!
I know his scarf!"—the sailors pass.

The hotel guests make joking bets,
And Mrs. Vane has turned, inquired
If Mr. Vane is feeling "tired."
He means to answer, but forgets.

She offers him binoculars:
A swift, light thing is slipping on
The bitter waters, always gone
Before the wave can make it hers;

So simply it evades, evades,
So weightless and immune may go,

The free thing does not need to know
How deep the waters are with shades.

It's but a trick; and still one feels
Franchised a little—God knows I
Would be the last alive to cry
To Whatzisname, "I love thy wheels!"

Freedom's a pattern. I am cold.
I don't know what I'm doing here.
And Mrs. Vane says, "Home now, dear."
He rises, does as he is told;
Hugging her arm, he climbs the pier.
Behind him breaks the triumph cheer.

There is a great deal of word-play here, and we must be selective in talking about it. But we are off into bewildering multiplicity already in the opening line. What are we to make of "pushed out"? Billowed, like the sails in the verse after? Or is it pushed away—suggesting either that our pleasant afternoon is gone, or that it is now made grander than it seemed? Or perhaps the wind pushes out the sky the way one pushes out an old-fashioned light switch, leaving everyone in the dark. In line three the sunlight "fails," probably because clouds have swept in, blotting the sun and making those deep "shades" in the sixth stanza. The rest of the quatrain gives us no help, only more possibilities, and no indication of how we ought to feel about this view from the pier. The wind "booms" in the sails of the racing boats, suggesting the deep, ambiguous noise of sheets puffing out, suggesting too the booms on the boats themselves swinging about in response to a freshened mind. If this is becoming a dark afternoon, it still is a fine one for racing. But what does "plummet" suggest, in conjunction with "fails"? We have no trouble with the connotations of light "failing," but if we read "plummet" carefully, we run into more ambiguity. The sunlight has dropped quickly, and the boats flying along the water's surface shine on the darkened seascape. "Plummet" does not, in that reading, seem to suggest trouble any more than does "pushed out." Furthermore, plummet means more than drop; it means to drop a plumb line, to take measure, to sound depths—meanings which also seem to work here. In darkness do we see something more clearly, something besides the darkness itself? Is it possible that light and darkness, order and disorder are reconciled here somehow, much as the pun on "pitch"—suggesting perhaps the dark hulls below the bright sails—denies the "brighten" of the fourth line and makes sense with it too? At this point in the poem, we have nothing but several alleys of ambiguity. But a little patience with "The Regatta" takes us someplace worth going.

In the second stanza we get a point of view, an elderly Mrs. Vane on the pier, doing the poet's job of bringing imagination to bear on worldly experience. Perhaps her imaginative involvement befits her name—one way or another; perhaps her "galleons on the Spanish main" are a vain fictionalizing of a dark, pitchy, flying disorder; or perhaps Mrs. Vane is a true "vane"— which by the spelling of her name seems a fair bet—a sensibility which in its fictions is responding rightly to obscure wonders in the landscape, to the winds, if you will, of truth. Mrs. Vane's eyes are "delighted," delighted by the failing of the light, or perhaps by age—and yet "delighted" in the normal sense, able as she is to sit among friends and see things truly, darkness or no. But the endorsement of Mrs. Vane is swift, evasive; it slips by us quickly in the reverberating of a word.

To save time, let us turn to the fifth stanza, in which we begin to look over the shoulder of Mrs. Vane's husband, a man apparently nearer his end and the end of his hope, and in which we hear the voice of the poet more clearly. Mr. Vane is offered the binoculars, but apparently he doesn't take them, out of senility, fatigue, or indifference. The imaginative vantage point is everyone's to take and use as he will, should he choose to pursue that "swift, light" thing which escapes human apprehension. The poem makes the meaning of "light" as elusive and yet as dimly sure as the elusive "thing" it modifies. The passing sailboat is "light" because it gleams on shadowy waters, light because it glides swiftly on the surface of waters, light because it is a mild and gay thing upon the face of "bitter" waters, a disordered and somber world over which, for the moment, it seems to win.

Every path we take in chasing the sense of the stanza ends up in the same place, somewhere off in a twilit distance. The poem is swept along by ingenious ambiguities—and yet it is not fair to say either that this is overdone, or even that these are the poem's finest moments. The race after meaning ends with "shades" in line twenty-four, the last mention of the boat race; the word which suggests every sense we customarily attach to it. But the next stanza brings us into the key ambiguity of "The Regatta."

What is but a trick? The boat race itself, using nature to defy nature? Or is it the trick of sight, the way these passing sails tease both the naked and the binoculared eye? Both of these tricks might be meant here—or something else. Wilbur also speaks here of the method of the poem itself, of the "trick" of the poet's language, the "trick" of making a regatta on a windy afternoon work as a metaphor for the human condition and the gounds of human hope. Wilbur feels "franchised a little" not simply by what boats do, but by what words do. The artist's own imagination does what Mrs. Vane is doing, looks carefully at the world and makes something greater out of it, which in turn gives the artist hope, however cautious hope has to be. But no sooner has Wilbur recognized his own trick of managed ambiguities than the delicate illusion is gone. For a second, creation has been *re*-created, a right blending of intelligence and fancy has made separate worlds seem one again; yet once that second is passed, mere artifice leads nowhere. The poet becomes self-conscious, and his imagination turns as "cold" as his body on this chilly day. In the company of the old couple, he takes his leave from the pier and from the poem. The tone now is colder too, almost mechanical; the word-play is over. For all the skill of the artist as a conjurer, moments of real imaginative engagement come quickly when they will, and pass as quickly away.

"The Regatta" ends with the poet doubting his own magic, having worked it. Perhaps, in this early poem, that cleverness Wilbur is often accused of is too obtrusive for us to feel how serious his intentions really are. There is much beauty in "The Regatta." It is not a game, but a rich, many-sided observation, and a compassionate look at people and nature. This "Regatta" which the imagination makes so much of is a fine boat race, painted for us in a lean, vigorous, loving way. The poem looks closely at nature as a realm of constant change and mystery, and finds cause to celebrate that mystery. It is easy to find a young man's unsure hand in what we already know is a young man's poem; but anyone who does so should be careful not to miss Wilbur's achievement in language here, and not to write it off as decoration.

Since "The Regatta," Wilbur's use of word-play has grown much less obtrusive; but in the years between *The Beautiful Changes* (1947) and *The Mind-Reader* (1976), the word-play continues to resound, and its purposes and its place in Wilbur's style grow ever more clear. "Year's End" (1949) and "Love Calls Us to the Things of This World" (1956) are two poems about flesh and spirit, time and eternity, life and death. One of these poems is elegiac, deliberate, liable to the old charge that Wilbur's thoughtfulness spoils his work. The other is one of the most admired lyrics in the past three decades, a poem full of vigor and spontaneity—yet it is even more astonishing, as far as language is concerned, than "Year's End." In both poems, words from which meanings spread wide are used to call separated worlds into a fleeting, miraculous union.

Most of the word-play in "Year's End" is outright punning. Here are the two opening stanzas:

> Now winter downs the dying of the year,
> And night is all a settlement of snow;
> From the soft street the rooms of houses show
> A gathered light, a shapen atmosphere,
> Like frozen-over lakes whose ice is thin
> And still allows some stirring down within.
>
> I've known the wind by water banks to shake
> The late leaves down, which frozen where they fell
> And held in ice as dancers in a spell
> Fluttered all winter long into a lake;
> Graved on the dark in gestures of descent,
> They seemed their own most perfect monument.

I count six puns in "Year's End," and two other words ("soft," and "shapely" in the fourth stanza) which seem broadly suggestive. This is not a poem like "The Regatta," about something always eluding us in the everyday world. It is about time stopped and held fast in a sudden eternity; and therefore the word-play here has a new task to perform. The object now is to transform "ends of time" into events of both destruction *and* conservation, and to suggest in that duality something of the mystery of eternity. Each pun must convey both temporality and eternity, the world of flesh, time, humanity, and everyday confusion, as well as the patient realities beyond time. "Downs" in the first stanza: the word means "fells" as a hunter fells an animal; or "sets down," as an artist sets down a recognition to deliver it from time and forgetfulness. Or, given the snowy evening, "downs" might mean "packs in down," wraps up snugly for safe keeping. Likewise, "settlement" suggests both a human settlement, a makeshift town made out of snow—and a *final* settlement, a conclusion to worldly turmoil. And "graved" in the stanza after: these falling leaves are both "engraved" and sent to the grave; their death is their transcendence into slow-time, their transformation into a kind of art. And "composedly" in the third stanza, "pause," and "fray," and "wrought" in the last, each make reference both to time and timelessness, to flesh or strife or passion on the one hand, and the creative act, the transcendence of time and flesh, on the other. Further, what is true of the puns in "Year's End" is true of "soft" and "shapely." The street is soft because it is snow-covered and quiet, because it is vulnerable and mortal, *and* because it suggests a "soft" untroubled world *beyond* the mortal. And "shapely": the astonished people of Pompeii lose in an instant their chance to give life artistic shape and finish, even as they are frozen by the ash and transformed into their own most perfect monuments. There is a wonderful melding here of diction, theme, and subtle observation of the natural world. The poem is a passionate expression of both intelligent anxiety and guarded affirmation, and an achievement of beauty and remarkable unity which leaves cleverness far behind.

Because "Love Calls Us to the Things of This World" is

Wilbur's most discussed poem, it needs only brief treatment here. The opening sixteen lines:

> The eyes open to a cry of pulleys,
> And spirited from sleep, the astounded soul
> Hangs for a moment bodiless and simple
> As false dawn.
>   Outside the open window
> The morning air is all awash with angels.
>
> Some are in bed-sheets, some are in blouses,
> Some are in smocks: but truly there they are.
> Now they are rising together in calm swells
> Of halcyon feeling, filling whatever they wear
> With the deep joy of their impersonal breathing;
>
> Now they are flying in place, conveying
> The terrible speed of their omnipresence, moving
> And staying like white water; and now of a sudden
> They swoon down into so rapt a quiet
> That nobody seems to be there.

People who like little else about Wilbur's work admire this poem for its gusto and its easy, spontaneous air—and I wish to look at the word-play in it for precisely this reason. The poem marks an important development in Wilbur's relationship with words, for here he succeeds as never before in making his word-play look easy. We readily notice the obvious puns on "spirited," "awash," "blessed," "warm," "undone," "dark habits"; but much less attention is paid to "astounded," "simple," "truly," "clear," "changed," and other words which subtly suggest that enduring and ever-changing harmony of matter and spirit which the waking man senses in his hypnagogic state, and which the poet celebrates with wakeful imagination. The sleeper's first look at the morning is giddy, solipsistic—and yet "simple" and foolish as he is in his drowsiness, he is worthy of the affectionate treatment he gets, seeking as he does after a "simple," pure reality beyond the maculate, turmoiled world. The angels on the wash line are "truly" there only to someone whose muddle-headedness has got the better of him—or is it that they *are* "truly" there, in some dimension to which the waking mind cannot find its way? The soul is indeed "astounded" in both senses of the word: it is both stupefied *and* struck with wonder; the dance of the laundry-angels in the sight of heaven is "clear" in all ways: simple and pure they are, as well as transparent to the point of nonexistence. The poem is full of affectionate word-jokes, all of which are serious, all of which are one with the theme of the duality of human existence, and the balanced, dual consciousness it takes to see our place in the world.

In an interview recently, Wilbur observed of the Russian poet Andrei Voznesensky, whom he has recently been translating, that "He likes to be playful in the midst of his greatest serious-ness or passion, and so do I. . . ."[5] "Love Calls Us to the Things of This World" shows us clearly what Wilbur means. The poem is at once perfect seriousness and perfect festivity, its language-founded ironies being play much as Huizinga defines it in its highest state, play as the exuberant celebration of mystery. The very gaiety of the play heightens the reverence; it does not profane the ceremony. The words we have looked at are more than expressions of contrast between worldly and unworldly realities. The energy and music here are as well-suited to holy festivity as their spreads of meaning are to the analytical mind. If the poem's reconciliation of playfulness and seriousness, energy and intellect is a trick, it is a trick which harkens back to the very beginnings of literature. Wilbur's theme in "Love Calls Us" is not a new one in his poetry; what *is* new is the grace with which he uses his rich language, a grace which shows that he has recon-ciled the play of words with that spontaneity and excitement which sacred play, ceremony, ought to have.

Festivity for the sake of seriousness, the word as a re-creative force, the transcendence of diversity and the recovery of lost union, shifting meanings which catch both the shift and the changelessness of the natural world—how far can this kind of poetry be carried? Probably there is a point at which even the most brilliant renewal of language ceases to be renewal, and the technique deadends in its own cliché. I am grateful that Wilbur has few imitators. I am grateful as well that in the last twenty years he has not taken to imitating himself. A verse style meant as a re-creative force must itself have constant *re*-creation, and

Wilbur's word-play has shown both a change and a continuity, like that change-with-continuity he so often admires in nature.

From *Walking to Sleep*, "In a Churchyard" is a sober rewrite of Gray's "Elegy," yet in the churchyard, too, puns and spreads of meaning have their role. Transformed again from "Year's End," Wilbur's re-echoing language gives his meditation that sober air it needs to avoid both banal gloom and cute artifice. His word-play here is one with his perceptions, his mood, and his place. The key to the poem's success is that the word-games are now more difficult and less obtrusive, the flow of one loaded utterance into the next being not rapid and easy as before, but deliberate, hindered, slow. The meeting of worlds, in both the landscape and the language, is again the theme; but here there are no swift, surprising recognitions. The truth of churchyards has to be found through hard imaginative work. The poem has been busy with the churchyard's suggestions of timeless, speechless realities, a "music innocent of time and sound," when the real world intrudes upon the visitor with even stranger mysteries:

> It shadows all our thought, balked imminence
> Of uncommitted sound,
> And still would tower at the sill of sense
> Were not, as now, its honed abeyance crowned
>
> With a mauled boom of summons far more strange
> Than any stroke unheard,
> Which breaks again with unimagined range
> Through all reverberations of the word,
>
> Pooling the mystery of things that are,
> The buzz of prayer said,
> The scent of grass, the earliest-blooming star,
> These unseen gravestones, and the darker dead.

If there is any sense—much less a manifold sense—to be made of "balked imminence / Of uncommitted sound," it does not lie as close to the surface as the word-play we have looked at before. Of course "shadows" suggests both the shadows in the twilit churchyard and the shadowing of the speaker's thoughts. But what about this "balked imminence," "honed abeyance" and "mauled boom"? "Balked" makes sense if it means thwarted; but it also means heaped up or ridged, like the mound of a grave. That would amount to nothing—except that "honed," besides its modern definition (sharpened) has an interesting archaic one. A hone is a stone marker, like a gravestone; and in a Northumbrian dialect it means hesitate, balk. There is a queer subsurface coherence here to enhance the usual meanings of these words. This meditation takes place in a churchyard, and the landscape of the churchyard enters the language of the meditation. Once more we are met with Wilbur's enduring theme, that the only way we can make sense of our timeless condition is to be intensely aware of the here and the now. The "mauled boom" is both the ambiguous summons of the unknown and the hammering ring of a real churchbell, in a tower itself suggested by the image of eternities towering at the "sill of sense." This is one elegy in a churchyard which does *not* leave the churchyard as the meditation deepens, but rather seeks its answers in the churchyard world. In this meditation, Wilbur's language has changed its sound, its pace, its strategy, but not its essential object: to be the means by which realms of reality are brought together. It shows the power which distinguishes genius from sheer style, the power both to transform itself and remain the same.

A look at *The Mind-Reader,* Wilbur's latest volume of poetry, demonstrates that the transformation is still going on. The title of the book is drawn from the dramatic monologue which concludes it. Wilbur has remarked that he finds himself increasingly interested in writing dramatic monologues,[6] and as one might expect, the shift in rhetorical strategies has caused more changes in his use of language. While "The Mind-Reader" introduces us to a clairvoyant—something of a charlatan—whom Wilbur says he met in Rome many years ago, the poem does not seek to catch anything of the language of its Italian persona. Rather, it is a mind-reading of a mind-reader, an attempt to penetrate to the consciousness pure. The theme is familiar: the true visionary, unlike this failed, unhappy one, must adjust his powers of imagination to a world of waking, rational perception, must reach his mystical awareness *without* forgetting the truth to be had from commonplace realities. The "mind-reader" is a gifted visionary, but because he has no use for temporal experience, his quest for the supernal leads him only into solipsism; and the frustration which results has nearly ended his hope.

Word-play in "The Mind-Reader" might therefore have two objects: to convey the duality of the mind-reader's characteristic hypnagogic state; and to underscore the pathetic irony of his condition. The mind-reader reads nothing because he reads himself too closely. The word-play we find in the poem is sparing, to be sure, perhaps because Wilbur must modulate his own familiar voice. But when the reverberating words turn up, as they do at crucial phrases, they serve precisely these purposes. They reveal both the mind itself and its fatal mistake.

The opening line of the poem ought to suggest immediately the difference in outlook between the poet and the persona he now assumes. "Some things are truly lost," the speaker assumes as a way of setting out—but that word "truly" should set us wondering, dangerous word that it is, and one of Wilbur's favorite loaded words. Already we are tempted to doubt all this assurance about what is "truly" lost, and not let this metaphysician off without proof. The sun hat, pipe wrench, and overboard novel he talks about show us that he equates true, absolute loss with removal beyond human sense and recollection, disappearance into an enormous, unfathomable natural world:

> The sun-hat falls,
> With what free flirts and stoops you can imagine,
> Down through that reeling vista or another,
> Unseen by any, even by you or me.
> It is as when a pipe-wrench, catapulted
> From the jounced back of a pick-up truck, dives headlong
> Into a bushy culvert; or a book
> Whose reader is asleep, garbling the story,
> Glides from beneath a steamer chair and yields
> Its flurried pages to the printless sea.

Of course we can never have this hat, wrench, or book back again; but still, they are "truly" lost only if we take reality to be the world we can see into, either with our eyes or our dreams. I am not splitting hairs. For thirty years, Wilbur's self-avowed "quarrel" with Edgar Allan Poe has focused on exactly this point: that the mind which responds solipsistically to the waking world and trusts too much to a world of dreams finds only madness when it seeks transcendence.

The rest of the poem shows us that the speaker lacks interest—and faith—in perceived reality, and that this is the cause of his misery. Consider the pun on "printless" which closes the opening stanza. The speaker's joke epitomizes his own dilemma. The sea is "printless" to him in three ways. The fallen book leaves no imprint, no track on the surface; the sea to him is printless, inscrutable; it is also "printless" meaning inexpressible, for no language, no quantity of print, will solve its mysteries. The mind-reader has given up on making sense of the world he lives in. His landscapes and seascapes, real and imagined, are disorderly, frightening, perfectly obscure. The play on "printless" is matched shortly thereafter with a similar pun on "groundless," as the mystic takes us on a trek through his own subconscious: we move from the water into the woods, but the effect of the pun, stressing as it does the bewilderment and hopelessness of too much imagination and too little insight, is something we have seen before. The mind-reader is Wilbur's foil, the poet as abject visionary, trapped in a world in which his powerful mind can find no peace:

> Whether or not I put my mind to it,
> The world usurps me ceaselessly; my sixth
> And never-resting sense is a cheap room
> Black with the anger of insomnia,
> Whose wall-boards vibrate with the mutters, plaints,
> And flushings of the race.

These "flushings" suggest the mind-reader's cheap and shabby world, the psychological torments he suffers and witnesses, and the emotional self-indulgence he is fated to hear over and over and make his own dismal theme. "Flushings" catches the predicament of the kind of artist Wilbur struggles *not* to be, in language which conveys the temperament and the ontological stance which holds such a poet in thrall—and of course, in its vividness, the fact that Wilbur has been here himself. There is no smugness in this poem, no hint that Wilbur is window-shopping among desperate sensibilities. If "The Mind-Reader" shows us nothing else, it suggests that Wilbur knows first-hand about the perils of the imagination, for he haunts us with the very condition of mind he warns us against. The word-play in the poem is meant as homage to a powerful consciousness gone wrong. We should note too that the word-play in the poem is used here not as it is used elsewhere, to celebrate the subtlety and the possibilities of life, but rather to illustrate isolation from life. Only one word in the poem suggests a recognition of underlying order; as one might expect, the word turns up as the speaker almost reaches a larger awareness:

> Sometimes I wonder if the blame is mine,
> If through a sullen fault of the mind's ear
> I miss a resonance in all their fretting.
> Is there some huge attention, do you think,
> Which suffers us and is inviolate,
> To which all hearts are open, which remarks
> The sparrow's weighty fall, and overhears
> In the worst rancor a deflected sweetness?
> I should be glad to know it.

Fretting: misery and music at once, a music born of misfortune, a music one might hear faintly if one listens closely to the real world, and not so fondly to voices in his own dreams. In the world itself resounds that reconciliation which the mind-reader should be glad to comprehend, but which his pathetic consciousness will not allow him to achieve. His monologue is a dignified, credible statement of the tragedy of the contemporary imagination, the tragedy which poetry in this century has been about. Here, then, is Wilbur adopting his word-play to fit voices very different from his own, specifically to the voice of that sensibility with which he has passionately quarreled for thirty years.

Wilbur, at this writing, is sixty years old—still young, as far as careers and reputations go in the world of poetry, and I do not offer these observations as a guide to what to expect from

Wilbur in years to come. He is a true poet, not a word-smith, and this achievement with reverberating language might be something he already moves beyond. I have sought only to show how Wilbur's relationship with language is not the comfortable, clever indulgence, or the artifice, or the mere vehicle, which many people assume it to be. Living as we do in a time which confounds crudeness with passion, drabness with authenticity, and coherent, thoughtful art with superficiality, we can easily forget that artifice and intensity can have much to do with one another. Learning to read an important and innovative poet is always difficult work, forced as we are to see the world—and the world of poetry—a little differently than we have before. Wilbur requires just that kind of readjustment, a broadening of sensibilities which could do us nothing but good.

NOTES

1. Herbert Leibowitz, review of *The Mind-Reader, The New York Times Book Review,* June 3, 1976, p. 10.

2. Calvin Bedient, review of *The Mind-Reader, The New Republic,* June 5, 1976, p. 21.

3. See for example Donald Hill, *Richard Wilbur* (New York: Twayne, 1967), especially pp. 167–74 [excerpts reprinted here]; Paul F. Cummins, *Richard Wilbur: A Critical Essay* (Grand Rapids, Mich.: Eerdman's, 1971), p. 7.

4. Wilbur, "Poetry and the Landscape," *The New Landscape in Art and Science,* edited by Gyorgy Kepes (Chicago: Theobald, 1956), p. 86.

5. David Dillon, "The Image and the Object: An Interview with Richard Wilbur," *Southwest Review* 58 (1973):247.

6. Dillon, p. 242.

BRAD LEITHAUSER

Richard Wilbur at Sixty

More than a third of a century has elapsed since publication of
his broadly praised first book of poems, and now, at sixty, with
five more volumes of poetry behind him, Richard Wilbur is
almost unanimously acknowledged to be one of the few living
American masters of formal verse. Such unanimity is unusual in
a world as diffuse and factional as that of contemporary poetry,
and it bespeaks perhaps not only a deserved admiration but also
a suspicion that the role is not widely coveted. In a world in
which free poetic forms loudly prevail and rhymed, metrical
verse is commonly perceived as old-fashioned, Wilbur's emi-
nence as a formalist can be conceded generously and without
envy. It is a somewhat singular position, then, that Richard
Wilbur occupies—a monarch in a realm which in the last few
decades has grown increasingly depopulated.

A great many of Wilbur's rough contemporaries who now
work chiefly in free forms—among them, W. S. Merwin, Louis
Simpson, Donald Hall—began as formalists and carried their
formal training into their freer explorations. This is generally
not the case with poets twenty or thirty years younger than
Wilbur. Free verse and its various half-disciplined siblings have
of course been around a great many years, but only now, for
better or worse, are we witnessing the ascendancy of the first
generation in the history of English-language verse never to
have worked seriously in form. Poets have always rightly re-
sented the way critics can, because they have little first-hand
experience with the demands of form, condescendingly dismiss
as "mere artifice" or "tour de force" what was achieved only by

Printed in a slightly different form as "America's Master of Formal Verse—
Reconsideration: Richard Wilbur" in *The New Republic,* March 24, 1982, pp.
28–31.

dint of vast emotional as well as mental labor. This unhappy gap now undergoes a poignant widening when poets themselves may have difficulty grasping how much love and skill has gone into the formalist's craft.

One last singular aspect of Wilbur's position, this one clearly unfortunate, is that because his long fidelity to form makes him something of a rarity, his critics commonly scant the contents for the package, or equate a "conservative" use of old forms with a conservative or narrow outlook. Although Wilbur's use of form is indeed what one first remarks in his poetry, he has, in the vernacular of a plain-speaking poetic age, "something to say" as well. Indeed, however one may ultimately evaluate his work, a careful reader must come away from it convinced that its creator is a man of large, lively and mettlesome intellect.

In the late summer of 1981, when I visited Wilbur at his house, I found him in the happy state of having recently completed his fifth translation from seventeenth-century French drama. After four Molière comedies he has turned to tragedy, Racine's *Andromache*, rendering it, as he did the Molière, in rhymed couplets. Having the play completed left him feeling ready to begin his fall teaching duties at Smith College, not far from his home in Cummington, Massachusetts, and also to work with greater absorption on his next volume of poetry, which he hopes to have amassed in two or three years. Five years had passed since the appearance of his last book, *The Mind-Reader;* he tends to work slowly.

Critics of Wilbur who have faulted his verse for not showing enough of the ravages of our age might also, and now somewhat jealously, note that these have not touched him physically either. He is a very handsome and an extraordinarily youthful-looking man, large (six foot two) and slim, his reddish brown hair all but untouched by gray. He likes daily exercise, for which his house, with its swimming pool, ping-pong table and tennis court, is well equipped. Located beside a dairy farm, this is an attractive modern house in what remains a somewhat rural landscape. The house, too, has its rural touches, including a large vegetable garden and a structure which is for a writer at once romantic and practical: a renovated silo, a kind of miniature and homely

Yeatsian tower, in which Wilbur can work in isolation. Winters are bitter here in western Massachusetts, and in recent years he and his wife Charlee (to whom his first book, like his most recent, was dedicated) have started migrating after Christmas to Key West.

Since his discharge from the army after World War II, Wilbur has chosen a life of great stability. He has passed nearly all these years in academia, mostly at New England colleges. (Interestingly—in this dispersive age—his four grown children all now live in Massachusetts too.) In this, as in many aspects of his poetry, he bears comparison with Robert Frost, who was an early friend. Charlee's great-aunt was Susan Hayes Ward, the woman who first published Frost, in the *Independent,* and offered him needed encouragement during the long gestation before his first book materialized. Frost as an elderly man once confided to Charlee that she'd made a good choice in marrying Wilbur, but that she should guard against his going mad. To readers who find in Wilbur the triumph of a dry rationality, this admonition may seem needless, but a close reading shows that for Wilbur as for Frost (who lived in such unsettling proximity to madness) the ordered form of a poem represents a "stay against confusion." Indeed, it may be tempting to see in Wilbur a desperation that probably is not there, for in fact Wilbur appears to have kept over the years not only his wits but most of his composure. Yet it is significant that the major tension in his work is the contrary, dissociative tug between the ideal and the actual, and the shuttling role the mind must play between the spirit's hunger for visions and the body's physical hungers.

It is a tension to be found in Wilbur's first book, *The Beautiful Changes* (1947), though not predominant there. Indeed one characteristic of that book is that little—save perhaps an affection for rhymed verse—predominates; it is a wise and expansive young man's miscellany, in which one encounters war poems and nature poems, religious meditations and light verse. The language ranges from a plunging colloquial ("God knows I / Would be the last alive to cry / To Whatzisname, 'I love thy wheels!'") to a formal rhetoric weighted by archaic inversions ("laundry white," "they dream and look not out"). The poems openly display a multiplicity of influences: E.E. Cummings in some of the diction ("Any greenness is deeper than anyone knows") and in the penchant for odd and often neologistic compound words ("herehastening," "fineshelled," "lightcaped," "muchtouched"); Marianne Moore in the many quirky leapings, linked only by "and," between the general and the concrete ("There's classic and there's quaint, / And then there is that devout intransitive eye / Of Pieter de Hooch"); Frost in some of the apothegmatic, seasonal reflections ("And doubtless it is dangerous to love / This somersault of seasons; / But I am weary of / The winter way of loving things for reasons"). Remarkable in *The Beautiful Changes* is the deft way such debts are acknowledged and paid; by means of a transmuting wit and affection, what might have been mere echoes become tributary extensions of beloved voices. Note, for example, how quietly the choice of "somersault" above, with its homonymous "summer" budded within it, enriches the line. Such delights are often so subtle in Wilbur's work that they could be taken for mere happenstance did they not arise so frequently and so neatly. Few of the poems, I think, in *The Beautiful Changes* are among Wilbur's best, but the work is flush with such bountiful promise as to leave little doubt of his future accomplishment.

It was a promise in large part met with publication of *Ceremony* three years later. A cleaner and more robust line had emerged, with no loss of the technical complexity and intricate music Wilbur had already unveiled in *The Beautiful Changes*. This second book offered new fields of competence—dramatic dialogue, narrative, some fine translations from the French, and an epigrammatic concision whereby large observations are delivered in compact boxes. Take for example this couplet, one of two under the title "Epistemology":

> We milk the cow of the world, and as we do
> We whisper in her ear, "You are not true."

In two lines Wilbur has evoked and wryly commented on that schism with which the philosopher must live—at once insisting that all surrounding objects may be illusions, and yet drawing from these illusory bodies his mundane but essential daily livelihood. (Wilbur may also be taking an offhand slap at men's impossible demands on women.) *Ceremony* also abounds in passages which exhibit a capacious gift for conveying action, as in the opening of "Part of a Letter":

> Easy as cove water rustles its pebbles and shells
> In the slosh, spread, seethe, and the backsliding
> Wallop and tuck of the wave. . . .

With his second book, Wilbur had manifested both so much promise and such achievement that even Randall Jarrell, a critic who found much to censure in Wilbur's early work, granted that "he seems the best of the quite young poets writing in this country." Other critics had fewer reservations; Wilbur was praised warmly by Louise Bogan, M. L. Rosenthal and T. S. Eliot—heady applause for a man who had published both volumes before turning thirty.

In one of his later poems, "Seed Leaves," Wilbur examines the philosophical implications of a plant recently erupted from the soil's "crusty rubble." It has not yet taken on any distinguishing characteristics, any "sure and special signature," and hence serves as a kind of universal vegetation—an everyplant, so to speak. As such, it wields a mystery and potentiality it can never sustain once having identified itself:

> This plant would like to grow
> And yet be embryo;
> Increase, and yet escape
> The doom of taking shape . . .

In the personification of the plant's dilemma we find a ready analogy to Wilbur's own poetic evolution. A variety of voices and tones sounded in his first two books, leaving his future development, like the plant's, unclear; with the appearance of his third, however (*Things of This World,* 1956), a favored tone, a distinctive voiceprint, had emerged. This is hardly to suggest that Wilbur hasn't altered since the mid-fifties, for he has indeed changed and, in some ways, gotten even better. Nonetheless, the poems of *Things of This World* are far closer kin to his most recent work than to his two earlier books.

What traits, then, can we say are characteristic of Wilbur? Most immediately evident is a breadth of language which comprises many sorts of words regarded suspiciously by most of his contemporaries. He is fond of long words, often latinate, that might be considered "overly poetic" ("quotidian," "invincible," "adamantine," "discarnate"); he employs a number of terms whose range of meaning has all but vanished—another kind of corporate "takeover"—behind their commercial connotations ("franchise," "office," "promotion," "revenue"); he plucks from the litter of advertising slogans a number of wayworn enhancers ("lovely," "gorgeous," "beautiful," "superb"). These salvages are not always successful, but the effect of such "tainted" language when fed into a matrix dense with music and wordplay can be aerating: one feels that a language's musty corridors have been purified.

Characteristic, too, is what might be termed an elevated grandness of both subject and style. In powerful, fair-spoken lines Wilbur confronts absolutely enormous questions, both timeless (the mediation of body and soul, the past's claims on the present) and temporal (nuclear weapons, the Bicentennial, the Vietnam War). His approach is usually direct, or as direct as a complex subject matter will permit (as he said in one of his essays, "If you respect the reality of the world, you know that you can approach that reality only by indirect means"), and he does not flinch from words like "death," "love," "blessed," or "ecstasy." His comment in a radio broadcast regarding his poem "Love Calls Us to the Things of This World" is revealing: "Is it possible . . . to speak intelligibly of angels in the modern world? Will the psyche of the modern reader consent to be called a soul? The poem I have just presented was a test of those questions." Though Wilbur has often spoken of his inability to write poetry on order for specific occasions, he has managed to bring his elevated style to bear on a range of events, both personal and societal. There are elegies for Auden and Dudley Fitts, a couple of Vietnam War protests, a wedding toast for his son, a birthday poem, a "Speech for the Repeal of the McCarran Act," a Christmas hymn. Just as Wilbur's language is broad, so is the scatter of events on which he has focused his talents; his verse, though elevated, is flexible enough to encompass an impressive sweep of life. (And it should be noted that in Wilbur all is not elevation; no one in America writes finer light verse.)

Implicit in much of this elevated verse is a repudiation of Auden's claim that "poetry makes nothing happen." A poem like "Advice to a Prophet" is not merely—though this would itself be ambitious—an attempt to portray something of the horrors of nuclear war; in contriving to set it in the form of advice to a doomsayer, Wilbur with unspoken optimism suggests that it is possible—through prophecy, through poetry—to transform the way people perceive the threat of world destruction. About this poem he has said, "It made it possible for me to feel something beside a kind of abstract horror, a puzzlement, at the thought of nuclear war; and it may so serve other people. I hope so." Wilbur advises the prophet to speak not of mankind's destruction, which we can hardly conceive, but of the destruction of the natural world, which through spoliation of the environment we know all too well. Nature, the poem says, has helped give us our humanity—and hence, indirectly, the poem speaks of mankind's destruction after all:

> Ask us, prophet, how we shall call
> Our natures forth when that live tongue is all
> Dispelled, that glass obscured or broken
>
> In which we have said the rose of our love and the clean
> Horse of our courage, in which beheld
> The singing locust of the soul unshelled,
> And all we mean or wish to mean.

Here warning blends, in a passage as affecting as any in Wilbur, into celebration.

Formal, elevated utterance is of course a hazardous enterprise that easily balloons into bombast, a danger Wilbur evades by a variety of techniques, perhaps most importantly through a punning lightness and a continual use of the colloquial. Lines dip frequently into bare and simple statement (e.g., "And all we mean or wish to mean"); as Wilbur has put it, "I don't like to stay aloft too long." It is characteristic that a spare image like "A toad the power mower caught / Chewed and clipped of a leg" would cohabit in the same poem with "Toward misted and ebullient seas / And cooling shores, toward lost Amphibia's emperies," or that an "open mouth / Banjo-strung with spittle" would room with "An unseen genius of the middle distance, / Giddy with godhead or with nonexistence."

Wilbur's success with elevated verse also derives from something harder to define and isolate, and which might best be termed a sense of proportionality. Stanzas fit together; asides remain subordinate to the thoughts they spring from. This is a talent Wilbur has commanded from the outset, as Louise Bogan observed in her review of *The Beautiful Changes:* "he can contemplate his subjects without nervousness, explore them with care, and let them drop at the exact moment that the organization of a poem is complete. This ease of pace, this seemingly effortless advance to a resolute conclusion, is rare at his age; the young usually yield to tempting inflation and elaboration." The result is that Wilbur conveys a sense of a mind whose supervisory inner eye has seen the poem as a whole. Or, to phrase this differently, one almost always senses that he is in control of his poem.

This control may put off certain readers, in search of a headlong spontaneity rarely present in Wilbur. To return to the image of the plant in "Seed Leaves," one must in fairness ask what losses he incurred in "the doom of taking shape." A reader who turns from later Wilbur to his first two books is apt to feel that a wildness has been tempered, an exuberance curbed; his poetry has lost none of its energy (Anthony Hecht, a poet of prodigious energy himself, has written that Wilbur's is "the most kinetic poetry I know"), but the poet who once placed a full stanza in capital letters, coined neologisms with a counterfeiter's abandon, and wildly prised words out of their fixed parts of speech (creating, for example, the verb "Veniced") has grown more circumspect. And with this circumspection has come, perhaps, some loss in the capacity to surprise.

Linked to this loss is Wilbur's tendency at times to be too articulate about what he confesses is ultimately ineffable. For to analyze a mystery, even in a spirit of humility and praise, is sometimes necessarily to diminish it. Wilbur is fond of excursions to the edge of the knowable ("the pitchy whirl / At the mind's end" in "The Beacon," "the furl / Of waters, blind in muck and shell" in "Conjuration," "the buried strangeness / Which nourishes the known" in "A Hole in the Floor"). The reader may be left with a feeling that such attempts finally are, though admirably bold, disappointing—that in *terra incognita* obliquity and implication are the poet's only satisfactory map and compass.

On balance, such reservations must be tentatively muttered, while praise should be sung in full voice, for Wilbur in a glum and occluded poetic age has kept his eyes open to acclaim beauty and the dignity of "the thing done right / From the clay porch / To the white altar" ("A Plain Song for Comadre"). And his work—though in recent years it comes with regrettable slowness—shows little sign of depletion; some of his more recent poems (his elegy for Auden, "The Fourth of July" and the title poem from *The Mind-Reader*) belong beside his best work.

Questions of depletion, of roads taken and not taken, arise naturally as a poet moves into his sixties. Gratified to have the Racine translation behind him at last, Wilbur now looks forward to working more concentratedly on his own poetry, but has set no new goals for himself other than a desire "to find out if there is anything I've been avoiding writing, and to write that." He is uncertain whether he wants soon to begin another translation. Though time-consuming, these translations offer him numerous appeals, among which is a satisfaction in knowing he does them extremely well. Wilbur himself, whose good-natured boasts are modestly couched in excessive qualifications, says, "There is a pleasure in doing something better than anyone else. And I translate seventeenth-century French drama into rhymed English couplets better than anyone else."

Wilbur's wife wants him now to devote his time to his own poetry and to put off another translation until, in his words,

"I'm in my sunset years." Most poets reaching sixty would find their sunset years encroaching fast. He and his wife speak of them as if they are decades off. To look at him swimming laps in the chilly water of his pool—or to look into his most recent verse—one can thankfully believe that the two of them are right.

POETS ON POETRY   Donald Hall, General Editor

Poets on Poetry collects critical books by contemporary poets,
gathering together the articles, interviews, and book reviews
by which they have articulated the poetics of a new generation.